MASTERS OF

SALES

MASTERS OF SALES

Secrets From Top Sales Professionals That Will Transform You Into a World Class Salesperson

Including:

Brian Tracy ⸱ Tom Hopkins ⸱ Martha Stewart ⸱ Harvey Mackay
Jay Conrad Levinson ⸱ Tony Robbins ⸱ Tony Parinello ⸱ Keith Ferrazzi
Jack Canfield and Many More!

BY

New York Times Best-selling Authors

Ivan R. Misner, Ph.D. and Don Morgan, M.A.

Ep
Entrepreneur·
Press

Managing Editor: Jere L. Calmes
Cover Design: Perlman Creative Group, www.perlmancreative.com
Composition and Production: Eliot House Productions

This publication is designed to provide accurate and authoritative information in regard to
the subject matter covered. It is sold with the understanding that the publisher is not
engaged in rendering legal, accounting, or other professional services. If legal advice or
other expert assistance is required, the services of a competent professional person should
be sought.

—From a Declaration of Principles jointly adopted by a
Committee of the American Bar Association and
a Committee of Publishers and Associations

Cover photo credit: Erich Lessing/Art Resource, NY. Painting titled Archduke Leopold
Wilhelm in his picture gallery in Brussels, c. 1647 by David Teniers the Younger. Museo
del Prado, Madrid, Spain

Library of Congress Cataloging-in-Publication
Misner, Ivan R., 1956-
    Masters of sales: secrets from top sales professionals that will transform you into a
world class salesperson/by Ivan R. Misner and Don Morgan.
    p. cm.
    ISBN-13: 978-1-59918-129-5 (alk. paper)
    ISBN-10: 1-59918-129-0 (alk. paper)
    1. Selling. 2. Sales personnel. I. Morgan, Don, 1946- II. Title.
HF5438.25.M587 2007
658.85—dc22   2007013847

Printed in Canada

12 11 10 09 08 07   10 9 8 7 6 5 4 3 2 1

Contents

Acknowledgments

The editors have a combined experience of about 90 years in selling. But the real acknowledgement goes to the more than 100 people around the world who contributed to our understanding about masterful selling . . . and who convinced us that the art of selling is undergoing a fundamental shift. The space in this book did not allow us to include every contributing author, but everyone added to this new world view about the shape of selling today. Each of our contributors is listed at our web site, www.MastersBooks.com, and would welcome your contact. This book celebrates our masterful contributors, but more importantly, it recognizes the combined efforts of each salesperson to distribute our technological advances and critical services to the world. Without dynamic, forward-thinking salespeople, our world would not be the same.

We also want to thank our respective BNI partners who "looked after the store" while we compiled and attempted to make sense out of the many techniques, strategies, and concepts submitted to us. Notably, we thank Ann Longanecker, who provided much of the early layout for us, and

Julien Sharp, whose tireless work with the background editing transformed our shaggy notes into streamlined text. Finally, we appreciate the time allowed us by our families, whose understanding gave us the time and focus to get the job done. Everyone connected with this project helped put together this work about masterful selling, which continues to evolve and move forward, led by the Masters of Sales. Selling, business, and life in general are all shifting toward a team effort, and we extend our heartfelt thanks to our team for helping to deliver this important message.

—Ivan Misner and Don Morgan

Preface

YOU CAN LIE TO A SALESMAN

You can lie to a salesman,
And still get to heaven,
Request their proposals, and make 'em dance.
'Cause a salesman will trick you, and take your money.
If you lie to them first, they never get the chance.

Oh, salesmen are useful,
Don't get me wrong,
They're fountains of free advice.
So, hook 'em on hope, and string 'em along,
And beat 'em to death on price.

Every night at sundown,
If you listen, you can hear it.
Like ghostly specters from beyond the pale
Digitized voices rising from their chambers
It's the spirits of salesmen trapped inside voice mail.

Hi, Fred, it's Steve getting back to you
I've got good news on that price.
Why don't you give me a shout
So we take the next step.
I've left this message twice.

—Lyrics by Stephen Josephs and Bill Joiner

The average person loves to buy . . . but hates to be sold to. And people really dislike the typical salesperson. This book takes a hard look at selling with integrity. *Sell* is not a four-letter word. (OK, it is, but you know what I mean.) Selling can be good for everyone. One of the goals of this book is to raise the bar for salespeople, who can sell in such a way that the above song does not apply to them.

The art of sales is evolving and now includes many contributions from the social and human sciences. Did you know that the mere mention of one wrong word or an incorrect emphasis can break or make a sale? Selling is a delicate art that evolves and adjusts to our tumultuous global environment. Three or four decades ago, the commercial world was totally different. In those days, if you bought a Ford car you were a loyal FORD MAN and certainly not an import car person. Today, you might buy a Ford car from a Ford dealer who also owns a Mazda dealership. Your new Ford could have parts built by Mazda, with engineering design borrowed from Jaguar in Great Britain, and an on-board GPS system from China. Old-fashioned buyer loyalty is not the same as in the past. Sellers, who used to include lessons on how to operate their product, might now be taught about special features in their product from a young buyer, who conducted extensive product research on the internet prior to meeting the salesperson.

Salespeople who sell effectively are aware of these changes, and are adjusting their strategies accordingly. The Masters of Sales practice their craft in a way that is most synchronized with the demands of our new world. These masters are pioneering the new sales paradigm.

You picked this book up because you are curious about finding the newest "magic" sales buttons. Our job is to guide you on a brief journey into selected techniques and strategies used by masterful sellers who push the right buttons at the right time with the right people, and thereby achieve success through selling. So, let's begin the journey at the beginning of the process.

A sale occurs when there is a transfer of a product or service for money—usually between two parties. Selling encompasses all those qualities necessary to make the sale happen. These are characterized in www.dictionary.com as being "persuasive, inducing, or merely causing the transaction to happen." This dictionary definition covers the waterfront, but doesn't give us a clear and exact picture about what sellers actually *do* to create a successful sales transaction. We want to give you a glimpse of the seller's magic.

Picture yourself shopping for a family gift and walking into an attractive, high-end kitchen store with thousands of products. Your mission is to get the perfect gift, but you're only vaguely aware of what might suit the occasion. Furthermore, you don't want to be distracted by a bored sales clerk, who appears to be only interested in hearing his cash register ring. In the end, you will either leave very pleased about having found just the perfect gift, or you will walk out empty-handed and dejected, vowing never again to step foot in that store. The interaction between you and the salesperson inside the store had a lot to do with the result, and even determined your destiny. (The destiny part is really true. As a result of your sales experience, you either go home to begin celebrating, or keep searching, getting more and more tired.)

Consumers want to be guided by masterful salespeople who can help them solve problems and overcome the challenges they encounter. Done well, this highly interactive process will convert the client from a totally unknown individual into one who shows long-term, sincere appreciation to the salesperson. A masterful selling job occurs when a product or service precisely matches the client's needs/interests/wants and an exchange is made.

Our commercial environment today is characterized by a plethora of products and services—and sales messages. Sellers have access to more sales knowledge and strategies, but so, too, do the buyers . . . who may like to buy but don't like to be *sold*. The masterful salesperson knows how to create an enjoyable buying experience for his customers.

Buying has always been a form of recreation for some; for others . . . not so much. This is why the master salesperson will even use personality profiling to help his customer find just the right solution. Sellers work with buyers in a one-on-one situation or in more complex corporate environments. The corporate salesperson must sort through a myriad of thoughts, needs, emotions, and circumstances of not just one person, but the many people involved in the buying decision. Each salesperson wants to close every sale, but the knowledgeable ones understand that a long-term relationship is preferable to a one-hit sale. It is much harder to get new clients than it is to keep existing clients loyal. This secret is pursued by only the most masterful of sellers. Part of the secret is to create a selling experience where the buyer says, WOW.

Plain and simple, our highly charged, over-choiced, and changing world requires a shift in selling that positions the seller as a member in the buyer's successful and problem-solving team. What is most interesting is how selling is now seen as a two-way street, wherein both the seller and buyer want to feel equal as partners in the transaction. The new sales paradigm places increased importance on two-way quality communication in a way that adds mutual value to a buyer-seller relationship.

The responsibility for distributing our societal products and critical services rests with salespeople, without whom our commercial engines would grind to a halt. Despite the important role played by salespeople, we still haven't established an institutional response for properly training these important individuals. Instead, these folks learn their craft through word-of-mouth, private training courses, or by attendance at the school of hard knocks. However learned, master salespeople use all the existing sales tools, and continue inventing new ones. It is important to select the right tool for the job, and in each of the following chapters we hope to show you a sampling of sales tools used by the masters.

Studying at the feet of the masters accelerates our learning by teaching us tips of the trade. These people are the ones who have already achieved success in the art of selling. True Masters of Sales move into community leadership roles because, as leaders in their own networks, they understand the importance of networking to their craft. As leaders, they are more effective at dealing with the most complex entities on planet earth—people. And people like to buy from leaders.

In the not-so-distant past, a profession in sales may have been at the bottom of our social acceptability scale, but this is rapidly changing. Professional selling is a vital vocation for high achievers seeking rewards associated with dedicated and focused effort. These new Masters of Sales fulfill an honorable, even critical, role in helping move the world forward. This book gives you access to many pieces of the selling puzzle. The chapters are laid out like the traditional model for selling: sales attitudes, sales goals, prospecting for clients, handling objections, product demonstrations, the close, and the follow-up. Within each chapter, you will discover new recipes for success that you can follow precisely and, once mastered, add to with your own ingredients.

Become a master . . . and then teach us!

The Master of Sales Attitude

Aligning Your Inner Self with Your Outside Personal Image

You judge yourself on your thoughts but others
judge you by your actions.

—FRANK DERAFFELE

T he masterful salesperson is ultimately judged by his or her sales volume, and that result is determined by the inner drive of each salesperson. It doesn't matter if you are born with masterful selling skills or doggedly learn the craft of selling from self-study and mentors. Either way, the foundation for success in sales starts with the alignment of your inner characteristics with an outward plan for achievement.

Gunther T. Verleger, a successful businessman and sales professional from Germany, describes the teaching of Matthias Pöhm, one of Germany's most successful sales trainers:

Mr Pöhm teaches sales strategy through an analogy to gardening. Pöhm teaches that the trunk of a plant or tree must be strong and straight so that it can produce beautiful fruits and leaves. He describes the salesperson similarly. The salesperson must have a strong and straight self-identity which is well grounded and self aware. Sales professionals need to be self-confident, courageous, faithful, bold, and believe in core values. All of the salesperson's beliefs must be consistent; otherwise their misaligned beliefs will be illuminated through spoken and non-verbal communications, which confuse the client. A salesperson's identity influences customers to be either gorgeous loyal clients or ones that wither and run away.

People (salespeople included) consistently display their values, attitudes, and opinions through their personal actions. These actions have an important impact on a selling career. Masterful sellers cannot afford to be plagued with inner hesitancy. He who hesitates is lost! These high achievers move through their selling activities with self-confidence, fueling their self-belief with each successful deal. Understanding that every prospect will not result in a sale, the masters are prepared to risk failure to achieve further success. The masterful sellers are proud of the critical roles they play as leaders in the distribution of products and services required by society.

The risk of losing a deal is not a concern because these people believe in the abundance of opportunities available to the high achievers. They balance their career with their personal life and are seen by others as "nice people." Treating their customers more as partners and less as adversaries, masterful sellers favor a team orientation over operating solo. They know that to be at the top of their game, they must work cooperatively with others in a marketplace that is forever changing through technological advances and increased competition. The master seller believes in the TEAM acronym: Together Everyone Achieves More.

The "art" of selling requires continual exercise of cognitive inputs and skilled behaviors, which blend and merge to achieve a sales transaction: A client exchanges his money for the seller's product or service. So, who are these masterful sellers in today's world? Is the sales stereotype accurate? In truth, Masters of Sales are not hard to distinguish. These are people whose identity is well-defined and whose human characteristics easily draw us to them.

Salespeople are amazing folks who work in a multitask, multifaceted world of dichotomies. They deal in high and low tech, interconnecting departments, and with all manner of customers, suppliers, and competitors. The multitalented Masters of Sales live and work in an environment that is well described by two acknowledged masters who brought us the concept and strategies of Guerrilla Marketing.

DIRECT SELLING

JAY CONRAD LEVINSON AND AL LAUTENSLAGER

Guerrillas know how to be proactive when it comes to direct selling. Waiting for a client to specify a desired solution and playing the competitive bid game is un-guerrilla like. Direct sales overcome this. Kevin Nations, who used to sell for a well-recognized *Fortune* 100 telecommunications company and is currently "The Six Figure Sales Coach" (www.kevin nations.com), found that even as he represented an industry leader, he and his company were always being edged out of a large local school district, primarily because of price. Together with several equipment manufacturers,

Target L.T.
↘ Needs,
Provide
Solns.

and by asking all the right questions, they designed a complete communications solution that answered the district's long-term needs.

This combined strategy placed Kevin and his partners into a position with a competitive advantage. No other company asked the same questions or could offer the complete solution with the relationship Kevin had developed. The client would never have known of the benefits, the advantages, and the complete solution had it not been for a well-planned sales approach. The client also wouldn't have had such a positive relationship had it not been for Kevin's aggressive sales attitude and approach. The result: Kevin and his company won a $30 million plus contract. Kevin Nations is a guerrilla seller.

Guerrilla marketers say nothing happens in a company until something is marketed. Guerrilla sellers say nothing happens until something is sold. All guerrillas know that both are right, and they work together.

Selling has often been called the distribution arm of marketing. Getting your marketing message out face-to-face to a prospect always wins out. One-on-one interaction allows for dialogue. A postcard can't answer a question on the spot. A radio commercial can't overcome an objection stated by a prospect. A sign can't supply additional information when requested. Personal selling can.

When the early caveman was asked about his wheel for sale, he could answer back. When asked, "What is that round thing that you are selling used for?" he could demonstrate. He could collect cave bucks once he answered, once he sold.

Personal selling, whether you are a caveman or a guerrilla, allows you to develop and adjust a message to satisfy a prospect's need for information or to answer a question. Developing and adjusting messages is marketing. Satisfying prospects' needs is guerrilla selling.

Dialogue happens when you are face-to-face with a prospect. Personal selling is dialogue between you and your prospects with the objective of getting them to open their wallets in exchange for your products and services, even if those wallets contain cave bucks.

According to the U.S. Department of Labor, more than 14 million people are employed in sales positions. Sales positions that first come to mind are real estate professionals, retail clerks, stockbrokers, representatives selling a manufactured product, automobile salespeople, and door-to-door salespeople.

Personal selling also allows for targeting the most promising leads. A newsletter, advertisement, or TV commercial can't always be as selective because they communicate to the masses.

The guerrilla drawback to personal selling is the cost. Typically, a business will spend a great deal more on personal selling than on any other form of marketing. High costs don't contribute well to guerrilla profits, unless guerrilla selling provides guerrilla revenues higher than these costs.

Nothing develops a personal relationship better than personal contact. Direct selling is personal contact. The telephone comes close, but did you ever try to read body language over the phone?

There is a lot more to personal selling than personally delivering a message to a prospect face-to-face.

First you have to identify to whom you should deliver your message. You already know that "everybody" is not a target market. Knowing those most interested in your product or service increases the probability of exchanging goods and services for cash. These people are candidates for your message delivery. These are the candidates for your one-on-one, face-to-face dialogue. These are your best personal selling targets and those most likely to be relationship-bound.

Preparation is part of personal selling. What to say and when to say something come with training and experience. Knowledge is powerful in all selling situations. Knowledge about the company, the person, the need, the problems to be solved, and the objections all prepare a personal salesperson to win the victory trophy of the selling contest.

Armed with knowledge, you are ready to deliver your message. This happens in the form of a conversation or a presentation. Presentations could be demonstrations, explanations, testimonials, or fact-finding. All deliver information. Guerrillas know that presentations can be exchanged for checks. All are designed to transact business upon completion.

Transacting business is the ultimate goal of personal selling. This happens when prospects have decided you can solve their problems or enhance their business, quality of work life, or profits. This also happens when you establish a high degree of trust with prospects. Trust leads to confidence. Combining the two leads to business transactions, the fruit produced by guerrilla marketing seeds.

You might not know the prospect's mind is made up until you ask him. This is what is known as a close. Identifying the next mutually agreed upon action is a close. Not doing so lengthens the selling process, leaves things to chance, and makes this already high-cost form of marketing even more costly; this is not part of the guerrilla success formula. Prospects need to utter the words "I'll take it" at some point. The focus here is one customer at a time. This follows all of the persuading and information provided by marketing and selling. It is a one-on-one personal selling effort that gets to these words.

Follow-up and relationship-building round out the direct personal selling efforts. Customers and prospects want attention before, during, and after their purchasing experience. Reinforcement and encouragement go a long way in providing this attention and building relationships. *Guerrilla Marketing* points out that guerrilla marketers concentrate on how many relationships are made each month, not just the amount of sales receipts received.

Half the cars sold in Japan are sold door-to-door. These guerrillas meet the right prospects to start and develop relationships, supply information, and act as a resource. Business transactions increase significantly when you and the buyer know and trust each other. This is exactly what happens in the world of Japanese car sales.

Loyalty

Building and maintaining relationships keeps the customer coming back. Traditional marketing focuses on always getting new customers. Guerrilla marketing focuses on getting more from existing customers. The personal selling relationships ensure this will happen. Your best prospect is still a current customer.

Listening

Guerrillas excel at listening. Guerrillas are active listeners. Learn how to listen well. It's very difficult for someone trained to present a message to keep quiet. Guerrilla salespeople are disciplined to do so. Listening shows intent. How do you know what problems need to be solved unless a prospect tells you? If you start in on a pitch to solve a problem that the prospect doesn't have, you will not sell anything. Guaranteed. Listening is a key skill in all sales calls.

Customers and prospects love to talk about their favorite subjects: themselves. Listening to them shows that you care more about them than yourself. Showing interest and caring leads to more completed order forms. Are you listening?

Asking Questions

Some of the best selling happens when you listen. Understanding what a prospect wants and needs and hearing it from them personally tells you what to target, what to sell, what problems to solve, and what challenges to overcome. This understanding comes from the dialogue in a personal selling situation. The dialogue involves asking questions.

Questions uncover needs, problems, pains, concerns, and objections. Questions move to create prospect commitment as a result of the information uncovered. Questions that will reveal the best information and make the dialogue flow best are in the general categories of:

- opening
- motivation/vision
- concerns
- current situation
- current supply
- relationships
- perceptions
- product usage
- communication
- referrals
- purchasing process
- final thoughts

There are many benefits to asking the right questions. Questions not only qualify the buyer, but also establish rapport, identify the real needs and challenges, and find the prospect's "hot buttons." Questions give you an understanding into most sales situations. The answers to all of these questions are important when establishing relationships and developing the proper sales dialogue.

Asking questions is nothing more than a form of interviewing. The end result is that you gain knowledge, build relationships, gather referrals, and ultimately generate new business. All of these are right up on that championship medal platform with all other guerrilla marketing values and principles.

Relationships

Just think of all the relationships you have in your life aside from your family and friends. You probably go regularly to the same store for groceries. Everyone has a favorite place to get his or her hair cut or styled. We all have our favorite restaurants. Businesses only buy from certain suppliers for a myriad of reasons. A good relationship is one of the most important. Marketing enhances all of these relationships: signs, mailings, radio ads, appearance, product and service delivery, and so on. All of this supports the personal contact that happens in the course of business transactions with these relationship partners. The marketing supports the personal contact involved in selling, which ultimately leads to the exchange of dollars for products and services. Ongoing communication keeps customers returning and loyal. Returning customers provide lifetime value to you. Understanding the lifetime value of those returning customers gives you the high return on your marketing and sales investment that guerrillas expect.

Selling isn't always having every prospecting, presentation, and closing technique down pat. It mostly is establishing trust, being credible, and making sure you are offering and communicating value to your prospective buyer.

Selling is a very important part of the marketing process, but it is not a replacement for it.

A sales rep or the selling process is part of your company's promotional and marketing communications mix. Conveying information about benefits to prospects and keeping them informed of new products, services, or ways to solve new problems all lead to customer satisfaction. Customer satisfaction generates revenue. Without satisfied customers you have no business.

Many consumer businesses rely on advertising and promotion. B2B organizations rely more on the personal selling arm of marketing. Much of this is related to the nature of the customer's buying process and the buyer-seller relationship.

Since communication is a two-way process, being face to face with a prospect in a sales situation also allows for prospect feedback. The salesperson can then communicate back to the selling organization in an effort to respond, solve, improve, or communicate more effectively.

Marketing will get you to the dance. Once you're at the dance you have to do your own dancing. Marketing generates leads, makes the phone ring, and causes people to ask for your product. Selling (dancing) convinces prospects to take money from their bank account and put it in yours in exchange for something.

Great dance lessons, looking sharp, and following the etiquette doesn't always make you the best dancer. Great marketing doesn't always make the sale. Marketing, advertising, PR, and promotions lay the groundwork, but the sale actually happens after all this marketing informs, persuades, and motivates prospects to visit with you, request more information, or try a test run.

Marketing communication materials and print collateral is often referred to as sales collateral. Sales collateral is as much a part of the marketing process as a sales person is.

Many guerrilla businesses don't have large numbers of salespeople, if any. As the owner, principle, or manager of the business, you are thrown to the prospect wolves in the form of a sales rep. Knowing and exerting the selling fundamentals will lead you to make more business transactions.

Guerrillas like to maximize their trips to the bank with deposits. Up-selling is one of these fundamentals. Guerrillas up-sell by being prepared—

prepared even when the customer says, "Yes, I'll take it." Kevin Nations, "The Six-Figure Sales Coach" mentioned above, states that customers who have just bought are in the most receptive state possible to make a buying decision (they've just proved it). Once in this state, up-selling can be done. His success and his coaching clients' success are due, primarily, to three direct up-sells. These up-sells will increase profits:

- Offer a premium version of the service your customer has just purchased at a reduced rate.
- Offer a subscription version of the services (i.e., if you are a carpet cleaner and someone buys cleaning, offer him or her a subscription cleaning service where you deliver and they pay many times per year).
- Ask for many referrals. Narrow your customer's customers to get your referrals. "Who do you know who has small children at home, pets, the cleanest home, or the dirtiest?" Also go overboard thanking them when a referral turns into a new business for you.

Figuring out how to win a customer's time, considerations, and money is the key to successful selling. Even with complexities related to products and services, there still are many times when subtle differences between your offering and the competitor's make a difference. The closer products in the market place are to parity, the better the salesperson has to be if the company is to succeed.

We are not in business because it's a hobby. We are in business to earn a living or provide a living for others. We can only do this if there are profits. We can only have profits if there is revenue and revenue comes as a result of selling. How's that for a crash course in business? Marketing supports and aids in generating a sale.

Sales is not marketing, and marketing is not sales. In fact the word sales is not even listed in the *Guerrilla Marketing* index, but it is an important part of the marketing formula.

Marketing can't exist without sales, and sales cannot exist without marketing. Though they have the same objective, the two require different strategies and tactics. These different strategies and tactics must be integrated to be effective. These integrated actions are the tools for finding the right prospects who are then converted to paying clients, with the final part of the process leading to returning customers and growing the resulting customer. That's sales. That's marketing. That's guerrilla revenue and eventual guerrilla profitability.

Excerpted from *Guerrilla Marketing in 30 Days* by Jay Conrad Levinson and Al Lautenslager, copyright ©2005. Used by permission of Entrepreneur Press.

———•◦•———

Years back, the common view held of the salesperson was of an assertive, loud, and somewhat pushy individual, with a style of cold calling, phone marketing, and expansive over-promises that earned him or her the name of "hawker." Hazel Walker, a successful businesswoman and marketing expert from Indianapolis, Indiana, teaches us about a new sales master who is emerging as appropriate for today's commercial environment.

———•◦•———

DEVELOPING HABITS OF A MASTER OF SALES

HAZEL M. WALKER

When I first met Linda Chandler in person, I was quite surprised. Here before me was a very petite woman, impeccably dressed in a white flowing dress, with the most beautiful smile that sparkled in her eyes and lit up her face. Eyes that made me feel at once at home and at ease. As I sat down with her for the first time three years ago, I felt as if I had always known her. Linda has a way of seeing beyond the business into the heart of every person she meets.

I had read her bio and the book she had written, listened to her audio books, and spent many hours on the phone with her. Before I actually met her, I envisioned a much different person . . . someone who was tall and commanding, dressed in a power suit, power-driven, with all the right stuff—after all, she is a legend in her industry. My first thought was that this does not look like a Sales Master. I was quickly reminded of the old adage, *Never judge a book by its cover.* Many sales have been lost precisely for that reason.

Linda, a former senior vice president of Sutro & Company, worked with the founders and senior management of companies like Rolm, Tandem, Apple Computer, Intel, AT&T, Lockheed, The Limited, Toys 'R' Us, Sun Microsystems, and many others. This is a POWERHOUSE of a woman. She personally sold over a billion dollars to retail clients. In one month, Linda sold over $30 million, breaking her 130-year-old firm's record and earning a commission of $250,000 for those incredible 30 days!

I've read many books and gone to many classes that have taught me how to close a deal, look for the buying signals, control the conversation, and bring home the money. Few have resonated with me. Being a master salesperson has always been important to me, but I never wanted to be one of "those salespeople." You know the type: pushy, hard-sale, more concerned with the bottom line than with the people they are dealing with. That kind of salesperson is not who I am as a woman, and I was concerned that I would never be a great salesperson, until Linda began to teach me. I have learned that I can be a woman, secure in my values, and a master saleswoman.

Linda Chandler taught me to pursue and apply ten habits to my selling. As a by-product, I have also found them to be extremely useful in all other aspects of my life.

Values

✗ Habit 1: Have a Strong Belief System

Having a strong belief system allows me to maintain a positive attitude. I do believe that I can achieve all that I set out to do. Even on those days when I have heard "no" multiple times, I believe that I will succeed and my next sales call will be a success!

Habit 2: Display Your Courage

Some days it takes all of my courage just to pick up the phone and make that first follow-up phone call; ultimately, I know it is all up to me. Masters have the courage to stand alone and the courage to look inward when things are not going their way. It doesn't do any good to blame others for our own lack of courage.

Habit 3: Loving Your Customers

I really enjoy people, so this habit is not hard for me. I truly understand that people are the most important part of selling and my customers are the most important people in my business.

Habit 4: Keep Score

Numbers don't lie, and they keep me from making excuses. The numbers lay out the picture in front of me. This habit is the one Linda helps me with the most. Personally, I work at looking at my numbers to keep myself on track. Good or bad, they are my compass.

Habit 5: Persistence and Perseverance

Doing those things other salespeople don't want to leads to the wealth and success that only the master will see. Those times when I feel like giving up and calling it a day, I sit down and write that one last proposal, make that last follow-up phone call, or go on that last appointment.

Habit 6: Constantly Learning

Deep down I know that learning and implementing what I learn is the hallmark of a master. This caused me to work with a personal mentor, read what other successful people do, and take classes so I can grow personally and professionally. Having that constant hunger to learn more, be more, and do more adds a tremendous quality to my life.

Habit 7: Stretching

We are like rubber bands: until we are stretched, we will never know how far we can shoot. Stretching is not always easy and is easily prevented by beliefs about not being able to accomplish high goals. This is where the other habits help keep me reaching higher.

Habit 8: Patience, Not Procrastination

I find it easy to confuse procrastination with patience. Unless I am acutely aware, I may put something off in the name of being patient when instinctively I know that it must be done. This commonly shows up in my decisions regarding following up on a sales proposal. Should I be patient and not follow up with the client regarding my sales proposal or is this merely procrastination? It's not always easy to differentiate the two.

Habit 9: Practice, Practice, Practice

Self-mastery requires constant and consistent practice. Just as with an Olympic athlete, the right practice is how mastery is achieved. Linda reminds me regularly that to continue on the path of mastery, I must practice my opening scripts, my presentation, my qualifying questions, the close, and follow-up until these sales techniques are second nature.

Habit 10: Dare to Be Unique

Dare to be yourself, not a carbon of everybody else. I've always felt a deep sense of the importance of being myself. I was gratified to hear Linda talk about salespeople who stand up for what they believe in with integrity. Each human is possessed of a unique mix of qualities, and optimizing our uniqueness is how we stand out from the crowd as leaders and masters.

Point yourself in the direction of your dreams and just go. Start practicing the habits of the masters, read about the masters, find out what it is that sets them apart. Find out what it is that sets you apart and then stretch! These same qualities helped me achieve a life in sales that I only dreamed of as a youth.

Imagine standing next to a highly successful salesperson. Does your image of a salesperson match the real person? It is not ironic that highly acclaimed sales trainers include the personal values of honesty and integrity in their courses. One icon of sales training, Zig Ziglar, teaches us that selling is a very interactive human endeavor where rapport, trust, and ethics are determining factors in a successful selling career.

SELLING 101:
WHAT EVERY SUCCESSFUL SALES PROFESSIONAL NEEDS TO KNOW

ZIG ZIGLAR

Important Skills for Today's Sales Professional

A primary reason I have worked so hard to grow Ziglar Training Systems into an internationally respected training company is so that we can SELL each other on the importance of the foundation stones of honesty, character, integrity, faith, love, and loyalty. In order to build on these foundations, we need to develop skills for learning, listening, communicating, and becoming dependable and credible. With these skills, we can build a business, a life, a family, a friendship, and a professional selling career while making a difference in the world in which we live.

Honesty and Integrity in Selling

Making a difference in the world depends upon honesty and integrity. Being ethical is not only the right way to live; it is also the most practical way to live. True selling professionals don't talk about ethics; they LIVE ethically!

Integrity, Honesty, and Ethics Pay Off

When Robert Davis was an outstanding salesman and sales manager for Terminix Pest Control in Baton Rouge, Louisiana, if you asked what he did for a living, he'd simply respond, "I kill bugs." His healthy self-esteem and belief in his company's services allowed him to excel personally and professionally.

At one point in his career with Terminix, Robert had a new salesman who got a little overzealous. Late one Friday afternoon, a client called with a serious problem. Bees were swarming around his home and placing the family in distress. Robert assigned his new man to the seemingly simple task, but as the salesman headed out the door, he called back, "Has anyone ever sold a $200 'bee job'?" The others smiled at his "bravado" and said, "No."

When the new man returned in less than thirty minutes with a check for $225, everyone was quite amazed. The telephone interrupted the excitement that bringing in a check for the largest "bee job" ever was generating. Robert answered, and the man who had signed the check was on the phone.

"I just wanted to call and thank you for responding so quickly and getting rid of my problem," the man began. "Those bees were a real concern, and your man certainly did the job."

"But I was wondering," he continued, "if $225 was normal for a 15-minute job."

"Are you going to be home for the next few minutes?" was Robert's immediate response. When he got an affirmative answer, Robert put the salesman and the check in his car. When they arrived at the man's home, Robert walked right up to the man and said, "Sir, I'm afraid we got a little carried away with our enthusiasm. Since I had not clearly explained the parameters of this job and how it should be billed to our new salesman, we overcharged you. (Notice that he did nothing to embarrass the salesman, though he had in fact explained exactly how to do the job and said that it was a $125 job at the most.) So this one's on us." With that, he handed the man his check.

"Well, that's mighty kind of you," the man said, "but I still have this problem with roaches and ants. Can you do that for me at no charge, too?"

They all laughed, even as Robert wrote out the contract for the $300 sale that resulted from his ethics, integrity, and honesty. Had they kept the check for the "record" (and unfair) bee job, they would have had a client who wondered if he had been "ripped off." By returning the money and doing the right thing, Robert's company was rewarded with a larger sale *and* a long-term client.

When you are honest and ethical and live with integrity, your rewards are guaranteed. They may not happen as quickly as they did for Robert Davis, but just like putting money in the bank guarantees a return, demonstrating the qualities of honesty, integrity, and ethical behavior will guarantee a positive return in your career.

Trust

The one thing that customers have *always* rated highest in the sales world is *trust*, which is a direct reflection of the integrity of the individual. The primary reason people will choose *not* to buy from you is lack of trust. When you make a serious promise to the prospect or a "casual comment" involving a promise, the prospect takes both as gospel. This is especially true if there is any difficulty during the sales process and even after the sale. If the person has any trouble in any phase of the relationship or use of the product, there is the distinct possibility that any "lack of follow-through" will be blown completely out of proportion. Even the tiniest matters become "deal shattering."

Listening

All successful sales professionals utilize listening skills to their fullest. Thus far in my career, I have never heard of anyone missing a sale because of listening to the prospect's needs, wants, and desires. Interestingly enough, the more salespeople know about their prospects' needs, the better position they are in to meet those needs. Not only that, but the trust factor goes up when the prospects see salespeople intensely listening to their needs and desires.

Listening is just *not* as difficult as we make it. When we are *not* talking or *preparing* to talk, we can listen. There are many steps and even week-long courses in developing listening skills, but for our needs here we can use the old saying, "Talking is sharing, but listening is caring."

Reciprocity

When we carefully "listen" to the prospect's elaborate interests, desires, hobbies, and other thoughts, we are putting them in debt to us. They then have a feeling they "owe" us something, and consequently, are more willing to "listen" to our story since we have given them the courtesy of listening to them.

Communication Specifics

Most people like to listen at the same speed they speak, so whenever possible adjust your speech patterns to conform to those of the prospect. Some exceptions to this policy are the following:

1. The prospect "loses his cool" and gets loud and abusive. When anger enters the picture, lower your voice and slow your rate of speech.
2. The prospect uses crude or profane language. Keep your language clean and professional. Chances are excellent that the prospect will judge you by a higher standard than he judges himself. The higher the level of moral dignity and integrity, the higher the level of trust and respect. The higher the level of trust and respect, the better your chances of making the sale.
3. The prospect speaks so quietly you must strain to hear every word. Keep your voice level at a comfortable volume so you are certain you are being heard. The prospect will not work as hard to understand you as you will to understand him.
4. The prospect speaks so agonizingly slow or so incredibly fast that if you emulate him or her completely, the distraction would be obvious. You should make some adjustment in the direction of the prospect's speech pattern.
5. Never conform to speech accents, bad grammar, slang, or speech impediments.

Today's Sales Professional

The successful sales professional knows that happiness is not pleasure, it is victory; that when you do what you need to do when you need to do it, you will eventually be able to do what you _want_ to do when you want to do it. And most important, the successful sales professional _knows_ and _understands_ the sales credo: _You can have everything in life you want if you will just help enough other people get what they want!_

Excerpted from _Selling 101: What Every Successful Sales Professional Needs to Know_ by Zig Ziglar, (pp. 9–15), copyright ©2003. Reprinted with permission by Thomas Nelson Publishers.

There is a certain aura surrounding a masterful seller that is hard to define. All masters exhibit a deep sense of self-worth, focus, and generosity that becomes integral to their success in selling. Called a "brilliant maverick," Kim George, coach, trainer, and author shows us how to measure this depth of character that up to now could only be vaguely sensed.

THE ABUNDANT SALES PERSON

KIMBERLY GEORGE

I introduced the concept of AQ (Abundance Intelligence™) in my book, _Coaching into Greatness: 4 Steps to Success in Business and Life_ (Wiley, 2006), as a new form of intelligence. AQ is different from IQ (Intelligence Quotient) in that we measure a person's ability to perform at his or her optimal level consistently and authentically. AQ measures masterful people by their prevalence of abundance aptitudes, patterns, and beliefs. It turns out that masterful sales people have a high AQ.

People with high AQs believe that that there is more than enough to go around. They have the ability to be who they are in the world, which is attractive and magnetic to customers. As salespeople, they believe they already have everything they need to make the sale. Not only is the proverbial glass half full—it is *overflowing*. These people are inspired and pulled forward by an internal conviction that they are on a path that is just right for them. They connect with success by visualizing a successfully closed sales transaction. Abundant sales people are more than just positive thinkers; they attract customers like bees to honey. They accept that life is not always easy and doesn't always follow the straight and convenient path. They don't fight changes encountered in their world, instead they adapt to those changes.

Abundant salespeople sense a distinctive inherent greatness as their birthright. These people demonstrate self-confidence, but not as arrogance or in a manner that diminishes people around them. Customers feel built-up and improved after interacting with abundant salespeople. Believing their inner beliefs, perceptions, and attitudes directly influences their directions and opportunities, their sales attitude is, "If you're not hitting your sales targets, your life targets might not be lined up properly."

By contrast, a person holding a "scarcity" attitude has a fundamental belief that there isn't enough to go around for everyone, so he thinks, "I have to get more than my fair share." This position holds that the person who collects the most will be the winner.

Often underachieving, scarcity people resist their own greatness because their limited vision fogs the view of how they fit into the future. Since they *think* in terms of lack, these people believe there is no sense in overachieving because they very likely won't get their fair share. Scarcity boxes us in and defines us according to external factors that are out of our control.

Based on in-depth work with hundreds of business owners, I have noted seven key aptitudes that clearly define a position of Abundance Intelligence™. Salespeople with these aptitudes excel at their craft by asking for more customers and closing more sales, while building their own social capital.

1. *Self-worth*. Abundant salespeople understand their uniqueness by how they add value to customers during the sales process. They confidently use sales strategies and tactics that allow them to comfortably express their values and beliefs to the prospective customer.

2. *Empathy*. Abundant salespeople do their best to understand and then serve their customer in any given situation. They know that if they are severely distraught, tired, sick, or stressed, they will not be able to give their best, so maintaining a healthy attitude is critical. They sustain themselves through tough times by networking with supportive friends who are able to empathically provide reciprocal support.

3. *Self-expression*. These people are convinced that they are the best with whom to do business. They retain a professional posture of sticking to their personal standards, which pulls people to them. When they ask for the client's business or referrals, their quiet inner confidence puts people at ease.

4. *Actualization*. Abundant salespeople don't sit on the sidelines, waiting for things to happen. They take actions consistent with their skills and talents. They accept responsibility for their own actions and don't blame others for shortcomings. If they face a barrier, they ask for help and support to find an acceptable solution for all sides. They comfortably give and receive.

5. *Significance*. Abundant salespeople are confident about their uniqueness, knowing they are the best person for a particular job. They demonstrate self-confidence when asking for business, building their social capital, and following up.

6. *Surrender*. An abundant salesperson doesn't view surrender as a form of weakness, rather a sign of letting go of old habits, attitudes, and behaviors that don't serve them in a healthy way. They see potential opportunity in everything that passes by.

7. *Inquiry*. High Abundance Intelligence means high openness to other points of view. Uncertainty is a reason to thrive and be curious.

Security in their curious and creative aptitude enables these people to move through all challenging situations. Learning while acting keeps them growing and improving while being pioneers in their industry.

Can you see any of the above characteristics in your own persona? Each of these abundant aptitudes contributes to purposeful actions and a well-defined goal orientation to the effort. Instead of being derailed by worrying about the past or the future, these masterful people find inspiration and forward momentum in their immediate surroundings.

———•·•———

Networking and building relationships are similar to growing a savings account: The more you put in, the more you can draw out later. If you want help from others, you must first make social deposits to your account. Myron Waldman, currently the founder of an internet marketing firm, got his start by building enterprises that invented industrial devices, and then selling them worldwide. He reminds us that being well-liked and getting great referrals is not the whole picture: you must also deliver the goods as promised if you want to be a good salesperson. Adding to quality capital is as important as adding to social capital.

———•·•———

SOCIAL CAPITAL + QUALITY CAPITAL = SELLING MORE!

MYRON WALDMAN

Selling efficiently begins with a promise of committing to developing excellent social and quality capital. Together, these two forces will help you close faster on many more new customers. Think of social capital as the lamp fixture and quality capital as the bulb. The lamp can be stylish, promising a bright, cheery room that draws people inside. But without a reliable and working bulb, the value of the complete lamp is discounted. When speaking of sales efficiency, we mean attracting more significant sales with expenditure of less effort and time to get the job done because we accumulated lots of social and quality capital.

According to Dictionary.com, social capital refers to the connections between individuals that are economically valuable, as a result of people or firms thinking about those individuals possessing high social capital, when the first party needs something done. In other words, building up one's social capital happens through the accumulation of strong, long-term, network-worthy relationships. This form of personal capital certainly helps you obtain new clients—many of whom come through word-of-mouth referrals.

Lilliane considers each of her potential mortgage clients "clients for life." Her concern for people is expressed even in her initial prospective-client interviews. An existing client referred to her a newly remarried couple who were close to retirement. The woman had excellent investing habits and built wealth, while the man earned a good income but neglected to accumulate savings. Their marriage would be the third for each one, and they wanted to buy a home together.

Lilliane produced a creative solution that had, as its first concern, protecting their new relationship. Lilliane was certain their diverse money management habits would collide and create dissention. To protect their relationship, Lilliane arranged an 80 percent mortgage for them, and for the husband (who didn't have enough cash for his equal share), she arranged a second mortgage to finance his portion of the down payment. He was to be solely responsible for this second mortgage. Both were very appreciative of her extra effort to respect their diverse financial habits and still achieve their mutual goal of home ownership.

Lilliane expects to gain future business from the couple's adult children and their friends, because she now has a new client for life. But she also has to be aware of accumulating quality capital. She must keep up her quality capital if she expects to gain their future business. Quality capital is something slightly different.

I discovered the existence of quality capital by listening to salespeople tell stories about "the big client that got away." Listening to these stories, I discovered that a sale can easily be lost through a lack of quality capital. This type of personal capital comes from consistency in the way that I sell and provide goods and services to others. Accumulating one's quality capital means ensuring that each and every product or service you provide is exactly as you promised. Quality capital is built on your own professional integrity or the integrity of your company.

Jerry owns and operates a gift shop specializing in regional goods. He maintains his quality capital by visiting his suppliers each year, even those 2,000 miles away. A high-tech company, knowing about Jerry's reputation for quality, placed an order with him for premium-priced custom promotional items. The order represented a new opportunity for Jerry, who never planned on being in the promotional products industry. Nonetheless, Jerry and his staff carefully checked each item received and delivered only the flawless items. Several months later, the company placed another order for even higher-priced items. Jerry knew that even one flawed item would turn the customer away—forever. He was quite aware that his investment in social capital was worthless without quality capital.

Together, social capital and quality capital create a strong selling force that accelerates your sales success. Let's look at how this works in a service business.

Steve is a young attorney who left a larger law firm so he could focus more on people. He knows that to gain clients he must sell his service, but because of Steve's high social capital, his prospects are almost always referrals from existing clients. As Steve says, "People seem to like me, and I clearly like people."

Steve went on to explain that his quality capital is silent while his social capital is loud. I asked him what he meant by "silent" and "loud." He said that "as a business lawyer my job is to prevent problems. If I can't solve a problem, that same problem creates visibility or "loudness," which could wipe out much of my quality capital as a professional lawyer."

He continues, "Some [prospective clients] just don't match up well with my strengths or personality, so I tell them that I'll take the time to find another attorney for them who will be compatible to their needs." By working to always provide a quality service, he also enhances his social capital. "Apparently, leading a prospective client to a more suitable attorney sends a powerful message about me, and it pays off by getting those same people to refer their friends to me later on."

Using social and quality capital to increase their sales efficiency, Jerry, Steve, and Lilliane have fast growing businesses, and they are respected for their sales achievements. Each found that quality capital was essential to making social capital work, and with their increased sales efficiency, they set the stage for more orders.

Attending to the above tips will influence your customers' buying decisions. The consumer may start by gathering facts about their preferred purchase, but the ultimate purchase decision is heavily influenced by the consumer's sixth sense about the seller. The consumer's intuition comes from their sense about your personal integrity, your quality capital, and your ability to help them.

Successful sellers appear to fully embrace life and people around them, acting like a magnet drawing even more potential customers to them. Ron and Joanna Stark intuitively understand and demonstrate this through their personal experiences in law, writing, and business. They illustrate the inseparable correlation between success in business, sales, and human relations through the following story.

THE ART OF MONUMENTAL SALES

RON AND JOANNA STARK

"Starving artist" is a common image because artists are seen as notoriously bad salespeople who can't sell their masterpieces. They may have tons of creative talent, but most artists can't make a living by selling their works alone. But some notable exceptions to the rule stand out.

One such exception is a talented businessman who, in his mid-50s, left a career with business and sales experiences to become an internationally acclaimed sculptor with solid financial success in a time span of ten years. John Kennedy delights thousands of people around the world with his graceful monuments of bronze illustrating the power and depth of relationships. His work is also representative of his own experience in selling and business.

His early career included a stint in the British merchant navy, a job in photojournalism with UPI, and time as a public relations director, author, inventor, nightclub owner, and manager of a major English rock-and-roll star. In the 1980s, John and his family moved to Palm Springs, where he pursued his passion for sculpting. Within a decade, his gentle, sleek bronze renderings were sought by collectors in England, Switzerland, Germany, France, and throughout the United States.

Asked how he became so successful so quickly, his immediate answer was, "You must pay as much attention to business as you do your craft. You must be able to sell your goods, and that begins with selling yourself. My sales technique, if you must call it that, is based entirely on relationships. It is very simple, really. It is about my relationship with myself, my family, friends, business associates, and my customers. Selling is an art unto itself—that begins with you."

The following is a list of steps that John felt most influenced his success (and that of others):

- *Believe in your passion and also your abilities.* As an artist, the product is the artist as well as the sculpted product. It's critically important to represent your product with conviction.

- *Identify the type of customer you need to be successful.* List the people most likely to purchase your products. Focus your primary efforts on your most likely target market, with a goal of discovering common experiences that can lead to a sense of camaraderie.
- *Regularly exercise your network of contacts; encourage word-of-mouth referrals.* Create personal connections between your customers and you. In John's situation, he often entertained in his home where his sculptures were also the featured décor. Guests "brought friends," thereby exposing more people to his product and giving John the opportunity to build new relationships.
- *Create winnable business dealings for all parties.* During your negotiations, be respectful of your customer and yourself so you always have a door open to future dealings.
- *Cherish your customer.* Let your customers know that you appreciate their business and enjoy the common relationship. Use the simple, powerful phrase, "Thank you for your business."
- *Avoid flippant sales clichés.* John never used the words "deal" or "close." (*"Save that for cars and cards,"* he said!) Be intelligent, thoughtful, and respectful, and use clear communication, avoiding sales rhetoric.
- *Be grateful and give back.* John embraced the philosophy to giving back to his community by donating sculptures for personal causes. His act of giving returned through increased recognition and sales of his work.
- *Take time to enjoy your business, your craft, the people in your life, and life itself.* It will show and is very contagious!

John embraced these ideals with his characteristic charm. He welcomed everyone into his studio and life, calling out equally a cheery, "Hello, my friend!" It made no difference to him whether that person was the housekeeper or a Hollywood celebrity. He understood the importance of selling who you are and what you represent while respecting your fellow man.

John's years of networking led to the pinnacle of his career: In May 2002, actor/singer/humanitarian Harry Belafonte and United Nations

Secretary Kofi Annan unveiled John Kennedy's work, the "Spirit of Audrey," a bronze, seven-foot, lyrical rendering of Audrey Hepburn. Commissioned by Robert Wolders, Audrey Hepburn's last love, the sculpture was positioned in the United Nations Plaza to commemorate her work with the children of the world.

Kennedy's belief in the power of relationships and the art of sales was clearly evident from the tearful, contemplative people in the pews at his memorial service in 2004. We all were secretly confident that we had been his very best friend.

———•·•———

Winning the game of selling takes full knowledge of the fundamental plays, and also takes the right tools, one of which is a winning attitude. This attitude predisposes one to always look for opportunities to enter and win another race.

Debbra Sweet, owner of a promotional company, knows how to increase sales volume with higher profit margins through a never-give-up mind-set.

———•·•———

MASTERING THE MIND-SET

DEBBRA SWEET

Knowledge, process, and enthusiasm alone are not sufficient to become a master at selling. While you do indeed need to master the fundamentals of selling, the competitive edge for a salesperson comes from having the proper mindset. Being mentally prepared to sell fits everywhere in the selling process, and especially with you, the seller. To illustrate the importance of mind-set, I will share two examples.

More Than Sales Technique

I was recently involved in training a new sales rep in my company to sell our marketing, advertising, and promotional products. Our sales process is very structured and easily produces consistent sales. My new rep understood the concept and mechanics, and she knew how to present the benefits of dealing with our company.

Believing in what we do, she consistently closed $200 sales. The problem was that most of the other reps walked away with $2,000 sales, using the same presentation and selling program. We coached her on all the mechanics of selling; finally, in frustration, we asked her: "What is a lot of money to you?" Her response was, "$200." It is not a coincidence that her sales averaged $200. The difference between us was that my mind-set for the sale started at $2,000, while her mind-set started at $200.

In her mind, $200 was a lot of money, so she assumed everyone else felt the same way. She never shared her opinion with us or our clients, yet her mind-set about money held her back. It prevented her from conveying the underlying conviction necessary for a more masterful sales result.

It took her a couple of weeks to make the mental shift, but once she shifted her mind-set, her $200 orders became $700, $2,000, even $5,000 orders! To increase her success, all she needed to do was shift her mind-set.

Much can be accomplished by a mere shift in one's mind-set. Mastering your mind-set is more than understanding the relative impact of price on customers. It also includes being open to existing opportunities, which are often within an arm's length. The following is a perfect example.

Embrace Unexpected Opportunities

I was driving to an appointment last summer when my truck blew a tire. I slowed to the shoulder of the busy highway, and thankfully a tow truck right behind me pulled over and blocked me from traffic.

As he volunteered to follow me to the nearest garage, I noticed his imprinted jacket (one of the products I sell). As I was thanking him 15 minutes later at a tire shop, I saw a potential opportunity. I opened a conversation about our respective businesses, during which he mentioned his possible need for imprinted items in the near future. We exchanged business cards, and he drove away. Because I was without transportation for a few days, awaiting the arrival of my specially ordered tires, I decided to follow up on the opportunity presented me.

First I called the tow truck driver and found out that he had an event for which he needed imprinted apparel . . . but it was in a week. Knowing I could help him in time, I went to work on getting what he needed. I also spoke to the manager at the tire shop, which was part of a national chain and got the contact information for the purchasing department of the tire company. I made my first sales call by cell phone. I ended my day spending $500 on new tires, and closing a $1,000 sale with the tow truck driver. I also started pursuing a major corporate sale with a large tire company. Not too bad for blowing out a tire on the side of the road!

Instead of giving into a demoralizing mind-set related to having to buy new expensive tires, I seized two new selling opportunities: one with the tow operator and the second with the tire shop guys helping me. Masterful sellers develop their mind-set of opportunity over time by looking for it, learning to recognize the opportunity, and beginning to follow through. Sales can happen anytime, anywhere, and under any circumstances—even on the side of the road. You just have to master the mind-set to make it happen!

A persistent attitude is mandatory for success in any endeavor, including sales. No one knows this better than Janet Attwood, a sales master who transformed her selling experience to master communicator, facilitator, and trainer. You may need to stop banging your head against the wall and change directions, but don't stop too early—you might be closer to success than you realize! Listen to your intuitions, and you can make lots of money.

PERSISTENCE PAYS OFF!

JANET ATTWOOD

I learned a lesson about following my intuition from an early experience selling print advertisement space. Our company president created an advertisement for our clients: a four-page environmental feature using remnant space at a greatly discounted rate. If we sold all the discounted space, we still would earn great revenue on the feature, while using up our unsold (remnant) ad space in *USA Today*.

As soon as the logistics were in place for the *USA Today* feature, we began cold-calling targeted corporations. When we connected with a targeted advertising executive on the phone, we asked them the simple question, "What is your company doing that is good for the environment?" Once the exec told us what their company was doing environmentally, we started selling them on buying remnant space in our groundbreaking environmental feature, premiering in the prominent *USA Today*. We told them about the benefit of being seen in the *USA Today* advertisement feature and how it would create a lot of goodwill for their company. "And besides," we said to them, "the ad space prices can't be beat!"

One client I targeted was *Discovery Channel*. Everyday I called its number and every day I got the same taped voice mail. I diligently left messages, hoping that a woman named Joyce would return my call.

Determined to finally connect with Joyce at *Discovery Channel*, I called once again and, upon hearing a real woman answer the phone, stammered for words. Before I could launch into my pitch, the voice said, "Is this Janet Attwood?"

"Yes, this is she," I managed to say.

"Janet" she said, her tone of voice immediately sharpening. "You called me over 34 times and left voice messages at least 15 times! You have been persistent to the point of having a bad taste in my mouth! Please never call me again!" **CLICK.**

Horrified, I knew my day was over. Any further effort was futile. As my thoughts calmed, I kept returning to the vision of how the *Discovery Channel* was a perfect fit with our *USA Today* environmental feature, regardless of Joyce's thoughts about me. I had to call Joyce just one more time! All she could do was hang up on me and, at worse, call my company complaining of harassment.

But . . . something inside of me said to just keep going forward . . .

Do the Thing and It Is Yours

The next morning I walked into work, headed straight to my phone, dialed her number, and by luck, Joyce said hello. "Joyce, this is Janet Attwood—please don't hang up!" I said hurriedly. "Can you just give me two minutes?"

"What?" Joyce said, with certainly the most annoyed voice she had.

"Last night I just couldn't stop thinking how this environmental feature is perfect for *Discovery Channel*. Your message will go out all over the world, sharing all the wonderful things your company is doing for the environment, and I know you would agree with me that the price is definitely right, giving *Discovery Channel* tremendous return on your advertisement."

I said all this in a single breath. Then I stopped frozen in silence. After what seemed like many minutes, Joyce, in her still aggravated voice asked, "How much is a quarter of a page?"

"$40,000" I replied.

"I'll take it!"

She hung up, and I felt my heart pounding in my chest. I was petrified that she would hang up the minute she recognized me. After all, she had every right to! Calming my heart, I closed my eyes and breathed rhythmically to get myself back into my body.

Each breath brought more color to my face, and soon a smile took over my being! "I did it—I actually did it!" I breathed a huge sigh of relief. My biggest fear of "rejection and abandonment" was emotional baggage following me everywhere in life. For the first time in many years, I felt fearless as a result of that one phone call.

I remembered a quote I had heard a few years back, "Do the thing you fear the most and the death of it is certain!" Those words took on an even deeper meaning after that phone call. The good-sized commission I would make was great, but even better was the feeling of satisfaction I felt for listening to my inner voice saying, "This is the perfect venue for them—GO FOR IT!" I learned then and there about the powerful role played by our intuition, or inner voice.

Mastering any activity brings pleasurable feelings, but mastering that which you fear most or is your biggest barrier to success is cause for celebration, especially if you don't quit just before success is about to occur!

Success in sales means adapting to an environment that continues to undergo dramatic changes. The shifting sales paradigm now favors building relationships between buyer and seller, enabling careful identification and alleviation of buyer issues. Linda McCarthy, a successful marketing franchise owner in California, gives us an allegoric view of the sales shift from an aggressive and manipulative approach to one of consultation and reciprocity.

THE OCEAN OF SALES

LINDA McCARTHY

The best tip I can offer about being a masterful seller in this vast ocean of sales is to remind you that sales is all about *you*. Inevitably, you are the hook to "reel" in your prospect, and your personal character is the bait. If someone likes and trusts you, she will buy literally anything from you because she knows that you will only steer her on the right course. Masterful sellers must have rich human characteristics.

I love everything about the ocean. In her book *The Wealthy Spirit* (Sourcebooks, 2002), Chellie Campbell talks about human character in relation to three kinds of marine animals—sharks, tuna, and dolphins:

> *Dolphins are wonderful creatures: Intelligent, happy and play-ful. They communicate well; they swim in schools. They've been known to ward off a shark attack and protect other fish. They are fun loving and beautiful, arcing in graceful leaps over the waves.*
>
> *Tuna fish are food. They don't know that the blood in the water is their own. They think everything that happens to them is some-body else's fault. They take no responsibility for their choices.*
>
> *Sharks are eating machines. It's not their fault, they are born that way. But their job is to eat you. If you find yourself in the water with a shark, get out of the water fast!*

Selling strategies can be related to these three animals. Sales "sharks" are constantly hungry. All they care about is the "kill." You have seen sharks swimming around at a business event such as a chamber of commerce reception, handing out brochures/fliers, trying to close the deal at the event, and avoiding meaningful conversation with everyone. Doing business with them is painful at best. There are many "successful" sales sharks around, but their customers often leave the sales transactions dissatisfied.

Tuna are neither aggressive nor team players. They are often found alone in their offices or cars wasting time working on non-income earning activities. Tuna avoid business networking events in favor of staying at home watching *Judge Judy*. They blame the competition, the economy, or the weather for their poor productivity. Tuna are energy suckers (leeches). Tuna are not offensive salespeople because they hardly ever have the energy even to call you.

When a sales dolphin swims into a shark or tuna client's life, that client nearly always switches their buying to the dolphin, who understands the importance of forming a selling relationship and is genuinely interested in others. Dolphins are more relaxed and appear less "hungry" to make the sale. Dolphins make prospects feel welcome at business events, and through their follow-up, they end up with happy, loyal customers who gladly refer their friends.

Sharks are loners, unwilling to share their prey with others, while dolphins swim in schools, network, and are great team players. Clients feel safe and know their best interests are being looked after with the dolphin seller. In effect, dolphins understand the idea of "Givers Gain" and that goodwill given returns to them in some form or another.

Chellie sums it all up in her incredible book by saying, "Sharks will steal your money, and tuna will leech money from you. Real money is made when you have dolphins on your team."

Selling Goals
vs. Life Goals
(Pssst . . . They're Related!)

---

*Goals are merely those dreams for your life that
are fueled with sufficient passion.*
—DON MORGAN

I can hear the groans: "Another discussion about goal setting. How boring!" Well, boredom comes from repetition, and without repetition, masterful achievement is not possible. Reading more, practicing more, and understanding more about goals bring this part of selling into a normal daily routine where it motivates and guides the Master of Sales.

Our lives are directed and pulled by conscious and subconscious desires, which when aggregated become our future vision. This vision (whether to lose 25 pounds and be athletic or to consistently earn $10,000 commissions and be wealthy) is directed by our destination goals, but the more finite process goals help us get there. Treat each daily detail as an important process goal to achieve, and indeed these small ones will accumulate so that ultimately our larger vision becomes our reality. It is easy to derail our dreams by self-doubt, other people, and external events, so the only way to keep the vision alive is to transform it into tangible, goal-directed behavior.

Most goal-implementation plans require getting other people enrolled in our personal program. This is where person-to-person selling comes into the picture. In this instance, selling means convincing other people to give us something they have in return for something we possess. In a traditional view of selling, the buyer exchanges her money for our product. But in the real world, every person sells continually—whether ourselves on a first date, our beliefs, or our knowledge. If we sell successfully, we might achieve a goal of having an enjoyable evening date, public recognition or personal satisfaction as a return from our effort.

Setting the right environment to complete a sales transaction might include bringing flowers on the first date or artfully crafting a storefront window to allow those walking by a glimpse of the buying opportunities to be found inside the shop. The sales trainer might say, "Your goal is to create an environment (a stage) that causes your customer to feel like a VIP taking delivery on his Rolls Royce." The sales process is a very social activity, one that creatively mixes the buyer's goal of owning a solution with the seller's complex goals of meeting company targets, earning an income, and personally helping the customer. Learning this craft of goal satisfaction is never ending and forever challenges the master seller.

During the compilation of this book, we heard from Joan Fletcher, who wrote us about a very successful young salesman. In spite of his sales awards, his corner office, and charismatic charm, he still felt he was just scraping the surface of success.

Even though dutifully creating written goals, his level of self-satisfaction was low, until he realized that the big picture was not just about how much money he earned, or the big house, or the number of sales he hoped to close. The big picture was his vision about what he truly wanted to achieve in all combined areas of his life. Once he discovered this realization, his renewed selling accomplishments became directly tied to setting aside money for his daughter's education fund, to have time to help coach his son's soccer league, and to work in his yard. Even with more personal goals than before, his sales results climbed higher.

Work goals, selling goals, and life goals are intertwined . . . and each influences the others.

———•———

An inherent law of human nature states that each goal achieved by a (sales)person will open a new frontier. Each new frontier requires our creative intelligence to overcome the new challenges and achieve positive results. Brian Tracy—with more than three decades of experience, and 42 books on the subject of human potential, sales, and business; and developmental consulting with thousands of organizations and people—fully understands the process for goal achievement.

———•———

SET AND ACHIEVE ALL YOUR SALES GOALS

BRIAN TRACY

*If I've got correct goals, and I keep pursuing them the best way
I know how, everything else falls into line. If I do the right thing,
I know I'm going to succeed.*

—DAN DIERDORF

Top salespeople are intensely goal oriented. In every study, the quality of *goal orientation* seems to be associated with high levels of success and achievement. The highest-paid salespeople know in advance how much they are going to earn each week, each month, each quarter, and each year. They know how many calls they will have to make to achieve a particular level of sales, and they have clear plans about what they are going to do with the money they earn.

It is essential for your success that you decide exactly how much you intend to earn each year. If you are not absolutely clear about your earnings target, your sales activities will be unfocused. You will be like a person trying to shoot at a target in the fog. Even if you are the finest marksman in the world, you are not going to hit a target you can't see. You have to know exactly what you're aiming at.

Your Annual Income Goal
Begin with your annual income goal. How much do you intend to make in the next 12 months? What is the exact number? Write this number down. This becomes the target toward which you orient all your activities throughout the year.

You need a goal that is realistic, but challenging. Take your highest income year to date and increase that amount by 25 to 50 percent, whatever amount you are comfortable with. Be sure to make your goal believable and achievable. Ridiculous goals do not motivate you; they demotivate you, because deep in your heart, you know that they are unattainable. As a result, you will quit at the first sign of adversity.

Top salespeople in every field know exactly what they are going to earn each year and each part of each year. If you ask them, they can tell you within a dollar what they are aiming at every single day.

Low-performing salespeople have no idea how much they are going to earn. They have to wait until the end of the year and get their tax forms to find out what happened. For them, every day, month, and year is a new financial adventure. They have no idea where they are going to end up.

Put Them in Writing

To be effective, your goals must be in writing. Sometimes people are reluctant to write their goals down on paper. They say, "What if I don't make it?" You don't need to worry. The very act of writing your goals down increases your likelihood of achieving them by 1,000 percent—ten times—and usually far faster than you expected. Even if you don't hit your goal on schedule, it is still better for you to have a written goal than to have no goal at all.

Your Annual Sales Goal

The second part of goal setting is for you to ask yourself, "How much am I going to have to sell this year to achieve my personal income goal?"

This should not be too difficult to calculate. Even if you work on a combination of base plus commission, you should be able to determine the exact sales volume required for you to earn the amount of money that you want.

Monthly and Weekly Goals

Once you have decided your annual income and sales goals, break them down *by month*. How much will you have to earn and sell each month to achieve your annual goals?

Once you have your annual sales and income goals and your monthly sales and income goals, break them down to *weekly* sales and income goals. How much will you have to sell each week in order to achieve your long-term goals?

Daily Sales Goals

Finally, determine how much you have to *sell* each day to earn the amount you want to *earn* each day. Let us say that your annual income goal is $50,000. If you divide $50,000 by 12, you get approximately $4,200 per month. If you divide $50,000 by 50, the number of weeks that you work in an average year, it comes out to $1,000 per week. Now you have definite, specific targets to aim at.

Set Clear Activity Goals

The final step in setting sales goals is for you to determine the specific *activities* in which you must engage to achieve your desired sales level. How many *calls* will you have to make to get how many *appointments* with prospects? How many presentations and callbacks will you have to generate to achieve a specific level of sales?

When you keep accurate records day by day and month by month, you will soon be able to predict with considerable accuracy exactly what you will have to do each day and each week to achieve your monthly and annual income goals.

Let us assume that you will have to make ten prospecting calls a day to get sufficient appointments to make enough sales to achieve your goals. Make it a game with yourself to make your ten prospecting calls before noon each day. Set this as your daily activity target, and then discipline yourself to follow through on your plan.

Get on the phone by 8 or 8:30 in the morning, or get out and cold-call, if you have to. Whatever you do, force yourself to make your ten calls before noon, every single day, until it becomes a habit.

You Control Your Sales Life

The most important part of planning your activities is knowing that sales activities *are controllable*. You can*not* decide or determine where a particular sale will come from. But you can control the *inputs*, the activities that you must engage in to achieve the sales in the first place. And by controlling your activities, you indirectly control your sales results.

Some days and weeks will be better than others. Sometimes you will make a lot of sales, and sometimes you won't make any. Sometimes you will have dry periods and sales slumps. Other times you will sell two or three times as much as you projected. But the law of averages is at work. It is inexorable. If you just keep on making the necessary calls, you will eventually make your sales, on schedule.

Your Results May Amaze You

In many cases, when you start setting goals for the week, month, and year, and start working toward them systematically each day, you will hit those goals far *faster* than you expected. Many of my students set one-year goals and hit them in six or seven months. Some people have actually hit their sales goals for the entire year in as little as three months.

Whenever you start setting clear, specific goals for every part of your sales life, you will be amazed at the results. Some of my seminar participants had worked for years selling a particular product in a specific market. But they had never set goals before. The first year after they began setting goals, their sales exploded. They suddenly started breaking sales records, even though they were still selling the same product out of the same office, to the same people at the same prices. Goal setting made the difference.

Tap into Your Subconscious Mind

This happens because the very act of *writing* a goal programs it into your subconscious mind. Once you have programmed a goal into your subconscious mind, it takes on a power of its own. Your subconscious mind works 24 hours per day, sleeping and waking, and starts guiding you rapidly toward the achievement of this goal.

Once you have programmed a goal into your subconscious mind, it takes on a power of its own.

Your subconscious alerts you to opportunities and possibilities around you. It brings you the right ideas for the right things to say, sometimes in the middle of a sales conversation. Once you program a goal into your subconscious mind, it continually motivates you into taking the actions necessary to achieve it.

Sometimes, your subconscious mind will help you read your prospect's face, giving you a better sense of what to say. Everyone has experienced being in a sales presentation where he simply couldn't make a mistake or say the wrong word. The sales presentation went smoothly from beginning to end and concluded with a closed sale. Whenever this happens, it is because your mind is perfectly programmed, at a subconscious level, to enable you to perform at your best in the pursuit of your goals.

The Right Words at the Right Time

When you feel excellent about yourself, your subconscious mind will give you exactly the right words at exactly the right time. It will make you sensitive to physical cues and verbal clues that will guide you to bring up a subject that you hadn't even thought about. But it will turn out, from the customer's point of view, to be exactly the right thing to say.

You might mention that your company has an excellent reputation for customer service and after-sales follow-up. You later learn that this was the prospect's primary concern and was exactly what he needed to hear in order to buy from you.

As previously stated, the average person uses only 10 percent of his potential. By programming your subconscious mind with clear goals, you gain access to the 90 percent of your potential that lies beneath the surface, deep in your subconscious mind. You program your subconscious and access it on a regular basis by deciding exactly how much you want to earn and precisely what activities you will have to undertake to earn that amount of money.

The Number-One Reason for Success

In my work with more than 500,000 salespeople throughout the United States and in 25 countries, I have found that the commitment to goal setting has been the number-one reason for the success of the top people. All the highest-paid sales professionals in every field are committed goal setters. They write and rewrite their goals every day. They continually add to their lists. They access and activate their subconscious and superconscious minds. They begin to attract into their lives people and circumstances that help them achieve their goals.

See Yourself as the Best

Continually imagine yourself as the very best in your field. See yourself as one of the highest money earners in your business. Model yourself after the highest-paid salespeople in your industry. Walk, talk, and treat others as if you were already a sales superstar.

When you see someone else driving a new car or dressed in expensive clothes and wearing an expensive watch, say to yourself, "That's for me!"

You decide that whatever anyone else has accomplished, you can achieve as well. There are no limits.

From _The Psychology of Selling: How to Sell More, Easier and Faster than You Ever Thought Possible_ by Brian Tracy, copyright ©2004, Nelson Business. Used by permission.

———•◦•———

Do you remember the children's fable about the fox not being able to reach the succulent grapes and then saying, "Oh they were probably sour anyway; I didn't really want them"? It is easy to lose sight of your dreams unless you allow passion to drive you forward. Julien Sharp transitioned her business solutions and consulting organization to a communications specialty firm, and certainly knows how to make things happen. Read on to discover her secrets.

———•◦•———

FROM MICKEY MOUSE
TO CRUISE SHIPS

JULIEN SHARP

As a child in the late '70s, I didn't miss a single episode of *The New Mickey Mouse Club*. And after each episode, I sobbed into my pillow because I wanted to be one of the kids on that show. I wanted to be a musical performer . . . more than anything in the world.

I grew up in a rural area near Indianapolis, and times were tough. But my parents fed my music passion with guitar, piano, and voice lessons, and drove the 15-mile round trip to school for my music and drama activities. Sadly, it was not enough . . . I would never get to be on *The Mickey Mouse Club*. We lived too far from California, and by the time I could get there, I'd be way too old to be a Mouseketeer.

Fortunately, as a teenager, I was able to perform at local events and built a small reputation as a singer. One year, our family took our most spectacular holiday ever, a Christmas cruise. While shipboard, I encountered a new dream: My longing to perform on *The Mickey Mouse Club* transitioned to a desperate longing to be a cruise ship entertainer.

My father was a Chrysler auto employee, and he had continually lived under the threat of unemployment during the company's hard times. However, under the guidance of Lee Iacocca, Chrysler's fortunes turned around, and my father's job was preserved. After being awarded a Chrysler Scholarship for college tuition, I was so impressed that I read all about the great man who made this possible. One of Lee Iacocca's quotes jumped into my very soul: "You've got to say, 'I think that if I keep working at this and want it badly enough, I can have it.' It's called perseverance."

This idea became my mantra, and it was put to a hard test when I decided to pursue in earnest my dream of performing on a cruise ship. That summer before college, I worked and saved all the money I could toward a single-minded project: selling someone on hiring me to sing on a cruise ship. My dream converged into my all-encompassing goal.

Research Your Client

It was 1986, before Google Search; even finding the name and address of a cruise ship company seemed impossible. But focused on my goal, I ordered Miami's white and yellow phone books and scoured them for cruise ship companies. Next I prepared a query package to send to my list of companies. *(I understand now that I was conducting target market research, prospecting for customers, and preparing a product presentation. But then, all I was trying to do was to get a dream job.)*

My friends scoffed at my diligence, saying, "No one is ever going to hire someone from Indiana to work on a cruise ship." My family, while indulgent, worried that I was spending my college money on a "pipe dream."

Rehearse Your Presentation

Lee Iacocca's words drove me forward (*"it's called perseverance"*). At a local record-it-yourself studio, I sang my heart into a well-worn microphone to create a demo cassette tape. Packaged up with the most professional photo I could afford, I sent my demo presentation with an introductory letter detailing my experience, education, and—going for broke—the absolute *passion* I had for achieving my goal. "A person who wants this as badly as I do," I wrote, "will make an excellent member of your team."

Enthusiasm Is Your Best Selling Tool

All my money and every ounce of emotional desire went into 12 demo packages destined for Miami. Four months after I started college, I received a letter from just one of the cruise lines. It had an opening for a youth counselor/entertainer to join its staff for a three-week cruise during the holiday season. It didn't matter what the job description was, all I saw were the words "might I be interested?" The most rewarding phrase in that letter was the staffing manager's comment that the company usually didn't hire based on unsolicited requests, but my letter, and the effort I had obviously put into my package, showed the spunk and drive that it wanted on its staff team! The company sent me a ticket, and that Christmas I was

singing and working in the Southern Caribbean. I worked for the line during summers and holidays throughout my college years.

Later, after completing a degree in business, I built a successful career in
the cruise industry as an entertainer, cruise director, and onboard entertainment manager. The lessons I learned from travel at sea had a powerful and
positive impact on my current consulting business. At an early age I learned,

1. to convert my dream to a specific goal,
2. how to research my target market,
3. to create an impassioned sales presentation, and
4. to sell with passion.

I have never forgotten in all these years the important lesson: to "think
that if I keep working at this and want it badly enough, I can have it." I had
to have the perseverance to finish what it took to achieve my goal, and I
had to realize that perseverance virtually never comes into play without
the first two words in the quote: "I think . . ."

Persist in Chasing Your Sales Goal

Translate "I think" to "I believe" *in the possibility of successfully achieving
my goal.* Your perseverance will not last without the intrinsic belief that
you have the ability to achieve it. Some folks never get to persevere because
they don't believe they could start something in the first place. They come
to believe in their negative self-talk.

"You'll never be able to do *that . . .*" or "I don't know the right people to
achieve *that . . .*" or "I can't do this, because of [insert any excuse here]."
Negative self-talk can seem to protect a person from having to do things that
are difficult or scary. Salespeople can be afraid of their inability to accomplish
an objective, and they can become afraid of rejection from the prospect.
Either way, negative self-talk destroys initiative and self-confidence.

To prevent negative self-talk, visualize a successful result to an ambi-
tious project. When I believed that hard work could get me on the cruise
ship, I put the ball in motion. A lot of steps (process goals) had to be
climbed up, but as I started making the demo tape, taking the pictures,
mailing the packets, and making dozens of follow-up calls, I also started to
enjoy the process. I didn't realize then that my actions were identical to a

selling cycle. The crowning achievement of getting my dream job was tremendously exciting. The excitement I felt then is shared by all salespeople everywhere when they land that big client!

———•◦•———

Comparing an Olympic high jumper to an average Joe is simple. Both can jump, but the Olympian makes a successful career from jumping by following a daily jumping regimen, while our average Joe may jump once a month. Similarly, the sales master follows a daily, goal-oriented routine each day, each week, each month, and all the way through the year. Ed Craine operates a successful marketing franchise and a mortgage business in San Francisco. He makes this point by telling us the story of a million-dollar salesman.

———•◦•———

MILLION DOLLAR SALES GOAL: HELP ENOUGH PEOPLE

ED CRAINE

Selling more than 100 loans a month for borrowers in Albuquerque, New Mexico, Greg Frost is one of the most successful loan agents in the United States. He closes one in every 11 loans for people buying existing homes, giving him a 9 percent share of the existing market. Considering the 689 mortgage companies, banks, and other lenders employing over 2,000 loan agents in his community, Greg is a masterful seller, known in his community as the the "Roger Bannister" of the mortgage industry. Bannister was the first person to run a mile in less than four minutes, and Greg Frost is believed to be the first loan agent to generate a $1,000,000 annual commission as a mortgage broker. Ranked consistently in the top ten highest producing mortgage brokers in the United States, Greg is also a highly sought after mortgage sales trainer.

Growing up in an East Los Angeles barrio, the son of Depression Era parents, Greg knew that if he were to go to college, he'd have to pay his own way. His parents were encouraging, but their income was subsistence. His first big lesson in goal achievement came about when he qualified for a football athletic scholarship. He had a small physical build, but in high school he bought a book on football, went out for the team, and dedicated himself to the goal. Hard, disciplined work allowed him to win an athletic football scholarship at the University of New Mexico.

I'm Poor but Don't Have to Be

In 1968, with his scholarship, a trunk containing all his belongings, and $47, Greg understood for the first time that he was poor. Instead of taking stock of what he didn't have, he focused on one overriding thought. "From this day forward, I can be anything I want to be."

A university football star, he was drafted by the Denver Broncos in the National Football League. Three and a half weeks after joining the Broncos in training camp, he was cut and sent back to Albuquerque, where he got a low-level job quarterbacking an ice cream parlor. Another employee's father was president of the nearby bank, and it didn't take long for Greg to go over to the bank and sell himself to the father and into the banking business, and later into his own multimillion-dollar sales organization. His story teaches us that masterful sellers are not born, but rather developed through a learned, goal-oriented process. The beauty of Greg's story is that we too can accomplish our goals.

Goal 1: Invest in Yourself

Part of Greg's success comes from a concept of investing in oneself. At an early age, Greg's mother introduced him to *Think and Grow Rich* by Napoleon Hill (Avetine Press, 2004). Greg still starts each year by reading this book and setting new goals. His standard annual goal is to close at least one more loan than the year before. To feed his mind, Greg never stopped learning. Realizing that real education starts after graduating from college, he attends a business training event every three months. He studies topics in his mortgage industry and sales training courses from other industries. He learns how other professionals sell in other industries so he can re-craft their techniques and strategies for his own benefit.

Goal 2: Disciplined Approach

Learning requires discipline. When Greg chose to become a football star, he bought a book on football and read it cover to cover. He practiced on the field and at home. He arrived at practices early and stayed late, to learn all he could from the coach. As a teenager, he was too light for football, so he went to the gym and lifted weights. His early disciplined behavior carries forward to his disciplined practice of eating breakfast and lunch with a client, prospect, or potential referral partner every day.

Goal 3: Build a Social Capital (Network)

Greg says, "Make friends with people you do business with and do business with your friends." Greg's daily one-on-one scheduled breakfast and lunch meetings feed his goal of building strong social capital with his clients. This discipline gives him an opportunity for two meetings for each of the 22 business days in a month, or 44 monthly quality sales calls! The social capital created through this sales habit helps mitigate the inevitable problems that occur during a long mortgage transaction.

Goal 4: Communicate Proactively

"Communication is the lubricant of every well-run organization," says Greg, himself a profound communicator. Never wanting a client to call in with a problem, his goal is to anticipate client needs and questions through a proactive approach to communications. He employs all manner of communication techniques, including face time, voice time, and automated communication. He uses it all to help succeed with his clients.

Goal 5: Help People

Sales is a "helping" business, and Greg Frost loves helping people. "If you love to help people, you'll have a rewarding and productive sales career," he says. If you don't, chances are you won't last long. There's an old saying in sales, "Help enough people get what they want in life, and you'll get everything you want."

Selling and acting are similar; both use staging and "players." The stage provides an overall environment for the players to act out the story. Staging the selling environment has a lot to do with directing the sales staff, who must then motivate and direct the buyers. Dawn Pastores brings an extensive adult educational background to motivating her sales clients with new word-of-mouth selling tools and her LTC (Leadership Teamwork and Customer Relations) approach.

SETTING THE STAGE FOR SALES SUCCESS

DAWN S. PASTORES

As a poor college student, I got a job in an outbound calling center soliciting cash donations for a state university. The call center didn't have a positive employee environment, and the management made the staff members feel incompetent. But it was the best-paying job on campus, and I had to pay for college, eat, and pay rent.

I knew how to sell, earning top awards at previous selling positions. This new job, however, challenged my ability. The management style at my job was known as "Theory X" (Douglas MacGregor): People are motivated by fear. To ratchet up our motivation, the sales managers threatened to lay off those who didn't reach optimal closing ratios.

One of our target markets was the parents of current students. The parents were not willing prospects, feeling that they already paid more than enough for tuition and educational expenses.

Money Kept Me Going

The call center took away all my joy of selling, but I stayed with the job because I needed the money. It soon became apparent to me that management by *fear* was going to fail because 50 percent of the staff, including me, was not even close to the required numbers. Ultimately, 60 percent of the staff left, whether voluntarily or otherwise.

From that experience I learned an invaluable lesson about the important role that environment plays in selling successfully. Salespeople will not meet high level achievements through imposition of tight boundaries and use of fear. This approach demoralizes them, and in this type of environment sales staff won't stay late to make the extra calls, or do anything that isn't bare-bones required.

My money-motivated persistence ultimately got me promoted to supervisor, responsible for hiring and training new job applicants. Drawing on my experience, I slowly discovered how to create a positive selling environment that empowered salespeople to achieve great results.

Finding Other Motivators for Top Performers

Management-imposed goals don't build Masters of Sales. After the basic income needs are met, other challenges are needed to inspire great achievements. I engaged my employees by allowing them to set their own goals within the center's parameters. I discovered that achieving a sales goal is directly proportionate to the salesperson's ability to set personally relevant goals. My job was to help salespeople get motivated from within and then reinforce that inner drive through external environmental reinforcement. This reinforcement included better training, improved management of time on the job, and the right word said at the right time

It isn't enough to just coerce or scare someone into doing his or her job. To achieve real success, people have to buy in to the job. I was able to achieve this in part by training my telemarketing sales team on the WHYs of calling. We talked about why we called a particular constituency and why we thought it would benefit the school. For the call center to be successful, each seller had to be clear about their message and WHY they were doing it.

Allowing sellers to change or modify their work environment and participate in activities that influence their performance releases their selling power. Our demoralized sales group was converted to a team that helped each other learn how to overcome objections and persuade clients to make cash donations. Each team member believed in the higher purpose of wanting to see academics become more successful through the cash infusions brought in from our work at the call center. Our new vision and energy replaced the days of low-energy-begging-for-money phone solicitations. This new team had passionate and grassroots understanding of university funding, and was committed to helping academics succeed. Part of our program also included a recognition program for the exemplary performers, and we gave out a lot of rewards.

Oh yes, about our results: we achieved our annual goal SIX months early!

Masterful salespeople are ruled by multidimensional human desires that pull and push them in different directions. Masters learn to be deliberate about using goal setting to sort through these desires to forge a lifestyle that balances sales and career goals with the rest of their life. Our next contributing author, Anthony Robbins, is a world-renowned expert on setting goals, and his words can be applied to salespeople working all around the globe, and in just about any market or industry.

CREATING A COMPELLING FUTURE

ANTHONY ROBBINS

What we are going to do now is take the first step in turning the invisible into the visible, in making your dreams a reality. By the time we are finished, you will have created for yourself an anticipation so great, a future so compelling, that you can't help but take the first steps today.

We'll be covering four areas:

1. Personal development goals
2. Career/business/economic goals
3. Toys/adventure goals, and
4. Contribution goals.

For each of these you'll have a set period of time in which to brainstorm. Write rapidly—keep your pen moving, don't censor yourself, just get it all down on paper. Constantly ask yourself, *what would I want for my life if I knew I could have it any way I wanted it? What would I go for if I knew I could not fail?* Suspend the need to know precisely *how*. Just discover what it is you truly want. Do this without questioning or doubting your capability.

Remember, if you get inspired enough, the power you'll unleash from within will find a way to manifest your desire. Also, initially, don't waste time getting overly specific with things like, "I want a split-level house on Nob Hill, in San Francisco, with all-white, contemporary furniture and a splash of color here and there—oh, and don't forget the Victorian rose garden." Just write, "Dream house. Big garden. San Francisco." You'll fill in the details later.

So right now, put yourself in a state of mind of absolute faith and total expectation that you can create anything you want. I'd like you to imagine that you are a kid again on Christmas Eve. You're in a department store, about to sit on Santa's lap. Do you remember what this was like? If you talk to kids before Christmas, they have no trouble at all coming up with a fun, outrageous list; they'll say, "I'll tell you what I want. I want a swimming pool. In fact, I want *two* swimming pools: one for you, and one for me!" An adult would probably turn to them and say, "What? You'll be lucky to get a tub in the backyard!" We'll get practical later, but for now, the point is to be a kid: give yourself the freedom to explore the possibility of life without limits.

For each of the four goal areas, complete the following steps.

STEP 1: On the chart provided, or on blank sheets of paper, write down everything that . . .
   a. you'd like to improve in your life that relates to your own personal growth,
   b. you'd want for your career, business, or financial life,
   c. you could ever want, have, do, or experience in your life, and
   d. will make a true difference in peoples' lives or contribute to your legacy.

STEP 2: Create a simple time line for each of the areas you listed for . . .
   a. personal improvement,
   b. your career/business,
   c. what you want, and
   d. your legacy.

Use a simple number beside each of the items in your list indicating the number of years you would like to take to achieve each item (i.e., 1 for one year, 3 for three years, 8 for eight years, etc.).

STEP 3: Select your single most important one-year goal in each of the four categories. This goal should give you tremendous excitement thinking about actually having achieved the goal and make you feel that your time was well invested. You should end up with a list of four very important one-year goals.

Now you should have four master one-year goals that absolutely excite and inspire you, with sound, compelling reasons behind them. How would you feel if in one year you had mastered and attained them all? How would you feel about yourself? How would you feel about your life? I can't stress enough the importance of developing strong enough reasons to achieve these goals. Having a powerful enough *why* will provide you with the necessary *how*.

Make sure that you look at these four goals *daily*. Put them where you'll see them *every day*, either in your journal, on your desk at the office, or over your bathroom mirror to look at while you're shaving or putting on make-up. If you back up your goals with a solid commitment to constant and never-ending improvement in each of these areas, then you're sure to make progress daily. Make the decision now to begin to follow through on these goals, beginning *immediately*.

How to Make Your Goals Real

Now that you have a set of compelling goals and clear-cut reasons for their achievement, the process for making the goals real has already begun. Your RAS (Reticular Activating System) will become sensitized as you constantly review your goals and reasons, and will attract you to any resource of value toward the achievement of your clearly defined desire. To ensure the absolute attainment of your goals, you must condition your nervous system in advance to feel the pleasure they will surely bring. In other words, **at least twice a day, you must rehearse and emotionally enjoy the experience of achieving each one of your most valued goals.** Each time you do this, you need to create more emotional joy as you see, feel, and hear yourself living your dream.

This continuous focus will create a neural pathway between where you are and where you want to go. Because of this intense conditioning, you'll find yourself feeling a sense of *absolute certainty* that you'll achieve your desires, and this certainty will translate into a quality of action that ensures your success. Your confidence will allow you to attract the appropriate coaches and role models who will guide you in taking the most effective actions to produce results quickly rather than the traditional trial-and-error method that can take decades or more. Don't wait another day to begin this process. Start today!

The Purpose of the Goal

Often as we pursue our goals, we fail to realize their true impact on the environment around us. We think that achieving our goal is the end. But if we had a greater understanding, we'd realize that often in the pursuit of our goals, we set in motion **processional effects** that have consequences even more far reaching than we ever intended. After all, does the honeybee deliberate on how to propagate flowers? Of course not, but in the process of seeking the sweet nectar from the flowers, a bee will invariably pick up pollen on its legs, fly to the next flower, and set in motion a chain of pollination that will result in a hillside awash in color. The businessman pursues profit, and in so doing can create jobs that offer people a chance for incredible personal growth and an increase in the quality of life. The process of earning a livelihood enables people to meet such goals as putting their kids through college. Children in turn contribute by becoming doctors, lawyers, artists, businessmen, scientists, and parents. The chain is never ending.

Goals are a means to an end, not the ultimate purpose of our lives. They are simply a tool to concentrate our focus and move us in a direction. The only reason we really pursue goals is to cause ourselves to expand and grow. *Achieving goals by themselves will never make us happy in the long term, it's who you become, as you overcome the obstacles necessary to achieve your goals, that can give you the deepest and most long-lasting sense of fulfillment.* So maybe the key question you and I need to ask is, *"What kind of person will I have to become in order to achieve all that I want?"* This may be the most important question that you can ask yourself, for its answer will determine the direction you need to head personally.

From: *Awaken the Giant Within: How to Take Immediate Control of Your Mental, Emotional, Physical and Financial Destiny!* by Anthony Robbins, copyright © 1991. Used by permission of Simon & Schuster New York.

———•·•———

Goal-setting prophets boldly proclaim that people can do anything they want to if their WHY is large enough (that is, why a person wants to achieve his or her goal). Put together an energetic and enterprising team of Australian students, led by student Krystle Edwards and guided by marketing franchise expert Barbara Knackstedt, and a Big Hairy Audacious Goal can be achieved in a blink of an eye.

———•·•———

IT'S IN THE BHAG

KRYSTLE EDWARDS AND BARBARA KNACKSTEDT

M y class of third-year engineering students formed a company. We sold stock; we created, manufactured, and sold a product; we then liquidated the company and gave a return of 400 percent to our investors. We did all this in just 14 weeks—while studying full time. Motivation was our secret. We were highly motivated by getting ourselves pumped up with a Big Hairy Audacious Goal, or BHAG. Once we did that, it was in the BHAG.

Engineering students don't often get hands-on experience with the realities of business by running a company themselves. Thanks to the collaboration between Young Achievement Australia (YAA) and the Engineering Department of the Australian National University, we did. We had four business mentors to guide us, but the work, responsibility, and the glory or failure was ours. Not only would our grades for this course depend on our results, we would also be competing for awards with other university student companies, both in our region and nationwide.

Our company, Hairy Yak, manufactured customized T-shirts, screen printing any slogan or design the customer wanted. Family, friends, and members of the university community held a vested interest in helping us generate enough sales to reach our BHAG in time.

I was elected as the marketing/sales director for our "Hairy Yak" company, and I realized that my most important sales pitch would be to my fellow company members. With all the other demands on our time, we needed a high level of motivation to keep going when things got tough. At first, we all laughed at the idea of setting a 350 percent return for our investors. Most YAA companies were content to break even and two for one was considered very successful.

But the more we kicked around this Big Hairy Audacious Goal, the more we began to believe we could do it. However, beyond the one-on-one sales, we needed someone to place a bulk order of at least 100 T-shirts to help us achieve our goal. We needed a corporate customer.

Even though we were motivated by our BHAG, we were not certain it would motivate a potential corporate partner. In kicking around ideas about how to find a corporate customer, we began to evolve a win-win sales rationale that concentrated on Hairy Yak T-shirts as a unique value proposition for a potential corporate partner. We visualized the creation of a service rather than having solely a "physical" product. The T-shirt would be a physical manifestation of our service, which turned out to be an advertisement service. Our strategy was to piggy-back off the strong, well-known reputation of YAA to help us gain free publicity and additional sales. We had to come up with a creative way to leverage the YAA brand.

Our first partnership was with Futons Express, a small furniture business with new owners and a limited advertising budget. After an initial meeting with Futons Express, we were given one week to develop a sales campaign that would create a win-win situation. Our strategy began to take shape through a second partnership with a PR and advertising company, Clarity Communications. Brainstorming with them produced the slogan, "I Sleep with Futons Express." Our sales program called for the slogan to be printed on 100 T-shirts given free to the first 100 customers to purchase a futon. A variation of the original slogan, "Hairy Yak Sleeps with Futons Express," would be printed on a huge poster along with our cartoon logo of Hairy Yak sleeping on a futon. These catchy slogans and logos could be used in future media campaigns.

Closing the sale for 100 Hairy Yak T-shirts was easy after our sales presentation presented all the win-win benefits this large purchase would bring Futons Express. With assistance from Clarity Communications, we organized a promotional launch at the Futons Express store with drinks and a free BBQ, and invited local media along. We also distributed mini versions of the poster across the ANU campus, raising awareness of Futons Express with university students, one of their major markets. Back at our Hairy Yak company war room, we continued to motivate ourselves through keeping our BHAG uppermost in our collective minds. There were only two weekends remaining until our final exams, but we worked around the clock one week to manufacture all 100 T-shirts needed for the promotional launch—and to deliver them on time.

We learned that successful sales depend on motivation; hence, we developed our Big Hairy Audacious Goal. We also learned that selling is made easy when a win-win for everyone is clearly communicated. Futons Express got a priceless full-page article in a citywide publication, an ongoing promotion with posters for their store, and exposure in the university student market. Their customers received a free T-shirt and the satisfaction of helping a Young Achievement Australia company. Clarity Communications was hired by Futons Express for further media work. Hairy Yak met its Big Hairy Audacious Goal, and paid its investors back more than four to one. As students we all got top marks in our course . . . and I was lucky enough to win the Marketing/Sales Award for the ACT Region of Young Achievement Australia!

Within the mantra of success is a simple acronym: KISS, which means "Keep it simple, stupid" (I know, it sounds a bit rough, but there you have it!). In so much of life and professional activity, the simple strategies and techniques can be the most powerful. Jack Canfield co-authored a book. He followed a KISS success program and sold more than 100 million copies of his book. Read on to hear his view on the "uncommon application of common knowledge" (Masters of Success, Misner and Morgan).

PRACTICE THE RULE OF 5

JACK CANFIELD

Success is the sum of small efforts, repeated day in and day out.
—ROBERT COLLIER (BEST-SELLING AUTHOR AND PUBLISHER OF *THE SECRET OF THE AGES*)

When Mark Victor Hansen and I published the first *Chicken Soup for the Soul* book, we were so eager and committed to making it a best seller that we asked 15 best-selling authors ranging from John Gray (*Men Are from Mars, Women Are from Venus*) and Barbara DeAngelis (*Real Moments*) to Ken Blanchard (*The One Minute Manager*) and Scott Peck (*The Road Less Traveled*) for their guidance and advice. We received a ton of valuable information about what to do and how to do it. Next, we visited with book publishing and marketing guru Dan Poynter, who gave us even more great information. Then we bought and read John Kremer's *1001 Ways to Market Your Book*.

After all of that, we were overwhelmed with possible marketing strategies to employ. We didn't know where to start, plus we both had speaking and seminar businesses to run.

We sought the advice of Ron Scolastico, a wonderful teacher, who told us, "If you would go every day to a very large tree and take five swings at it with a very sharp ax, eventually, no matter how large the tree, it would have to come down." How very simple and how very true! Out of that we developed what we have called the Rule of 5. This simply means that every day, we do five specific things that will move our goal toward completion.

With the goal of getting *Chicken Soup for the Soul* to the top of the *New York Times* Best-Seller List, it meant having five radio interviews, sending out five review copies to editors who might review the book, or calling five network marketing companies and asking them to buy the book as a motivational tool for their salespeople. On some days we would simply send out five free copies to people listed in the *Celebrity Address Book*. As a result of that one activity, I ended up meeting Sidney Poitier—at his request—and we later learned that the producer of the television show *Touched by an Angel* required all of the people working on the show to read *Chicken Soup for the Soul* to put them in "the right frame of mind." One day we sent copies of the book to all the jurors in the O.J. Simpson trial. A week later, we received a nice letter from Judge Lance Ito thanking us for thinking of the jurors, who were sequestered and not allowed to watch television or read the newspaper. The next day, four of the jurors were spotted reading the book by the press, and that led to some valuable public relations for the book.

We made phone calls to people who could review the book, we wrote press releases, we called in to talk shows (some at 3 A.M.), we gave away free copies at our talks, we did book signings at any bookstore that would have us, we asked businesses to make bulk purchases for their employees, we bought a directory of catalogs and asked all the appropriate ones to carry the book, we visited gift shops and card shops and asked them to carry the book—we even got gas stations, bakeries, and restaurants to sell the book. It was a lot of effort—a minimum of five things a day, every day, day in and day out—for more than two years.

Was it worth it? Yes! The book eventually sold over 10 million copies in 47 languages.

Did it happen overnight? No! We did not make a best seller list until over a year after the book came out—a year! But it was the sustained effort of the Rule of 5 for over two years that led to the success—one action at a time, one book at a time, one reader at a time. But slowly, over time, each reader told another reader, and eventually, like a slow-building chain letter, the word was spread and the book became a huge success—what *Time* magazine called "the publishing phenomenon of the decade." It was less of a publishing phenomenon and more of a phenomenon of persistent effort—thousands of individual activities that all added up to one large success.

In *Chicken Soup for the Gardener's Soul*, Jaroldeen Edwards describes the day her daughter Carolyn took her to Lake Arrowhead to see a wonder of nature—fields and fields of daffodils that extend for as far as the eye can see—a literal carpet of every hue of the color yellow, from the palest ivory to the deepest lemon to the most vivid salmon-orange. There appear to be over a million daffodil bulbs planted in this beautiful natural scene. It takes your breath away.

As they hiked into the center of this magical place, they eventually stumbled on a sign that read: "Answers to the Questions I Know You Are Asking." The first answer was "One Woman—Two Hands, Two Feet and Very Little Brain." The second was "One at a Time." The third: "Started in 1958."

One woman had forever changed the world over a 40-year period one bulb at a time. What might you accomplish if you were to do a little bit—five things—every day for the next 40 years toward the accomplishment of your goal. If you wrote 5 pages a day, that would be 73,000 pages of text—the equivalent of 243 books of 300 pages each. If you saved $5 a day, that would be $73,000, enough for four round-the-world trips! If you invested just $5 a day, with compound interest at only 6 percent a year, at the end of 40 years, you'd have amassed a small fortune of around $305,000. The Rule of 5. It's a pretty powerful little principle, wouldn't you agree?

Here's a suggestion for applying the Rule of 5 that can radically accelerate your career success. First ask yourself, what is a goal that if I were to achieve it in the next year would quantum leap my career. By quantum leap, I am referring to an achievement that would be a major breakthrough, not just a small incremental achievement. For Mark and I it was to write a best-selling book that would get us celebrity status, national media attention, and increase our speaking business. Taking one year to write that book and another year to drive it to the top of the *New York Times* list has earned Mark and me tons of millions of extra dollars. It was well worth the effort.

What would be a quantum leap breakthrough goal for you? Landing a big national account? Securing a huge line of credit for your business? Getting your MRSA degree? Learning a new language? Writing a monthly column in your national trade journal? Whatever you choose, the next step is to apply the Rule of 5 to its fulfillment. Every day take five specific actions to move your goal to completion. If you do this every single day, no matter how difficult, no matter what the obstacles, you will reach your goal . . . and take a major leap forward in your career.

Getting Clients
Prospecting the Old Way to the New

Successful people surround themselves with a
well-developed, sophisticated network.
—*MASTERS OF NETWORKING*, MISNER AND MORGAN

Throughout this book you will hear us talk about an evolution that is taking place within the sales profession. There is clear movement from older strategies of finding and selling customers to a newer approach that is more in sync with today's commercial world. This newer method for getting clients is borne out of dramatic world changes that influence virtually all facets of the selling experience: how sellers find buyers and buyers find sellers; how products and services are sold; and how buyers make buying decisions differently compared to the past. Perhaps the most dramatic changes are illustrated in the prospecting phase of finding clients where, in some jurisdictions, there are even local laws forbidding "prospecting" the old-fashioned way.

To begin a sales cycle, we need a prospect to sell to, and this is where the salesperson comes into his or her element. Marketing activities can help pinpoint areas ripe for prospecting and advertisements can warm up a cohort of buyers, but ultimately it's the seller who has to engage the prospect in a conversion process that results in a happy owner. To "get" clients, sales managers still rely on tactics they were taught years ago. These include cold calling by door knocking or telephoning, print and electronic ads to pull customers through the door, and PR campaigns, which really are just another form of advertisement. For example, the classic PR program might include a local barber shop that sponsors a little league or children's soccer team, and provides sport uniforms with the name of the barber shop on the back of each jersey: "Pete's Barber Shop." (Of course, the kids all get their haircuts at Pete's.)

Old habits die hard. As late as the 1990s, sales trainers taught the "three-foot rule." Karin White, one of our contributors, described this rule while talking about a friend, Deb Hoffmann. "Deb can make a cold call turn warm in a matter of seconds. Her tactic is to start a polite and friendly conversation with anyone within three feet of her. With her warm engaging conversation, she soon is able to turn the conversation around to her product. Wherever she is, in person or on the phone, Deb knows how to turn the tides to her advantage and find a new customer."

There are some sales heroes who are amazingly efficient at quickly turning a complete stranger into a warm, loving customer, but successful cold-calling strategies exist mostly in our sales dreams. To effectively make a sale, we have to find people who happen to be in the market for our product now. Cold-calling strategies rely on a lot of misses to get a few hits of hot, willing prospects.

A better approach for getting clients is referral selling. This method is rapidly gaining popularity among both novice and expert sellers, even though versions of the method have been around for eons. Recently referral selling has begun to be codified and organized to the point that it is nearly considered *mainstream selling* by those in the know. You might even consider referral selling to be a social movement gaining grassroots support.

Social changes are not typically characterized by a clear line of demarcation from the old to the new. Instead, social changes tend to evolve, and our shifting sales paradigm is no different. Cold calling, while still used, is being pushed aside in favor of referral selling. But since we're not fully into this new era and because many sales are still obtained through cold calling and telemarketing, we want to begin this conversation about getting new clients with the colder cold-call approaches and gently move you toward a warmer word-of-mouth strategy.

If you want a selling career, you have one very important need: customers. For years, sales professionals were taught to find customers by cold calling. Stories from those years are now part of our romantic sales lore. But that was then. Today we are just beginning to learn new ways to find—and land—our customers. Shelli Howlett's early selling career is part of that sales history. She tells the real story of those romantic years and how she learned a better way to land clients, which has culminated in her developing a highly successful, Texas-based marketing business.

COLD CALLING IS . . . WELL, COLD!

SHELLI HOWLETT

*A*fter *trudging from building to building in downtown Chicago, selling typewriters on a cold, snowy, windy day, I arrive at yet* *another high rise, hoping for a sale. I stop at unit 140, a business called The Sentinel, a Jewish publishing company, and I introduce myself to Larry, the office manager.*

Larry is short and soft spoken, with a ruddy complexion and short, curly hair. His slow movements suggest old age (but in my youth, everyone over 40 looked old!). He is really nice, and obviously wants to help me. I think of him as my kindly old grandfather, especially after he agrees to see me fire up my hi-tech AP400 Canon typewriter. Cold calling works: He agrees to buy four typewriters! My day is complete and so is Larry's, considering the productivity my machines will provide his company.

I assumed that cold calling was the only way to find new clients because it was the only way that I was taught to find new customers in those early years. It took a number of years and a number of cold-calling sales positions, but slowly I learned my lesson. As I advanced to more senior level sales positions, I began to understand more about consultative selling and how this form of selling required a longer-term trusting relationship between the buyer and the seller. In this instance, the seller is seen more as a problem solver.

In July 1993, I saw a publicity piece about BNI, an organization that helps salespeople get new customers through referral networking and building great business relationships. Wow, what a great concept! Liking people and building relationships was easy for me, and I wanted to be part of that group. I called to find out how to get involved, and by November 4, 1993, had launched my first referral network under the BNI banner. I was so impressed with the program that I became a BNI franchise owner two months later. I thought I was in heaven—or at least out of cold-calling "hell." I soon learned that heaven is not a smooth walk in the park, but by comparison to cold calling, referral networking is a great way to get new customers.

My task was to sell memberships in this organization. I remember in particular the time I drove 35 miles from Ft. Worth to Dallas to meet five people who wanted to start a referral network. Our breakfast meeting was scheduled for 7:00 A.M., but half an hour later, I was still having breakfast alone. No one knew about BNI. There was no brand recognition of my new franchise business, and no one understood the benefits of referral marketing.

I had to sell this new business just like my other product lines, but now I was learning how to get clients without cold calling. Soon, I discovered the fun and excitement that comes from being around positive and supportive people who all wanted to share referrals with each other. I found referrals for my new clients, they referred me to their associates, and we all looked for business for the other.

Eventually, my sheer persistence helped me break through the barriers. Since those early days at that hotel, BNI-DFW has grown in excess of 75 referral networks, with more than 2,000 client members. The success I had in selling memberships to my new business has taken me to the BNI Platinum Club, a group made up of the top 20 percent of franchisees in the United States. New franchisees from all over the world now ask me for advice about how to build their BNI businesses.

Here's what I tell them:

1. Cold calling in a territory does produce new customers, but only if you persistently knock on one more door, even though your knuckles are already bloody.
2. It is very important to discover a way to keep your attitude positive even when everything in your environment is negative.
3. Understand the distinct culture of your area, and adjust your approach to fit the area you are working.
4. As soon as possible switch your client-getting method from cold calling to the network referral approach. It's warmer, nicer, and gives you more leverage.

The telephone: Everyone has one (or four!), and cell phones are firmly planted on the ears of salespeople, many proudly displaying Bluetooth devices hanging from their ears like jewelry. Salespeople couldn't survive without a phone, and yet it can be a most fearsome instrument. Called "the Queen of Cold Calling," Wendy Weiss, a sales trainer, coach, and author, teaches us how to perfect cold calling on the phone. If mastered, it makes any phone call a snap.

MASTERING TELEPHONE TERROR

WENDY WEISS

Call reluctance can keep an otherwise talented sales representative from becoming a superstar, but there is good news for those who suffer from call reluctance (or, plainly stated, telephone terror). Using the phone in your sales career is a learned communication skill that you can master. Your call might be to an unknown prospect or a little-known client. Regardless, if you experience telephone terror, the call will feel COLD. The good news is that there are many tips to help sales professionals overcome phone discomfort and go on to be true telephone sales masters.

Make Terrifying Telephone Calls

Few things are more terrifying than the unknown. The fear you manufacture in your mind is far worse than the reality of actually making a cold phone call. Once you start making telephone calls and continue making them, it all becomes easier and not scary at all. You overcome fear by doing that which causes you the most fear.

Make a Lot of Telephone Calls

If you have only one prospect to pursue, that prospect becomes overwhelmingly important, because if you fail you are left with nothing. But if you have hundreds of leads to call, no one prospect can make or break you. The more calls you make, the more success you will have.

A client continually rode the boom-and-bust roller coaster with his sales activity. His busy times drove him crazy and the slow times were agonizing because of worry about sustaining his business. Because he had no time to prospect during his busy time, he only prospected during slow times. Once he learned to schedule phone prospecting even during the busy times, he stabilized his sales cycle.

Prepare

Prepare for cold calling the way you would for any major presentation. Know what you want to say, how you want to say it, and how you want to represent yourself, your company, and your product or service. Have a goal for each telephone call.

"Help!" cried another client. "I've made hundreds of calls and don't have a single appointment." We listened in on some of his prospecting calls. He was smart, articulate, and personable and did many things right . . . except he did not ASK for the appointment. Sometimes it's as simple as saying, "Would later this week or next week be a good time for us to briefly get together?"

Practice

If cold calling is new and uncomfortable, you must practice your pitch out loud. Role-play with friends or colleagues. Practice various sales scenarios. Through repetitive practice you will worry less about what you are going to say and be able to pay more attention to the client's responses. These responses will direct how you will conduct the phone call.

A sales representative was resistant to practicing with a prepared script. He thought he got better results by remaining "free" and more spontaneous. However, his results did not match with this belief. When he finally agreed to use a script, he discovered that it actually made him more comfortable in the call. By using the script, he didn't have to worry about his words, and instead he started to hear the concerns and interests of his prospects for the first time.

Start Where It's Easiest

The less important leads are the place to start because they are less stressful and give you practice. Once you feel comfortable, start working on the more important leads.

One client never used the phone for cold calling because she was afraid that her prospects would be annoyed, be angry, or might even hang up on her. She was convinced that instead of getting client opportunities, she'd lose out by phone prospecting. We started a list of her less important "C" prospects. As she worked through her list, she was surprised and thrilled to find that prospects were quite receptive to her words. With that experience, it was much easier for her to begin calling her "A" prospects.

Your Priorities Are Different from Those of Your Prospect

You want an immediate "yes"; your prospect may want to finish a report or a conversation, or may be ready to start her vacation! Be very careful not to read negative or extra meaning into early conversations with your prospect or prospect's secretary. If, for example, the secretary says that your prospect is "on the phone," "in a meeting," or "out of the office," that does not necessarily translate to, "My prospect knows that I am calling and is avoiding me."

One client had trouble separating her insecurities from her prospects' responses. Frequently she felt rejected by her prospects, when in fact they might only have been really too busy to take her call at that specific time. We worked on a "reality check" to determine, in any given situation, what was fact compared to emotional fiction. Soon she could accept that her prospect's responses may not be sheer rejection, and she continued phone prospecting with successful results.

Some Things Are Out of Your Control

If a prospect ultimately says "no," that is out of your control. But still under your influence is the ability to move onto the next call (and the next, and then the next . . .). It is also within your control to learn ways to improve your cold-calling methods.

Have Fun!

This is not life or death—it's only a cold call. The fate of the world does not rest on you and your telephone. You will not destroy your company or ruin your life if a prospect says "no." Loosen up, be creative, have some fun, and you will find the "YES" responses will far outweigh any "NOs!"

———

Selling is a numbers game that demands seeing lots of people to close on a few. Not everyone you sell to will want or be able to buy from you at that precise moment. Salespeople understand that many "nos" lead to that wonderful "yes." Don Mastrangelo mastered this concept by discovering a centuries-old principle. He turned this understanding into a best-seller book as well as a successful sales consulting business in southwestern United States.

———

GETTING FROM ZERO TO SALES HERO

DON MASTRANGELO

There is an 80/20 Rule in sales (the well-known principle stating that in every sales organization, 20 percent of the salespeople win 80 percent of the sales, while the remaining 80 percent split up 20 percent of the revenue). It's easy to know which category you want to be a part of: The top 20 percent, or what I refer to as the Sales HEROES.

The 80/20 rule was developed through the studies of 18th-century Italian economist Vilfredo Pareto. He postulated that in any endeavor, 80 percent of the productivity comes from 20 percent of the efforts.

If you want to be a Sales HERO, use Pareto's Law to your advantage! Meetings, crisis management, phone calls, office chat, or getting your ducks lined up in a row are NOT the 20 percent of your activity that is attributable to creating new business. There is only one task proven to directly lead to achieving your sales objectives: *prospecting*. Millions have tried to get around Pareto's law, and none has succeeded. Accept the reality. You cannot change the numbers game. You either sell by the rule or stop trying because you will not be successful. One way or another, you will have to get your selling influence in front of enough prospects to find those relatively few who are ready right now to buy your product. If you want to succeed in sales, your sales plan must generate enough sales to meet your income objectives.

To begin your planning process, first determine your financial goals. Record all of your monthly expenses, including vacation fund, charitable contributions, and savings/investments. Add to this any other desires for which you might need a contingency fund. You now know exactly how much money you need monthly to live the lifestyle of your choice. This becomes your monthly Personal Income Objective, which differentiates you from 80 percent of all salespeople because only 20 percent of all salespeople take the time to set specific future goals! Take it a step further by writing in clear terms exactly what you want to achieve.

Your next step is to determine what level of sales revenue you need, or how many units you need to sell, to earn your Personal Income Objective. Based on your average deal size, determine how many deals you need to close to achieve your desired level of sales.

Once you've determined how many deals you need to close each month, figure out how many prospecting calls it will take to achieve your plan for closed deals. Use Pareto's Law to calculate the number of calls necessary to land paying customers. Let's assume you need to close four deals per month. Following the logic below, you will discover that about 100 prospecting calls will result in four closed clients.

According to Pareto's Law, you must walk through five doors or make five phone attempts to actually reach one decision maker (20 percent of the total). Therefore, you will make 500 attempts to attain your goal of completing 100 prospecting calls. Of the 100 decision makers you actually speak with, 20 percent will have a genuine interest and stay in your sales pipeline for your further follow up. But 80 percent, no matter how good you are at selling or how much they need what you offer, are simply not going to be interested.

Now, through appointments, proposals, and follow-up calls, you will find that 80 percent (or 16) of the 20 prospects that are still in the game are not going to buy (at least not right now).

Don't worry, they may get back *in* the game later, but you do have four decision makers who will buy now. Congratulations, you just achieved your objective! At first this may seem like a small reward for all your efforts, but you will learn that it is a good, solid formula that will always help you get from sales ZERO to Sales HERO in 90 days! Here's a short-cut—simply divide the number of deals you need to close each month by .04 to determine the number of prospecting calls you need to complete.

Try investing 80 percent of your productive time for three straight months prospecting for new customers. If you do, you'll find that from there forward you will never need to invest more than 20 percent of your time prospecting to keep your client getting momentum going. Whenever you find yourself in a slump, start a 90-day action plan that embraces Pareto's Law—and you'll be back on your way to becoming part of the top 20 percent of all salespeople in the world.

To get clients you have to create a direction, persist, and you may need to adjust your product to your target audience. Trey McAlister is a referral marketing expert in the San Francisco area, whose story about a highly-acclaimed speaker ends with a unique twist that has nothing to do with creating a discounted price— in fact, just the opposite.

—•◦•—

A WORLD-CLASS FUNNYMAN SAYS:
"PERSIST AND SET HIGH EXPECTATIONS"

TREY MCALISTER

Hailed by the *New York Times* as a "modern-day Will Rogers who qui-etly became one of the most influential people in America," Andy Andrews is an internationally known speaker and novelist whose works *Tales from Sawyerton Springs* and *The Storms of Perfection Volumes I–IV* have sold millions of copies worldwide. His newest book, *The Traveler's Gift*, became a publishing phenomenon, coexisting simultaneously on the bestseller lists of the *New York Times, Wall Street Journal, USA Today, Publisher's Weekly*, Barnes & Noble, and Amazon.com.

Mr. Andrews spoke at the request of four U.S. Presidents, addressed the entire U.S. Air Force senior leadership, received a personal invitation to meet with the (then) 91-year-old Bob Hope, and worked with the entire LPGA Solheim Cup Team in their winning effort against the European Team.

Not bad for a guy who dropped out of school to become a comedian, and had to learn a few things himself about success through selling. As I was building my consulting business into what it is today, I relied heavily on the selling knowledge Andy Andrews gained while on his determined path toward being a world-renowned comedian and modern spokesperson. His advice is helpful to the modern-day salesperson.

Have a Dream and Be True to It

I always knew I wanted to be a comedian, but didn't know how to go about that. Everyone knows how to become a doctor and a lawyer, but how do you become a comedian? I mean there weren't any of the comedy clubs back then, so I went to school to be a veterinarian. Actually I wanted to be a veterinarian and a taxidermist, so I could say, "Either way you get the dog back!"

So, I went to Auburn to be a veterinarian, and I remember being in Organic Chemistry one day and looked up and saw that the teacher was packing up and the students were leaving. I looked down at my notebook and there were all these joke ideas all over it. It seems that I was more destined to be funny than look after someone else's pet.

At that point, I asked myself, "What are you doing here?" I mean, I was spending MY OWN money for school and supporting myself by working as the night manager at a ZippyMart. I mean I was the manager, but it was the night shift, so who was I managing? So I thought, "This is obviously where I don't belong," so I just left. Some people ask me, "So, you quit?" No, when you quit, you have to fill out paperwork and sign forms, etc. I just left and never came back!

I started my career as a comedian. I didn't know what I was doing or how I was going to do it, but I started. I looked everywhere for gigs. I began begging bands to let me perform between sets at the Holiday Inn and playing at horrible places, mostly for free. And many of these places, YOU would have gone in and said, "Wow, a good coat of FIRE would do wonders for this place!"

Never Give Up (or the Numbers Game Works . . . If You Work at It
I had a hard time at first, but I learned some lessons early on that would help me later as well . . . I learned that the law of numbers worked—if you worked it. I got on the phone a lot trying to book me as a comedian and got the "No. No. No. We don't know you. We don't book comedians. No. No." So then I figured every good comedian has an agent. Therefore, I would call as Ron Williams the agent, but would still get "No. No. No. We don't know him. We don't book comedians. No. No." I would get so depressed or discouraged that I would stop calling. But after a few months, I would get so mad or so excited that I would start calling again.

This went on a long time (months and months) until finally I got so mad that I said that I was going to call until I booked something. I made a lot of calls and I finally booked a $25 gig at a Steak and Ale in Birmingham, Alabama, five hours away. I drove up, stayed in a hotel, did the gig and left. It was horrible AND I lost money on the deal, BUT I had established a couple of things (which allowed me to "turn the corner"). First, I would persist until something happened, no matter what. Secondly, I knew I had to make a certain number of calls to book something. Over time, as I continued to make the calls, this ratio continued to appear, which allowed me to know the number of calls that I needed in order to sell the bookings I wanted. The good thing was that I was getting booked, but I still needed more to achieve true success.

Peer and Above—Raising the Bar by Association

Thankfully, at that point I stumbled onto the concept of "peer and above" (the concept of working better than your present level of achievement, for—and with—people who expect a lot of you). I was at the stage where no one was booking me consistently and when I was booked the venue and audience would end up just blowing me off. This is when working "peer and above" happened with a single idea.

In one frustrated moment, really as more of a lark, I raised my price to $1,000 a night. Incredibly, PEOPLE STARTED BOOKING ME . . . and treating me great when I got there. It was unbelievable. I guess what happened is that people stopped thinking: "A $25 comedian? How good can he be?" Now, I was performing for people who thought: "At $1,000 a night, this guy must be incredible!"

Because I was performing for a new caliber of people and at the same time associating with a more successful crowd (people who could pay $1,000 a night for a comedian, and who expected to get what they were paying for!), my own abilities developed further than they ever would have if I had continued working the $25 per night gigs.

Over the next 20 years, Andy's lessons in passion, persistence, and peer association continued to take him to larger audiences and greater heights, including being awarded the Entertainer and Comedian of the Year award in 1985 and 1986, and then to entertaining presidents and celebrities. His early sales lessons served him well as he moved into his new public speaking and writing career.

I am often asked by budding salespeople about how to ensure success, and invariably, I rely on Andy Andrews' wisdom. Carefully and truly define your dream, be loyal to achieving it, remember the numbers game, and—perhaps most important—set your standards high.

———•—•———

These next contributions describe techniques associated with a "new" form of selling that dates back to before recorded time—referral selling. This method of selling involves finding new customers through a referral system in which one person tells another about you and your product or service. Following are several very basic techniques related to referral selling. Master just one of the techniques and your business volume will pick up. Master them all, and you have begun a systematic client getting program—so read on!

Masterful sellers have secret phrases that get them clients. We call them "memory hooks." What's interesting and fun is that their secrets are really simple. Everyone can use these simple phrases, and Sherry Steiman's expertise as a word-of-mouth marketer puts them to the test.

———•—•———

THE SHORTEST SALES PITCH

SHERRY STEIMAN

I find that the best way to capture someone's attention is with a catchy phrase on how he or she can be helped.

My husband is a chartered professional accountant (CPA) and is extremely neat in appearance. Whenever I start speaking to a potential new client for him, I might say something like "Look at him, not a hair out of place, don't you think that's how he will do your accounting?" This is accompanied by a warm smile and a sincere voice.

It's short, sweet, and most importantly, gets the point across that he is a perfectionist and will be extra careful when taking care of his client's work. It is amazing how many new clients we have gotten with that phrase.

Recently, we landed a major landscaping-exterminating company in this same manner. The owner's wife, who ran the office, was complaining to me about her current CPA always being late in reporting back to her and never explaining the effects of the financial aspects of their business. She was obviously looking for someone that was going to dot every "i" and cross every "t." My phrase got that point across to her, and they are now our clients.

Psychology gives us a basic understanding about how to build short selling phrases. The objective is to tie a characteristic of your product/service/person to a common object, phrase, or phenomenon that is widely known. You want your phrase to create an association between the commonly known phenomenon and your less known product/service/person.

Most courses on memory use the strategy of associating the object to be memorized (for example, a personal name) with a more common object. Sometimes the more common phenomenon can be as simple as a sound. For example, the drug company Bayer HealthCare, uses "plop, plop fizz" sounds to refer to Alka-Seltzer®. When the catchy phrase is said to the right person at the right time, it helps direct a prospect to a seller.

The short phrase, which some call a "memory hook" (see *Seven Second Marketing* by Ivan Misner, Bard Press, 1996), will be remembered first. Next the name of the seller is remembered, and a prospect can now find the appropriate seller. All the phrase does is act as a memory jog to help qualify the buyer as a good match for the seller and bring into the conversation the name of the related seller.

As a seller of goods or services, it is important for you to find the phrase necessary to grab the buyer's need for your goods or services, or at least to ignite their imagination for future purchases. As soon as you say your phrase, be quiet and let the client mull it over. Let the phrase sink in. As you and other people begin using your simple catchy phrase, you'll be surprised at the results. Your catchy phrase will truly "reach out and touch someone."

"I get my best customers from satisfied customers!" This comment is most often heard from sellers who provide good customer service, but the Masters of Sales will take the process one step further. They build a system to get a continual flow of referred customers. Sue Henry is a real estate professional in Minnesota who uses a systematic referral system to get a constant flow of warm referred clients. Sometimes the simplest idea is the best one.

TEACHING YOUR CUSTOMERS HOW TO REPLACE THEMSELVES

SUE HENRY

I remember clearly the time when I was a new mortgage broker struggling to help my husband support our six kids and needing clients. I advertised in the newspaper and the real estate buyers' guide, and asked customers once or twice for referrals. Nothing seemed to work well, and my clients forgot me after their deal was closed.

Armed with the knowledge that about 90 percent of home buyers don't do repeat business with their original real estate agent or mortgage lender, I became determined to find a method for teaching my customers to "replace" themselves. My system involves asking for a referral at every opportunity.

Right at the beginning of the sales process, I let the customer know that I would be asking them for referrals. This begins programming their subconscious mind for who they know who might want my service. Once the original transaction is closed, I can move to the next referred client without losing time or sales momentum. This skill can be learned and implemented by anyone wanting a better way to find clients. Through use of this simple system, I cut my advertisement costs and increased my business 35 percent in the first year!

My Client Referral System

First and foremost, I always follow up on every referral received within 24 hours with a handwritten thank-you note to the person who gave me the referral. When I started this, it alone increased business by at least 17 percent per year!

But I don't stop there. I put in place a specific communication system that asks for referrals throughout the sales cycle:

> **Initial meeting.** *"I truly enjoy my career helping people realize their dreams. I am very lucky because I get to choose who I work with. Do you ever wish that?"* (We laugh because they immediately think of someone they wish they didn't have to work with.)
>
> *"When you bought your last car and started driving it around, did you suddenly notice how many other cars there were just like yours out there? Well, it's the same thing in real estate. Now that you are involved in a property purchase, as you go through your day, you are going to hear more conversations about people wanting to buy a different home or an investment property than you ever imagined. I am going to ask you for referrals as we go through the home-buying process."* I look the person/people in the eye, nodding my head as I ask, *"Is that OK with you?"*

While putting my intention of asking for referrals up front, I don't ask for specific names at this meeting. This helps clients feel more comfortable about sharing names later on because I haven't seemed "pushy." Remember, people like to buy; they don't like to be sold.

During the sales process. At any time during the sales process, I consistently ask, "*Are you happy with my services so far? Who have you talked to that would like to buy a home in the next six months?*" (If they tell me they aren't happy with something I am doing, I fix the problem before asking for referrals.)

Continue to ask the question. The same script must be used after writing up the purchase agreement, when their offer has been accepted, when closing is scheduled, when they get final approval, final walk-through, and at closing. At first, it will likely seem horribly repetitive to ask the same question over and over again. But, effective advertising relies on repetition to be effective, so consider your repetitive questions as advertisement for new clients.

At 30 days after the closing. I send out a questionnaire with a stamped, self-addressed envelope, asking clients about their home-buying experience and what we could do to improve it. I also use the opportunity to ask again for referrals.

If a customer lists a complaint on the 30-day survey, I address it immediately. If the complaint is something within our control, we fix it. For instance, one of my customers didn't receive a copy of their appraisal in their closing packet. We called the title company, mentioned that the borrower didn't have a copy, and asked if we could stop by and pick up a copy. I mailed the appraisal along with a $10 gift certificate to a popular coffee shop and a brief note thanking them for letting me know about the problem. A few days later I called to make sure they received the package. They were surprised and pleased that we took care of their complaint and went the extra step in giving them a gift certificate. Now I get two or three referrals a year from this satisfied customer.

If the complaint is due to circumstances beyond my control, I show sympathy and understanding. I give them a call and spend some time listening as they talk about it. A few minutes of uninterrupted listening or justifying what happened will surprise and help to satisfy them. After they have talked through their complaints, I then find a way to change the subject, such as asking them about something they mentioned they wanted to do to the house right away. I then see if I can help them with their project by referring an appropriate preferred vendor I know will do a great job for them.

I also ask them if they still get a thrill each time they pull into the driveway of their new house! By providing help and reminding them of the positive emotions that they first felt about the house, their negative emotion will usually settle down. Now (you guessed it) is a good time to ask for a referral and end the conversation in a positive way.

At the client's one-year anniversary, I sent out another questionnaire, asking about lifestyle changes. Had they been promoted, were they getting married, or had a child been born? Did they know someone who was thinking of buying a home in the next 12 months?

The results I experienced when first using this simple referral system caused me to want to improve my system: 80 percent of my customers gave me at least one referral, and 40 percent of those referrals did business with me. So, using simple math, about 32 percent of my customers referred successful business to me!

Take a serious look at where your new business is coming from and how much you spend on finding new clients. Wouldn't it make sense to implement a proven system that creates warm leads, increases business sales, and decreases one of your biggest costs—finding new clients? All new systems feel uncomfortable at first, but with regular practice, you will see consistent referrals from the people you are already working with.

When a client says "no" to giving you a referral (this will happen from time to time), that's OK. You'll hear "yes" often enough to make asking worthwhile. Remember, this process can be adapted and used regardless of the product or service you are selling!

———•◦•———

We want to direct your attention to a critical component of this new sales paradigm of relying on referrals to find clients. The fuel that powers this modern system of getting customers is a solid set of trusted and reciprocal relationships. Bob Burg is an acknowledged expert on networking and referral selling. An author and speaker, he teaches networking and use of persuasion skills to organizations and companies.

GIVING REALLY DOES LEAD TO RECEIVING

BOB BURG

There is a great misconception of how networking and selling interact. The concept of networking as it applies to selling often conveys a negative preconceived notion (i.e., shove as many business cards into people's hands as you can while telling them all about yourself and your products or services).

I define networking in this way: "The cultivating of mutually beneficial, *give* and take, win/win relationships." Note the emphasis on the "give" part. This might cause some to wonder if this is simply Pollyanna-type thinking that might not work in the real world.

It's actually quite realistic—giving works! Giving works both from a practical, as well as spiritual side. But let's just look at the practical side.

I have what I call "The Golden Rule of Networking." This rule is simple: All things being equal, people will do business with and refer business to those people they know, like, and trust.

When we give to (or do something for) someone, we take an important step toward causing those "know, like, and trust" feelings toward us in that other person. I've often said that the best way to get business and referrals is to first give business and referrals. Why? Because when someone knows you care about them enough to send business their way, they feel good about you. No, they feel *great* about you, and desire to give back to you.

Of course, it doesn't have to be actual business that you give. It could be information, whether that information is something that would help them in their business, personal, social, or recreational lives.

One example from my personal life illustrates my point. There was one corporate client I had been trying to "land." However, it was a big corporation with many divisions, and I could not seem to get a foot in the door. Not only that, I couldn't even find the door to try and stick my foot in!

At a convention, I met an experienced professional speaker and struck up a friendship with him and his family. Several times, when I was already booked for a speaking engagement on a certain date, I referred him to the person in the company that had invited me to speak. As a published magazine columnist, I also referred him as a contributor to the editor. This was appreciated by all parties, of course, and didn't take anything away from me. That's one of the great things about giving: it helps everyone and hurts no one.

A couple of years after meeting him I found out, through a third party, that the prospective company I had unsuccessfully pursued was a major client of this speaker friend of mine. I said, "I know this is a huge client of yours, and am not in any way asking for you to make a connection for me. I'd love to know, however, what you suggest would be the best way for me to contact the person myself. That way I could at least begin the relationship-building process."

He said, "I'll have the person there who is my main contact call you." And he did. And that client, together with all the spin-off engagements I've had from that company over the years, accounted for several million dollars in revenue for my company.

That was certainly not the first, nor was it the only, time that giving first has paid me big financial dividends. This is now the way I run my business and my life. It is also the philosophy of a great number of other people with whom I associate. The more successful a person is, the greater the chances are he or she is a giver, a connector of others, and a person who is always and forever attempting to "add value" to the lives of others.

Giving first works. The rewards do not always come quickly or directly from the person to whom you gave. It doesn't matter. Make giving first an ongoing part of your life and business practice, and you'll see terrific and long-lasting results. Give because it's the right thing and because you enjoy adding to the lives of other good people, and do it without the expectation of (or emotional attachment to) direct reciprocation. If you do, you'll find the principle of giving to be one of the truest of all universal laws, and you will get plenty of new clients and high-quality referrals.

———•◦•———

Cold calling and telephone terrorizing still produce new prospects, but this method is part of an older age. Today's marketplace demands innovative methods to get and keep clients. It's a different century—and a different world.
Business referral networks are now the preferred way to get clients, and networking experts Stephanie O'Hara and Tom Gosche, from the Chicago area, are master sellers, using network referral methods to keep their sales pipelines full.

———•◦•———

CONSTANT CONNECTIONS

STEPHANIE O'HARA AND TOM GOSCHE

The old school of selling can be offensive as we attempt to cope with an intense and highly charged world. Daily we encounter an overwhelming array of messages and inputs, each with the desire of capturing our undivided attention. Our memory and patience are taxed and have room for just a select few preferred messengers. Getting to be a preferred seller is the name of today's sales game. Masters of Sales know that becoming one of the selected few preferred vendors will require a mutually beneficial relationship between client and seller. Because relationship building consumes the seller's time and energy, the trick is to leverage those few people closely related to the seller into a wide net that captures many customers—through referrals.

Referral networking relies on a relatively small number of people, who represent, in various spin-off relationships, tens of thousands of buyers, and refers them to an appropriate seller at an opportune time through a face-to-face personalized process. This new focus on getting clients calls for building a manageable number of strategic, long-term relationships with key people each of whom agrees to find us referred clients. And we return the favor. Methodical use of this process multiplies our results far beyond the most energetic traditional methods of getting new customers. Masters of Sales are quickly learning to maintain a manageable referral network, and are rewarded with a steady flow of qualified prospects who consider us their vendor of choice.

Constant Connections

Our small group of referral partners keeps an eye and ear out for people in their respective networks, people who might need the other's product or service. Interacting with hundreds of people in the buying public, each referral partner keeps in constant connection with the people in his or her respective network, all of whom are part of the buying public. The result is an order book full of sales.

It works this way: Tom, a member of our company, and Dennis, a business acquaintance, work in the same building, and each belongs to a formal referral group of 20 business people. Each member of the two referral groups knows about 500 people, which means that every sales member of the group has access, through network connections, to about 10,000 members of the buying public. The objective is to create a buy/sell connection with each of those people when the service/product is needed. Tom and Dennis are getting good referrals from their own group, and now that they know each other in the same building, are able to take advantage of their own referral group as well as each other's group.

To build referral partnerships, we first have to meet the right people. This is easily accomplished by joining a structured professional referral marketing program like BNI. Here the seller joins a tight-knit group of other sellers, each of whom agree to abide by their membership agreement of finding referrals for the others. Whether you join a formal referral network or start your own, the job starts with meeting good potential referral partners. This means we have to interview them to make several determinations.

During this initial conversation, we look for signs suggesting that our new contact is someone that we want to connect with later. We want to know a little about their goals and objectives so we can assess whether we would be able to refer him or her to one of our existing referral partners and people in our personal networks. The side benefit is that it's really nice to help people meet their own goals and objectives and even more interesting when these same people find ways to repay your favor later.

The method we use to find clients might best be understood through a comparison with the traditional sales prospecting and selling method.

Traditional Model	Constant Connections Model
Transactions	Relationships
Write on business cards	Look for common denominators
Shallow	Deeper
Rapid	Slower, so a longer time to know clients
Depend on high volume	Cross-sell into more diverse services
Quantity vs. quality	Quality vs. quantity
Cold calls	Referrals
Impatient, a sense of urgency	Patient, in this for the long haul
Instant gratification	Long-term development
Casual connections networking	Closed connections networking
Customer	Client
Attend lots of events	Discriminating choice of events
Work hard to build business	Work smart to build business

We must stay closely connected to our network partners and to our personal network, which is comprised of people like you and me whose lives are influenced by hectic and sporadic demands. We use modern contact information systems (such as ACT, Goldmine, MS Outlook) to organize our lists and maintain constant communication with everyone on our team and in our networks. We continually assess when a client might be ready for a referral to us or to one of our partners. The objective is to become a buyer's resource for every person in our database, matching buyer appropriately to seller.

Natural laws governing social networks create incredible opportunities for our constant connections system. Making 20 focused phone connections per week creates 240 spoken connections during the quarter. This, combined with 400 strategic personal e-mails per month, gives us about 1,500 connections per quarter. These actions help keep us top-of-mind with our referring partners, who remind buyers to come to us when they need to be referred to a new selling vendor. We are secure in the knowledge that as we do these things, so also are our referral partners, with us uppermost in their collective minds.

As a BNI executive director in northern Illinois, I (Tom Gosche), send out at least one e-mail per month to each president of the 30 chapters in the Chicago area. In turn, they forward that e-mail to an average of 20 members, giving me a personalized connection with 600 people per month. If the message is strategically worded so the members want to pass it along to ten others, I am "reaching out and touching" 6,000 people monthly.

Through the use of the constant connections model, clients appear almost as if by magic. In reality, our model requires intentional effort of adding value to a few strong relationships in a formalized referral process. Once the system is started, referred clients emerge, but in truth they emerge as the result of methodical adherence to a long-term development approach for getting new clients. The real measure of your success with this program will be how well you handle an increasing book of business professionally, in a manner that continues to add value to others.

Starting a sales career as a model, then stockbroker, then homemaking guru, author, TV personality, and business magnate, this lady knows how to sell. Martha Stewart started selling her many varied products, and now her products' brand, "Martha Stewart" is selling her. This amazing woman shares a few key strategies to start a word-of-mouth buzz about you, the seller, getting you in front of more buyers.

PROMOTE YOURSELF AS AN EXPERT

MARTHA STEWART

1.

Is there a common problem people face that your business helps solve or a seasonal aspect that you can use for promotional purposes?

Everyone loves it when his or her problems are solved and solved well. And few people dread a season of the year more than "tax time." If you have opened an accounting firm and are trying to promote its business, develop a creative way of talking about it, such as offering the local media the chance to discuss "the five most common mistakes people make during the year that will come back to haunt them at tax time" or the "five often-overlooked deductions that can save you thousands of dollars." You might even offer to prepare a reporter's tax return for his story to illustrate these points. Concentrate on basic, universal problems to help connect your solutions with other people's problems.

Stories tied to a holiday are another great way of generating news coverage. For example, by mid-November, newspapers are printing stories with suggestions for unusual and unique holiday gifts. If you feel that your handmade craft would be a desirable gift, a well-prepared press release with photographs is one way to get the reporters' attention. Another good way is to send the product itself with an explanatory letter and an excellent photo that the papers can reproduce. If you can have the photographs scanned and send the press release in an electronic format to make the information more accessible and editor friendly, all the better. Let them know why your product is special and why it makes a good gift. Keep in mind that holiday stories are written well in advance of the holiday, and the papers need lead time.

2.
What are the social dynamics that have created the opportunity for your business?

One of the reasons I wanted to create *Martha Stewart Living* magazine was because I perceived a social trend: It was perfectly clear to me that women were hungry for information to help them run their homes more efficiently, entertain with more ingenuity and style, and learn all the clever homemaking techniques and tips that their mothers may not have taught them. I made it a point to discuss and promote the notion that "living" encompassed much more than just decorating and cooking—that it also embraced crafts, collecting, gardening, cleaning, organizing, and inventive child rearing. Raising the notion of homemaking to an art rather than treating it as a chore, made me different and interesting and worth covering for the press. In the beginning, reporters treated me a bit skeptically, trying to understand the multitasking I talked about, the joy I experienced, and the enthusiasm I exuded when I discussed what I was working on. But the more I talked, the more books and magazines I sold, the more I became known as an expert in homekeeping and all subjects related to living well. In the process, amazingly, homekeeping was elevated to the art form it deserved to be.

3.
Can your product or service be effectively demonstrated on television?

Television has extraordinary reach and power, and with the ever-increasing number of cable channels, there are more—and more specialized—

programming options available than ever before. Appearing on television is also an effective way to promote services, such as career coaching, particularly if you have an animated, friendly, jargon-free manner when illustrating your methods and their potential value to customers. Viewers love to see that you enjoy and believe in what you do. And they love success stories.

As I became increasingly well-known through my catering business, my early books, my magazines, and later my products, I traveled widely, giving speeches on my areas of expertise. Sometimes I donated my time to a charitable organization to help them raise money, and sometimes I charged a speaker's fee. These events created a national audience for my subject matter, increased my customer base tremendously, and created demand for more Martha Stewart-related products. That, in turn, led to regular appearances on the *CBS Morning Show* and NBC's *Today* Show. The exposure generated interest in my magazines and books and, later, my daily television show. I have mentioned the idea of "teach so you can learn." You must also remember the concept of "teach and the press will help promote you!"

Get Personal

Another thing to keep in mind is your personal story and whether it has ingredients that reporters will find intriguing, novel, offbeat, or funny.

I believe that each phase of my career has been intriguing to people in part because of what preceded it. When I was a stockbroker, people were interested to learn that I used to be a model. When I became a caterer and author, local media found it compelling that I had been a stockbroker. My image developed as a person who was willing to take risks and try new things. There are so many people who dream about changing their lives; the media know the public loves to be informed about someone who has dared to go out and do it.

One tried-and-true way to attract the media's attention is to put the focus on you as the "face" of the brand. This has worked beautifully for Ralph Lauren, Donna Karan, Sean "Diddy" Combs, and Oprah Winfrey, to name a few—as well as for me. Becoming the face of your own brand is a very effective way of connecting with your customers. A friendly, attractive face attached to a brand is a powerful selling tool.

Tell Your Story Well

Before you start sharing your information with the press, polish yourself by practicing on family, friends, or employees. Do this in a talk show format where the "host" grills you with questions. Develop your own question-answer script, but encourage your interviewers to be spontaneous, as well. This will familiarize you with listening carefully to interviewers' questions so you can grow more confident with practice. Remember to look the interviewer in the eye, try to relax and smile, and keep your answers relatively short and to the point. Do not underestimate the importance of your first interview with a small, local newspaper. Facts, figures, statistics—all of these should be as accurate as possible because the first printed interview in a local newspaper will often lead to interviews in bigger newspapers and magazines and eventually to radio and television, so you want to ensure that everything you say, everything that is reported, is true and not misleading.

At first, you will likely be the sole voice of your brand. As you expand and take on more employees, however, keep in mind that building a strong brand and accomplishing your goals means that you must be diligent in keeping your message consistent. Your goal is for customers to associate your enterprise with a few important and memorable characteristics that only change if you deliberately decide to change them. The more you and your employees sing the same song, the easier it will be for your customers to remember the principal melody.

Speak to be Heard, and Hear to Know How to Speak

*The most important thing in communication is
to hear what isn't being said.*
—PETER DRUCKER

The human relationship factor in selling is mentioned by virtually all contributors to this discussion of masterful selling. The reason for talking about sales communication is that relationships are formed through communication. The reality is that the quality of our relationships depends on the quality of our communications.

QR = QC

Of course, not all sale transactions require incredible relationships or even much communication, but this new emphasis is gaining momentum in modern selling. Even big box stores like Wal-Mart—not known for warm customer relations—illustrate the value they place on communication and relationship by employing a visitor host to greet customers at the entrance of their stores.

Within the sales process, we are reminded by Sara Minnis of a phobia many salespeople face. She coaches salespeople who are afraid of being rejected by a prospect or customer. She says, "Sales 'phobics' might have an unrealistic fear of being rejected during cold calling, during the closing phase, or on a phone conversation." Sara suggests that phobic salespeople tend to focus their communication on the emotional fit between themselves and the customer. She says, "The real business of selling can't begin until the sales phobic feels that the prospect likes him or her." To avoid this, she says, "The professional seller directs her communication toward finding a fit between her product and the buyer's need. Focusing on being liked only enhances fears of personal rejection, while attending to the customer's needs drives the transaction toward a closed deal."

Sellers in a strong relationship with their clients have a competitive advantage because the client feels connected or bonded to the seller. The single most important tool sellers use to establish a connecting bond with another person is communication. In fact, building a bonded relationship is *completely* dependent on having quality communications with another individual.

The art and science of communication is more than talking and hearing words. There are many strategies and techniques aimed at earning the right to have your message heard. If you can communicate at a level that matches the customer's style rather than your own, you will be on the way to masterful sales conversations.

Masters of Sales today assume more of a consultative perspective to their selling work. In fact, many box retail stores use the term "sales consultant" to describe the store clerk of yesterday. Master sales consultants know that their ability to communicate is critical to selling client solutions, because rapport and trust, the cornerstones of selling, are built or lost based on communication.

Susan RoAne, known as The Mingling Maven™ and renowned keynote speaker on networking, shares her knowledge about sales communications. She teaches us simple fail-safe techniques for using our communications to foster great relationships between the seller and the buyer. Sales transactions that conclude with a tremendous positive result are indicative of good communication between seller and buyer.

SUPERNATURAL SELLERS

SUSAN ROANE

Professional selling means having full product knowledge, understanding your customer needs, and knowing how each customer will benefit from the product. Masterful sellers are also able to **engage** their customers in comfortable but controlled conversation. The conversation usually starts small and seems to move in a myriad of directions, but in fact is intentionally directed toward establishing a common ground and a connection between the seller and buyer. These conversations appear casual, but in reality are deliberately designed by the seller to achieve a specific result.

In *Reinventing the Corporation* (Warner Books, 1985), authors Naisbitt and Aberdeen discovered that people do business with sellers they know, like, and—most importantly—trust. The actions, deeds, and words of the masterful seller are designed to establish rapport first, followed by trust-worthiness, all leading toward establishing a positive connection with the client. Think about it: We don't want to give our money to the hairstylist, mechanic, consultant, or personal trainer we find annoying or who we believe is *not* concerned about our best interests.

Casual Conversation: The Heart of Warming Up a Prospect

The "supernatural" salesperson converses easily, listens to what is said (and not said), and responds accordingly. I once featured an interview with our local music store manager. From him, I learned the essence of sales success. When asked what part of sales was based on conversation, he succinctly spoke these words of wisdom, "Conversation isn't a part of sales . . . it is the heart of it."

A national bank in New York engaged me to teach its managers how to "work a room" as part of its business development series. In preparation for this task, I interviewed the organization's top salesperson, who had won the organization's sales award for the previous four years. After intro-ducing myself on the phone, I mentioned her achievement as the out-standing salesperson. Her response startled me: "I've never sold anything."

"Yes, I won the award," she said. "But I don't 'sell' anything."

At my perplexed silence, she went on to explain, "I chat with my cus-tomers at bank-sponsored events and when they come into the bank. When I see them in the community, we always take a moment to talk and catch up. I get to know them, and *I let them get to know me so they know a real person and not just a bank employee selling them a service.* When I call with a new product, they take my conversation seriously, knowing that I don't waste their time on something they don't need."

Focusing the Sales Conversation During the Sale

Once engaged in a serious sales conversation, the seller's focus moves from one qualifying comment to the next, followed by the presentation and closing sequence. During this time, the seller needs to learn if her product is a match for the buyer's unique needs. Jean Miller successfully sells big ticket items, but never pushes the bells and whistles that her clients don't need. "When you oversell and persuade people to buy, you risk losing the client. I know that happy clients produce my commissions and spread word-of-mouth endorsements about me." As a former librarian, Jean is well versed in researching her clients and continues learning about their needs by carefully listening to what they say and don't say. She frames her conversation according to what she hears or doesn't hear.

Master Salespeople Follow Up in a Timely Manner

The smart and savvy salesperson has extraordinary follow-up, knowing when it's most appropriate to take that next action step. Carl LaMell drove one car for six years and finally wanted the newest model. At the showroom, he met a new salesperson and specified the car he wanted to buy. The salesperson had to do a little research, locate a car, and call Carl with details on how to finalize the purchase. The salesman didn't follow up and apologized for "not getting around to it" when Carl called some time later.

The next week, Carl went to the competitor Lexus showroom, was pleasantly greeted, and again indicated what he wanted. Soon, after a little sales research, the very thorough and pleasant salesperson found him the right car and a new car deal was completed in less than 48 hours. Follow-up communication with a prospect is part of the sales job, and yet often is neglected by novice sellers. It's no wonder they aren't making money.

Master salespeople have some specific traits:

- *Listen and talk.* Don't for a minute believe that great salespeople only listen and say nothing. "Conversational selling" is not a game of 20 questions but a give and take in which information and concerns are shared and addressed. The buyer always feels respected and understood, and the seller is always in control of the conversation.
- *Prepare.* They prepare for business and sales events by reading journals, web sites, and newspapers, and have three to five topics that relate and add to the selling situation should there be a conversational lull that needs bridging.
- *Use a conversational tone and pace.* That puts clients at ease and makes them comfortable about buying the object. This allows

customers to BUY the object rather than feeling as if they are being sold to.

- *Stay in touch.* They communicate with clients even when there is nothing to sell, which strengthens the relationship between vendor and future buyer.

Master salespeople know how to mingle, network, and converse in every room they enter and with every prospect or customer. They don't prejudge individuals and treat everyone with respectful conversation because "you never know" where the next customer will come from.

The psychology of people is funny. We are all people, but it's often hard to open a conversation with someone who doesn't want to say much. "Can I help you?" "No thanks I'm just looking." This is a real dilemma for salespeople. Harvey Branman is a professional photographer who paints a clear image of how to open a conversation that can move a sale forward.

SELLING IS EASY WITH COUSINS

HARVEY BRANMAN

Based on the theory that a small group of humans who could speak started a worldwide migration, we are all related, somehow. "Hello, cousin!"

Everyone we come in contact with might be a distant cousin from our past. Adopting this perspective can certainly influence our attitudes about others and the interactions we have with them—including our clients.

For example, when attending a family reunion, you might meet a distant relative and find it easy to ask a lot of questions about his or her history and experience. Usually we are quite interested in knowing more about our distant relatives and look for common areas of interest. The common bonds we discover help cement our family relationship.

This concept can work beyond "family" ties. When approaching people that I've never met with, the perspective that I'm meeting a long-lost cousin mentally takes any awkwardness out of our beginning relationship. The other person seems to feel that I care about them, and often we have the start of a great new friendship!

Engaging a stranger in conversation feels uncomfortable, but is highly likely to lead to positive opportunities. Think back. Most great things started with an original conversation with another person. Opening conversations are essential in selling, but most prospective clients don't easily open up or clearly describe what they want to buy. Either they mistrust the seller or the environment, or they simply don't yet know what they want. The salesperson's job is to help prospects explore their desires and then move directly to the selection and purchase of product. This necessitates opening a sales conversation.

Open-ended questions are great ways to start an initial conversation. I rely on a systematic approach, which I describe with the acronym FORM: Family, Occupation, Recreation, and Motivation (or Money).

My question for Occupation might be: "So, what do you do?"

Everyone wants to talk about what they do, and over time they will stop describing their business or interests and ask you about your own business.

My questions for Family might include:
- "Where are you from?"
- "Are you a native of Southern California?"
- "Where did you go to high school?"
- "Are you married? Do you have kids?"

It's amazing. I run into many people from my hometown Chicago, and even those who attended the same high school in East Rogers Park. Sharing a common place of origin allows people to subconsciously trust each other more, and allows more personal information to be shared.

Then I might ask them what they do for recreation:
- "What do you like to do on vacation or on the weekends?"
- "What are your hobbies?"

Two long-time members of the same business association discovered that each liked riding their bikes each morning before work. Soon they started riding together and joined the same cycling club. As their biking relationship grew, they began referring more business to each other. Discovering a shared recreational passion can positively influence your sales volume.

My last question to my new cousin is usually: "So, what made you decide to go into your line of work?"

Get people to share what they like about their work, and they will appreciate the interest you show in them. The potential for sales increases exponentially when we demonstrate a personal interest in other people. Remember, your competition is always right around the corner. The buyer will approach you or flee from you, based on how they interpret your communication as being interested or ambivalent toward them.

Approach everyone you meet with the feeling that they are a long-lost cousin with whom you can find common bonds. Use the FORM method to learn more about your "cousins" and discover common areas of interest. Create a bond between you and the buyer because this will help the rest of the selling process go smoothly.

Too few sellers are masters at listening to what the customer really wants. Listening is more than an art form, it is a serious tool used by many communication specialists, notably professional counselors and sellers. Stuart Mitchell, a sales and marketing pro from Brisbane, Australia, offers insight into the secret world of the professional listener. Those with these skills are more able to close the deal or solve the problem.

EARNING THE RIGHT TO BE HEARD

STUART MITCHELL

Two of the strongest criticisms about salespeople are:
1. They are only interested in selling me something.
2. They don't really care about me.

By contrast, I listen to my prospects and clients and win national sales awards year after year, while consistently doubling my sales targets. My claim to fame is that I actively listen to my prospects and clients.

"Active listening" is like a bank account. The more active listening deposits you make, the more sales withdrawals you get. It works this way. When you listen well to your prospects—AND THEY KNOW IT—they will, in return, listen to what you have to say about your product. This leads to more sales.

Salespeople communicate for a living and succeed through establishing a rapport and connection with an audience. Master sales communicators learn a special type of communicating that includes listening actively. Often called *attentive listening,* this skill is practiced by counselors and sellers alike to achieve rapport with their clients and a deeper understanding of their expressed or nonexpressed needs. This listening tool can be so powerful that it sometimes causes a classic challenge for successful counselors: having to deal with clients falling in love with them. Imagine having our buyers fall in love us, the sellers! This would be one of those good problems to experience.

When you can demonstrate a genuine interest in the other's well-being, that person will want to give you business—and often go out of his way to do so. This hard-won position of trust is developed over time and is started through being a good attentive listener.

While learning a career in sales, I discovered several common obstacles to mastering this skill. The following is my hard-earned wisdom.

Filtered Listening

Filtered listening means judging people based on your own opinion and worldview. Good listeners have the ability to "walk in another person's shoes," to understand (and accept) the other's perspective. It is easy to pre-judge people in areas such as race, gender, personal appearance, sexual preference, age, social status, and group affiliation. When you are the object of a pre-judgment, you know it.

Salespeople who demonstrate an attitude of acceptance are the winners. So don't filter people through your own preconceived views. Allow the new person to express his inner side before you make a qualifying judgment. All Masters of Sales know that sometimes the best sale comes from the most unlikely person.

Rehearsing the Response

During a conversation, the listener often isn't really listening but instead planning what to say next. Thinking about the words we need to use will block our ability to hear the other person's words. If we are truly to understand the prospect, we have to hear his words and emotionally be present during our discussion; otherwise we miss vital information that leads toward mutual understanding and success.

If customers feel that you are asking questions that are not relevant to their needs, they will not give you their confidence, trust, and respect—and they certainly won't give you their sales.

Interrupting

Interrupting a speaker to paraphrase or reflect on what they are saying can work because it offers a moment to ponder their own feelings and thoughts. But interrupting to give your opinion is less than helpful. Sure, do it if you are running out of time and you can skillfully interrupt. But do this only in a way that does not disenfranchise the client.

Self-Talk

Your customer is talking animatedly to you about his needs and concerns. You are talking with yourself about work, paying the bills, your family, or whatever. Self-talk is read by the customer as you not caring or their being unimportant to you. This feeling certainly will kill any growing rapport with your client.

You can overcome these barriers to active listening with the following active-listening techniques of mirroring and reflecting feeling.

Mirroring

This concept involves matching your body language with the client's, and includes your facial expressions, eye contact, tone level of voice, even your breathing. This is especially important when you first meet someone. Remember that people make up their mind about you in the first three minutes, so in these first minutes you must validate their opinion.

The objective is to develop mirroring skills that allow you to deal with a rugged truck driver one minute and an upper class, refined, elderly lady the next. In both instances, you want these people to feel as if you fully understand them and can relate to their issues. Do this, and you are a master of attentive listening. But, more importantly, your buyer will feel that you are similar to her own style, personality, and mannerisms, and therefore will be more prone to buy from you.

Reflecting Feeling

When I can pick up on both the spoken and unspoken feeling my client is experiencing and reflect those emotions back to them, I establish a deeper emotional connection with that client. This deeper affective level of understanding (rapport) accelerates my sales process with him. Through empathic or attentive listening, I can learn about the unspoken fears, concerns, and general emotions of the client. If I read anxiety, I know there might be a strong objection.

It's difficult for many salespeople to actively listen to the emotional side of a prospect, and yet this is exactly where the buy/no-buy decisions are made. The effective salesperson listens attentively for the emotions experienced by the customer because these simple feelings will block or accelerate a sale.

I have learned that manipulating or controlling customers is not effective in today's marketplace. To be a master seller, replace the old selling notions with a win-win expectation that starts with attentive listening and ends with a perfect match of client needs and product—even if your product isn't accepted, you will build a great long-term experience for you and your customer.

———•◦•———

Arranging and completing a big million-dollar sale becomes more intricate when the buyer successfully persuades one of Canada's wealthiest men by selling him a better deal. It's called negotiation and is a critical component of selling, especially in large ticket sales. Darrell Ross, from Vancouver, continually adds to his expertise as a professional trainer in sales and marketing by getting to know successful people. As a result, his successful marketing franchises are well-known.

———•◦•———

ASK THE RIGHT QUESTIONS AND WIN THE SALE

DARRELL ROSS

The first impression blew me away as I gazed at a huge wall filled with a variety of magazines on display. I was to meet with Peter Legge, CEO of Canada Wide Magazines and Communications Ltd., to find out how he became a sales master.

During his career spanning several decades, Legge successfully turned his small television listings magazine, *TV Week*, into the largest independently owned publishing company in Western Canada, producing more than 35 titles, with annual revenues in excess of $25 million. In addition to his media empire, he is an acclaimed professional speaker and author who is constantly booked for speeches and continues to sell one book after the other.

Legge believes that salespeople must have a vision of what is possible and then be prepared to do what it takes to realize their goals. In 1991, he heard that the *BC, Alberta, Saskatchewan,* and *Manitoba Business* magazines were for sale as a packaged deal. The $3 million (Canadian) price tag was beyond his means, but he didn't give up. Peter offered to buy only the *BC Business* magazine, because instinctively he knew what this one magazine would do for his company. He sold the owner, Jimmy Pattison (one of Canada's wealthiest men) on selling him the single magazine for $1.1 million, interest free, paid over four years.

In order to get that deal done, Legge had to ask a lot of questions. Even though he was the buyer, technically he had to "sell" Pattison on the idea that he only wanted part of the package for a lower price. His strategy was to divest Pattison emotionally from the product. So he asked questions like, "Why do you want to sell?" "What is wrong with the magazine?" "Why don't you want it?" "Why can't Jimmy Pattison make it work?" Through careful questioning, Legge got Pattison to realize that he really did want to sell just one magazine, and that the offered price was fair given Pattison's lack of interest in that particular business.

Legge maintains that the way to move all sales along is to ask enough questions until the true needs of the client are discovered. His method is to create a qualifying question based on each of the client's statements. For example: "So, what you're telling me is that if this product can help you achieve this goal, then you're willing to sign a contract?" Often the response will uncover another objection, such as: "Well no, we have to be sure that it can be delivered by such and such a date." Keeping to his system, Legge would then ask, "What you're really saying is that if we can help you achieve this goal and deliver on or before such a date, then you'll be prepared to fill out the contract?" And so on. These qualifying questions are what separate a sales master from those who struggle to make their quotas. The master is completely aware how his product or service will help the customer and is willing to ask the questions to close the deal.

The trick is to pick the best questions to uncover the real needs of your client:

- What are you hoping to achieve (by using this product, buying this advertising, etc)?
- How do you think you want to achieve that?
- What have you tried in the past?
- How well did that work?
- What is it that you are really looking for?

Taking his advice, I asked, "So what you're telling me is that sales success comes down to being able to ask the right questions?" With a twinkle in his eye he replied, "Well, sort of. You have to be able to ask the right questions of yourself as well." Every day he asks himself winning questions, such as:

- "How do I make a sale today?"
- "What is it going to take to write an order today?"
- "How do I get the contract signed today?"

In sales, as in life, one makes choices. Choices we make today affect our results tomorrow, and next week, and next year. These choices are merely questions that we ask of ourselves. Consider Peter Legge, the questions he asks, and how they set him up for success. Have a vision, and act on it. Take risks, research your customers, make everyone you meet a client, friend, or acquaintance, and don't take no for an answer. Most importantly, learn the right questions to ask, and ask yourself the toughest questions of all.

———•◦•———

The words used in our conversations of yesteryear may be politically incorrect or ineffective in today's world. Language changes as we evolve through the ages. Two Floridian professional sales trainers, Greta Schulz and Sandy Donovan, show us how to transform old sales scripts into ones that more effectively match the needs of today's buying public.

UP-FRONT SELLING

GRETA SCHULZ AND SANDY DONOVAN

There are visions that make us cringe when we think about "traditional" salespeople: White shoes, gold chains, and the ultimate, *"If I could show you a way . . . would you buy today . . ."* Yikes! Most of us know that looking and acting like Herb Tarlek from radio station WKRP in the1970s is not appropriate for today's sellers. Even so, I continue to see the majority of salespeople using these same outdated selling methods, even if in slightly toned-down styles. True Masters of Sales should leave the old selling communications styles to history and learn a style that more appropriately fits the modern consumer.

Old Method 1

The prospect asks you why they should buy from you and not the other guy. And you proudly answer, "Well, we are the number-one widget dealer in the Southeast. Our prices are competitive and we have excellent service . . . Blah, blah, blah . . ." (Wow, how interesting; sign me up!)

First of all, stop talking! No one is interested in all of the facts and figures about how great your company is. They are only interested in how this pertains to them. And how will you find this out? Great question!

The Master of Sales would answer:

> *Mr. Prospect, that's a good question, and I'm not 100 percent sure at this point that you should buy my product. But if we could take some time today and ask each other enough questions, we will probably discover one of two things: either we are a match and why, or we're not. That's OK, too, because what we do isn't for everyone. How does that sound?*

Establishing a process goal up front about the expectations of the meeting and the meeting process makes everyone feel at ease. If everyone feels comfortable about the interaction, the truth will come out.

Old Method 2

At the end of the meeting the prospect says, "Well thanks, leave me some information on your company, and I'll get back to you if anything comes up." You say, "Sure," leaving your fancy brochure. Then you put them in the "tickler file" for phone calls once a month to "check in." Pretty soon your days will be full with "follow-up" calls that lead to nowhere, but boy, you're busy (and broke)!

The Master of Sales would start his meeting this way:

> *Mr. Prospect, before we begin, would it make sense to set our expectations of the meeting? First of all, we discussed on the phone to allow about 45 minutes, has anything changed with the time? No? Great. Since we only touched on a few things over the phone, I would like to ask you some additional questions about your business, its challenges . . . etc. Of course, Mr. Prospect, you will have some questions for me about our organization and how we may be able to help. At the end of our 45 minutes, typically one of two things will happen. You might not see a fit between our two organizations, and you'll tell me no. And that's OK, because what we do isn't for everyone. Or, we will discover that it makes sense for us to move forward and we can make a decision today about our next steps. Sound fair?*

When you set expectations up front, there is almost no chance for an unclear communication. People are not uncomfortable making a decision; they are uncomfortable being given only one choice. Let's roll back to the beginning of this meeting. The prospect never would have said to just leave the brochure if you had set clear expectations at the beginning.

This approach allows you to avoid the biggest sales nightmare— Indecision. Masters of Sales know that by allowing their prospects the option of saying no, the pressure is lifted. As a result, they are more comfortable. In addition, they pay close attention. Wouldn't you, if you knew you had to make a decision?

"Wipe that frown off your face!" "Don't use that TONE OF VOICE with me!" Did your mother ever scold you for the scowl on your face or the tone of your voice? If so, join the crowd; we've all experienced this. The Tropicana Twist of communications, Anne Warfield, shares a few secrets about a communication that mirrors our verbal speech—or does it? As a Certified Professional Speaker and ranked in the top 7 percent of her field, we need to hear her advice.

YOUR BODY SPEAKS VOLUMES ... WHAT'S IT SAYING?

ANNE WARFIELD

A considerable message is delivered by one's body language. We respond to the total combined message sent, one that includes both verbal and nonverbal information. In fact, we seem to react stronger to what we think a person meant, than to their actual words. Masterful sellers know the importance of matching their body language with their words so their message is as straight and consistent as possible. If a supervisor says, "You are doing a great job," and displays a big warm smile and a relaxed body, you will probably believe them. On the other hand if a person says, "That suit looks great on you," and their teeth are gritted, they have a half smile, and a stiff body, you won't be sure if they think the suit is too tight, is the wrong color, makes you look funny, or what!

Consciously reading and sending messages through body language alone is an underpracticed art, even though everyone has experienced it. Think about the last messages you heard and observed. Did you pick up on the emotional undertone of the message? Did the words match the body's emotional set? By merely changing the tone of our voice and set of our body, we can alter the meaning behind our words. Put on a huge smile, hands on hips, tilted head, and say with a modulate voice, "That suit looks fabulous on you!" Now stand slumped, faced sideways to the person with your hands clenched, and say in a monotone quiet voice, "That suit looks fabulous on you." What's the difference in believability? In a nutshell, Masters of Sales know that controlling their body language sets them apart from the novice sellers.

Different interpretations can result merely from words given a different tone and emphasis, and the set of your body. If you raise your voice in a question while stating your pricing, it will sound as though you don't believe the customer will pay that price. Your message is that price is negotiable. If you shift your eyes and frequently look away, people will not trust the message being given. To achieve a great sales result, ensure that the message conveyed through your body language coincides with the message conveyed by your spoken words.

John came to us in frustration because one of his lead clients hadn't given him more business for the past three years, even though this customer sold $10 million of his product with high gross margins. The customer wouldn't give him an inch more shelf space.

I asked John how his client displayed his body language during the presentation. John said, "He usually sits with his arms crossed, leans back, and often squints his eyes at me. He seems to grab objects off the table as well." These are classic signs that his customer is upset and has shut him out.

John learned how to read the client's message while also opening his own body language. We taught him to use an *Outcome Focus* process of presenting, which helped to draw the customer into a closer relationship. This process teaches the seller how to present from a buyer's perspective or to identify how the buyer sees and hears the seller. Through this process, John customized his message to his unique customer issues, and increased the ability of his own message to be well received by the listener/buyer.

Once he grasped this method, John called to say that he used all he learned and walked out of his last meeting with an *additional* $10 million of business! The most amazing part, he said, was that by learning how to read body language, he put the client at ease and was better able to focus his energy on the needs of this client. He stopped telling his client what he thought was needed, and instead listened to what was of real importance to the client.

A Master of Sales knows how to present positive messages with body language by making eye contact, smiling, nodding occasionally during conversation, leaning slightly toward the customer, and tilting her head to one side as she is listening. People want to know that you will do whatever is possible to help them, and this message is vividly expressed through your body language.

How you are perceived is up to you. Get feedback on your own body language. Once you better understand the real message you are sending, you can work to get in control of the nonverbal signals you convey. Did you know that you can even send a smile, or a frown, through the phone? You will be surprised at how much you say . . . without saying a word!

Asking the buyer to purchase your product is the ultimate question in your sales conversation. Everything in the sales process leads up to the close, at which time the buyer confirms that he or she wants to buy the product (or service).

Don Morgan realizes, after many decades of selling professional psychological services, water filters, boats, scuba gear, cars, and professional consulting services, that it doesn't matter what you are selling if you don't ask for the sale.

DO YA WANNA BUY?

DON MORGAN

To successfully close a deal, you have to invite the prospect to buy several times during the sales process. Other than low ticket retail purchases, most prospects tend to avoid saying, "OK, I'll buy it" on their own initiative. They have to be coaxed to make this commitment. Master sellers know how to ask for the sale, and they don't interpret a customer's "no" as a personal rejection.

Closing a sales process is really very simple. All that is required is to learn a few simple closing questions and then practice them until you are a master closer. The closing phraseology used during this phase of selling is simple but carefully worded.

To truly master closing scripts, it's important to grasp the key communication principle of allowing the customer choice within the interaction. The choices are pre selected like a multiple choice test.

Communicating Options

Get in the habit of allowing the customer optional responses at the onset of the sales interaction:

> *When would be the most convenient time to meet for you?*

> *Morning or afternoon?*

> *Early or late morning?*

> *The beginning, middle, or end of the week?*

> *Would you like a more complete presentation that will take 45 minutes, or should I plan on a 15-minute overview at first?*

By offering options to the customer, you give him partial control over your meeting. This signals your desire to respect his needs and to be a partner in his buying venture. As the transaction progresses, there are other ways to offer customers a choice, such as:

1. Which color do you prefer?

2. Will the product be mainly for business or family use?

3. Will your full staff or just senior staff take the course?

4. What is a better time to deliver the product, morning or afternoon?

Selling cars taught me that customers have very definite ideas about preferences, even if they can't articulate these at the outset. When we give our car customers a choice in selection of their new car (fabric, color, transmission, style), we convey our desire to share in the responsibility of getting just the right product to satisfy the client's special requirements. Giving them choice also makes them feel like a VIP, which certainly helps close the sale!

To communicate choice, sellers must have full product knowledge and discover how to match the product's features to the client's desires, which are often not articulated. Building choice into the sales interaction helps to draw out the client preferences.

Master Selling Scripts

Use sales scripts that communicate choice from the meet-and-greet phase right through to closing, product delivery, and follow-up. A simple sequence of three closing scripts is useful to close a sale for most products and services. Once you memorize the questions and practice using them, your closing ratio will improve. The questions are easy to insert into a sales conversation, yet they still allow the customer choice of three optional answers.

These questions get inserted into your directed sales conversation that bounces back and forth between casually and formally discussing many topics related to the customer and to the product. After your product presentation is completed, casually inject in the conversation the closing question. Following are some examples.

Closing Question 1

Do you feel this product/service/program/organization/concept would be of benefit to/enjoyed by people?

The response will be some form of yes, no, or maybe.

A "yes" means the client sees the merits of people owning the product, and is likely to be considering the idea of owning it. This signals to the seller that it is OK to move forward.

A "maybe" means the person is thinking about issues or features of the product that may not fit his immediate needs. The seller must discover if the prospect does not understand some aspect of the product or service, and then answer these questions or objections with the proper information before moving forward.

A "no" means that the client does not like the product and sees no personal application for it or anyone else in his organization. The way to move forward is to thank the client and (if you feel that a rapport was established) ask, "Although you cannot see merit in this product, might you be able to refer a friend or colleague who might like it?" You can also try to refer the customer to some other vendor who might better meet his needs, thereby doing a friendly deed that will come back to you . . . sometime. (What goes around comes around.)

With a "yes" answer (or a "maybe" that has been converted to a "yes"), you can move along in your sales script. If you have a firm "no," you will want to move on quickly to the next prospect in line.

Closing Question 2

Do you think that this product would be beneficial to your business?

You can substitute the word "business" with other terms as applicable (life, family, organization, or program) depending on the circumstances.

With this question, you are getting a little more familiar with your client, and are seeking to build on her general interest and turn it into her commitment. Again, you will get one of three responses (yes, no, maybe).

If you get a "yes," then the customer feels the product will not only benefit people in general, but will also directly benefit her or her business. At this point, you almost have the customer's agreement to own the product. Her only other concern may be with the price or some other logistical issue that will show up in a "maybe" response. But you are getting close, and you need to help your client overcome any final reasons for concern.

If the client feels your product or service will benefit people and it will benefit her own life or business, very little remains to separate her from agreeing to buy.

If the answer is "no," then ask when she might want to reconsider owning your product and work toward scheduling a follow-up meeting. Once you get such a meeting scheduled or noted in your calendar, now is the time to ask for a referral (covered above).

Follow the formula. If you have a "yes" or have overcome the "maybe" response, move right into the final stage.

Closing Question 3

Would you like to fill in the paper work so you can begin using the product?

If your interaction and communication was more formal, you will use more formal wording to the question; alternatively, a more casual exchange should be used if you have had a more informal, comfortable sales exchange. "Charlie, shall I roll it out for you?"

You will have to decide on the exact words to polish off the deal, but with practice you will soon master the best scripts.

Using three semi-open-ended closing questions will allow you to direct the conversation toward a conclusion to your business. As the seller, you remain in control of the professional task of selling, while respecting the client's time and integrity.

———•◦•———

Relating to Your Corporate Clients

I think it's about juggling . . . you've got to keep your eye on all
the balls; you have to give each ball energy, and you've got to
catch them all, especially the one about to hit the ground.
—PROFESSOR HOWARD STEVENSON, HARVARD SCHOOL OF BUSINESS

The highways are clogged with corporate sales representatives going from one sales presentation to another, all focused on landing their next deal. You can see them by the droves in airports across the globe, usually attached to the latest wireless communication devices, waiting for their flights (and hopefully a first-class seat to get there in style or to get home relaxed). It's not by accident that the corporate sellers like to travel first class.

First class is classy, for sure, but it so happens this is also where they can network with people, many of whom could be their future clients (or who might *know* their future clients). The corporate sales professional relates to issues and concerns of senior corporate executives, whose currency is highly specialized information and issues. Getting to meet these people is only a part of the battle, however.

Selling effectively in the corporate environment is roughly the same as selling consumer goods one-on-one with a single buyer, with one consuming exception: There are more details spread among a greater cast of highly specialized players, all of whom have a hand in the corporation's ultimate buying decision. Selling a car to a single person, or even a couple, requires only a basic understanding of the buyer's situation and desires to create a sales exchange. The corporate seller needs more than a basic understanding, because the mass of information is greater and the selling cycle is much, much longer.

Corporate products exchanged between one corporation and another range from computer software, to industrial cleaning products, to heavy equipment, to financial consulting services. Selling huge volumes or extremely intricate technology means the financial stakes are high. Lots of money is transferred in exchange for products, and one person (the sales representative) is in the middle. Like an orchestra conductor, this professional arranges the timing for each detail connected with the sale. The corporate seller understands the importance of timing the details, using the right tool at the right time, and understands how to engage a host of different people whose egos and questions need satisfaction for the sale to progress.

A corporate sales representative works with a sales team, especially when the nature of his or her product overlaps other sophisticated products. In sales at this level, one person usually doesn't have sufficient knowledge or expertise to handle all product-related issues. Mistakes are costly and have mega-implications. Corporate sellers must use their leadership skills to know when to bring in other actors in the show, which also means letting others take the glory for the good of the project.

Corporate salespeople, like all sales professionals, must keep their morale high, because grumpy salespeople won't survive in any situation.

Driving toward the goal, attending to all the details, and celebrating the win are all part of the life of the corporate sales professional. The masters are those who want the top-dog spot just a little more than the rest, and who understand getting to that top spot is a team activity. These high-achieving people know the secrets of the master networker and the master of success, and they use it all to achieve their goals in the corporate arena.

Everyone is busy these days, but senior corporate decision makers, who ultimately decide to buy or not to buy, have even less spare time, are more harassed, and place greater expectations on the seller. Jill Konrath, author, speaker, and recognized expert on selling to large corporations, shares a few secrets about cracking into the big accounts.

SELLING TO CORPORATE ACCOUNTS

JILL KONRATH

If you're like most sellers, you have visions of lucrative long-term contracts sold to big companies that net you big paychecks. Landing that high-profile firm will propel your business to the next level, in turn making it easier to reel in the next corporate client.

Turning that dream into reality is really tough! Corporate decision makers rarely answer the phone, let voice mail answer unknown callers, and almost never call back. Once you crack open the prospect's door, he seems more intent on dismissing or "price whipping" you than hearing how you can help his organization. It's almost as if there's a methodical system to eliminate us corporate sellers, and this can be downright discouraging.

An elite corporate seller is well founded in the realities facing the radically changing world of the corporate decision maker. Corporate decision makers are pressured by Wall Street masters to maximize the value of their shares. They must balance their expenses against revenues, are constantly downsizing, rightsizing, and reorganizing to get it just right, and sit through endless meetings that consume most of their time.

These senior people live daily with escalating expectations to do more, faster . . . and with fewer resources. Every single day they receive hundreds of e-mails, take part in dozens of phone calls, and have their focus interrupted nearly every three to five minutes with something else to consider. They are overwhelmed with work, and the last thing they are interested in is more work. You may have the most timesaving thing out there, but at this level, they evaluate everything against demands from their current processes, ROI considerations, alternative options, and contracts currently under negotiation, and if they buy, it means implementing a new operational method. Often it's more expedient to live with their less-than-perfect status quo.

If it seems like a struggle to catch their attention, you might be relying on traditional selling strategies that no longer are effective. Corporate decision makers have little or no tolerance for sellers who make old-time mistakes:

- *Don't waste their time.* These senior people protect their most precious commodity—time. Their primary concern is how you can help them with their business, so focus on this when you initiate contact.
- *Don't use self-serving verbiage.* The nicer you talk about your product, the less believable you are. Everyone's product is the best—just ask the sellers. Experienced corporate people are jaded from assaults by invasive marketing messages. They've heard it all before.
- *Don't assume they understand your value.* Articulate your value proposition clearly so there is no doubt about the business outcomes realized if they switched from their status quo. These people don't have time to figure out the impact of your product on their operations.

- *Don't try to be their friend.* Personal relationships are important to selling, but they must be earned. Friendships result from your helping them achieve their goals or eliminating their issues.
- *Don't expect them to tell you about their business.* The price of admission to large corporations is your research and homework. If you don't invest time learning about them, they're not interested in giving you time.
- *Don't "product dump" on them.* Once you've landed a meeting, the worst thing you can do is to tell them all about your entire product line or every service your firm can provide. Their worst fear is sitting in front of a product-pushing peddler running off at the mouth.

You can achieve success selling to big companies by implementing the following strategies consistently:

- *Personalize every contact.* Corporate decision makers expect you to know about their business, so demonstrate your knowledge by mentioning a key strategic imperative or a recent acquisition related to their firm.
- *Show them how to make a quantifiable difference.* Corporate decision makers don't have much time to reflect on cost-saving mechanisms. Sellers who can offer ways to streamline operations, reduce costs, or achieve objectives will become trusted advisors.
- *Show them others' results.* You speak with other firms who struggle with the same challenges. This knowledge is your asset that can be converted to corporate problem solver.
- *Act and sound like a peer.* Act like a peer who is fully grounded in the business value of your offering. If you are intimidated when speaking to them, it's highly unlikely you'll land an appointment.
- *Be a provocateur.* Get them to think, and you've got their attention. You must be a specialist in your field. Introduce new information necessary to their decision making. Point out potential unintended consequences of their current direction. Do it graciously, and you will earn their respect, and lots of business.

Use the following questions as a litmus test to gaining an appointment:

- *Will your message interest them enough to grant you time during their busy schedule?*
- *Will your message be interpreted by the decision makers as a way to improve their operation?*

If you can answer yes to both of these questions, then you're on the right track. If not, rethink your strategy. Corporate selling today is less about your product or service and more about providing the right tools to help companies achieve their desired results. Keep your focus on that and you'll land lots of corporate clients.

———

"The customer is always right" takes on a new meaning in the corporate sales arena. Whether the customer is right or wrong, he is the one making (huge) buying decisions. Steve Kaplan knows selling from the bottom up. As front-line seller for his own business ventures, and having owned and sold several million-dollar businesses, Kaplan knows the balance between respecting the client's needs and earning respect for his expertise, and together moving the corporation further through use of the right product.

———

FACE-TO-FACE WITH YOUR PROSPECT

STEVE KAPLAN

If your telephone and mail efforts have hit pay dirt, you're about to go face-to-face with a potential client. Just as in any other aspect of life, first impressions are crucial. You want to come across as perceptive, experienced, and confident—a professional who works with big companies every day. The following tips will help pave your way.

Get Your Act Together

Don't prepare a one-size-fits-all sales spiel that can be rattled off in any meeting. To the extent possible, go into the meeting with a discussion plan tailored to that particular prospect. Your earlier contacts with the prospect should have given you the information you need. If not, go back to your reconnaissance of the company. Be ready to discuss whatever you specified during the meeting setup call. In addition:

SET PRIORITIES. Before every important meeting, I make a list of specifics I hope to accomplish. This helps me stay focused when I'm face-to-face with my prospect. I sneak an occasional peek to make sure all my issues have been addressed, and having a written list helps me avoid getting distracted by issues the prospect raises. These have to be addressed, of course, but not at the risk of forgetting the things that can make the difference between a good deal for the prospect and a good deal for me.

ANTICIPATE YOUR PROSPECT'S CONCERNS. What questions is he likely to ask? Be ready to provide answers. Better yet, prepare documents that can help answer these questions, as well as others that can clarify your answers. These documents could include sell sheets, product specifications, process explanations, and so forth.

One question a lot of my prospects used to ask when considering using one of my products was "How will I know that the people I specify are actually receiving the marketing materials?" Rather than giving them vague reassurances, I always came prepared for this question by drawing up a detailed flow chart outlining the procedures my company followed to make sure it happened.

PREPARE. Above all, never give a prospect reason to think that you are not taking the meeting seriously. If you haven't gathered all the information you were supposed to have obtained in your first phone contact, it's perfectly acceptable to contact the prospect before the meeting with any questions on the products or services you're going to discuss. Preface your call by saying that because you value his time, you want to learn about your prospect's needs so that you can focus on what's most important to him during the meeting.

In the Arena

Why is it important to be prepared before you walk onto the playing field for your first meeting with the prospect? Because your self-assurance is a major factor in how well you will do in the negotiation, and preparation is the key. With the assurance of knowing the answers to the most likely questions, you can approach every negotiation with the attitude that you're the experienced professional, the master of your game, the essential ingredient in the big company's success. (But don't let your self-confidence grow into arrogance; you bluff the prospect at your peril.)

FOCUS ON THE PROSPECT. Don't make the common mistake of talking too much about yourself or your business. Your time is limited—usually less than one hour in which to win over your prospect and get to the next level. Don't waste it all on matters of no importance to your audience.

Do establish rapport by using a pleasant conversational tone; tell an amusing story. Before explaining what your business does and how you can help, get your prospect to tell you something about her business and its needs. The more you can get her to talk, the faster you'll figure out the best way to sell to her. Then you can tailor your material and use your time more effectively.

If your prospect is serious, she'll ultimately be using information from your proposal in her own internal analysis. If you can give her a proposal or quote in a format that's easy for her, you're miles ahead of the game.

TEAM UP. Your odds are better if two or more of your people are at the meeting. In fact, you can greatly increase your advantage if you and the others know how to play a team game.

One way to leverage your person power is to use a variation of the legendary "good cop, bad cop" ploy. I would sometimes play the seasoned pro and bring along a younger sales rep as a wet-behind-the-ears type. The "kid" would ask a lot of naïve questions and be answered with patient explanations. Later, I would explain to the prospect privately that my associate was new to the industry and I was helping him learn the business. Not only did this make me look like a good guy, we obtained a lot of useful information—things an experienced sales rep might not know but might be reluctant to ask.

On the other hand, teams must be careful not to monopolize the discussion. When I took others to a meeting, we had an understanding that no one was to interrupt or shout down the prospect in the heat of negotiation. We also used a code: If one of us started talking too much, another would scratch his nose as a cautionary signal. You'd be amazed at how quickly I could shut up when informed by a team member that I was off base.

FOLLOW THEIR FORMAT. Remember what I said about bureaucracy? Imagine having to conform to a detailed internal analysis sheet and needing to extract pieces of information from a confusing proposal. This is tedious at best; at worst, it simply won't happen, and you're out of luck. Now put this same person in front of a proposal that clearly outlines the information pertinent to her internal document. I'm sure you see the advantage.

Once you know the format and information needed, make sure to submit every quote and proposal in that style. I've asked prospects for a copy of their company's internal analysis document, explaining that I want to make their life easier. First, however, find out what your prospect's company calls this form. This makes you sound knowledgeable about her company and makes it easier for her to say yes to your request. Most prospects will say no, citing internal confidentiality, but all you need is for one person to say yes, then you're all set for the rest.

If you can't get a copy of this document, make sure to ask specifically what information she requires, and whether she prefers a short summary or a long, detailed proposal. Because she's busy, she'll actually appreciate your doing much of the work. Once you have her input, be sure to follow her suggestions. She might tell you to keep your proposal to one page and avoid any hype, she might want you to lay out the benefits of the product, or she might want something else entirely.

After the Meeting

The game doesn't end when the meeting is over. In fact, it's just beginning. The only sure sign of success is the prospect's signature on the bottom line.

FOLLOW THROUGH. If you've stirred your prospect's interest, you'll come out of meetings with questions or requests to address. Don't fall into the common trap of forgetting to respond because you have too many other meetings to attend or phone calls to make. Take a minute after each meeting to write up a quick "recap and to do" list. Then get whatever information your prospect needs right away. If you're having trouble responding quickly to a request, let the prospect know you're working on answers to his questions. He'll take your response speed and accuracy as a prime indicator of your quality of delivery.

SEAL THE DEAL. All this goodwill and advice isn't worth much if you haven't closed the deal. Don't be afraid to ask for what you need. Establish time lines and stick to them. At the same time, avoid such transparent tactics as the "impending doom" close (claiming that after such-and-such date, your service won't be available or the price will go up). Hackneyed techniques like this usually backfire and can make you look amateurish; most high-level prospects can see right through them. That said, you can and should apply whatever legitimate pressure you can muster. Ideally, you'll find yourself in a favorable situation—perhaps one of the prospect's biggest competitors wants to buy your service—that can provide leverage to encourage your prospects to close.

A Few More Tips

Here are several more pointers that can help you get the ink on the dotted line:

GET YOUR PROSPECT VESTED. The more time and energy your client has involved in your getting the order, the better. After all, she doesn't like seeing her efforts come to naught any more than you do. Involve her, but don't harp. When you call, make it for a good reason, one that's relevant to the project.

SIMPLIFY THE PROSPECT'S LIFE. Often your prospect will need to plug your numbers into a payout model, compare your services to the competition, or even reformat your proposal into a style desired by his management. I once had a client who had to take all the information from all the suppliers and aggregate it into one-page overviews. These overviews included such topics as strategic rationale (why the prospect should use them), cost, and payout.

BURNISH YOUR CREDIBILITY. When you first start to get business, perhaps the most difficult hurdle is trust. Your prospects have careers to worry about, so they might be reluctant to try new suppliers. Seek to boost your credibility in any way possible. Send examples of your work, especially if it's for other large companies, or send articles about your business—anything to eliminate the perceived risk of doing business with the new guy.

CULTIVATE RELATIONSHIPS. People generally like to help other people, especially when it's someone they like. Don't be afraid to ask for help when you need it. This includes asking who does what, when the budget season starts, what's the correct proposal format, how results are evaluated—even where your price should be in order to be competitive. You'll be surprised at what you hear.

INTRODUCE THE FAMILY. As you spend more time with your prospect, bring some of your operations people along to visit with people they know only by phone. This will help them feel they're a valued part of the organization. It will also give them better understanding of the company's situation and motivate them to respond to your requests.

WHO MAKES THE CALL? Make sure you know who influences, who buys, and who kills the deal. Ask your prospect if there are any other issues or concerns you should address.

MAKE IT PERSONAL. Ask for the order. Don't sound desperate, but convey a commitment to doing a great job for your prospect. Make it known that you'll babysit the project to ensure its success. By so doing, you also forge a tighter relationship with your prospect, who now feels that he has gone to bat for you. Then make sure that the project comes off well.

MANAGE THE INTENSITY. Come across as professional and dedicated, but not fanatical. Balance the desire for the sale with the need to enjoy what you're doing. If the prospect says she'll have an answer for you on Wednesday, don't call on Monday and Tuesday to see if she's made a decision—you'll just seem desperate. Wait until Wednesday, then call to see if she needs any more information.

LEARN FROM NO. If you don't get the business, ask why. Make sure the prospect doesn't feel any need to spare your feelings; let her know that she'll be helping you by telling you the real reason, no matter how harsh. Don't get defensive, argue with her, or try to explain. You can ask specific questions to get more info; for example, if she says she wasn't sure you could deliver on time, ask what gave her that impression. Thank her for her input, learn from it, and go get the next one.

Excerpted from: *Bag the Elephant* by Steve Kaplan, pp. 96–102, copyright © 2005. Used by permission of Bard Press.

——•◦•——

 *We know rapport and trust are important to successful selling, but to the corporate client these ingredients are essential because reputations are on the line and the stakes are high. Anthony Parinello started a revolution in sales training, and is now a highly sought after keynote speaker for what he describes as "enter-trainment."*

——•◦•——

THE FIVE KEYS TO WORKING WITH VITO
(THE VERY IMPORTANT TOP OFFICER)

ANTHONY PARINELLO

R apport is one of those overused words in our profession. Rapport means "having a reciprocal relation" or "to be in close communications with." That's why words like model, mirror, and pace are touted by the gurus as surefire ways to build rapport. If you remember the process and follow their advice, you will have a much better chance at building rapport with other individuals. But beware! For those of us who want and need to build unshakable confidence when dealing with the VITOs of the world, there must be an understanding of the many differences between "personal" rapport and "business" rapport. The differences are profound. If you can build effective business rapport, then your career, financial horizons, and overall success in business will be as good as guaranteed. If you master the art of building personal rapport, then you'll widen your social circle of influence and interpersonal network, and you'll find greater opportunities, resources, and personal fulfillment in just about every corner of your life. Let's take a closer look at this.

Business Rapport. When you build effective business rapport with VITO, you're building skyscrapers where two-story buildings once existed. You're tapping into VITO's greater influence and authority and you're multiplying your results accordingly. One of the key operative words here is "effective," which should not be confused with the word "efficient." Being *efficient* is having the ability to do whatever needs to be done as fast as possible. Being *effective* is making sure that whatever needs to be done is being done the best it can be. The difference is vitally important in a business relationship. For instance, if you try to build business rapport too quickly, it will not have the critical ingredients of loyalty and strength needed to withstand the many ups and downs that business relationships typically face. Inadequate rapport built in haste simply will not last.

Personal Rapport. Good, solid personal rapport is built on a basis of mutual understanding and appreciation for another person's point of view, culture, feelings, and whatever else that person stands for or happens to be headed to. A great deal has been written on the topic of personal rapport; it's almost impossible not to find this topic covered in books about success in sales and personal fulfillment. Many (if not all) of these books suggest that you attempt to be "like" the person with whom you're trying to build personal rapport—that is, model your behavior on theirs and mirror what they do. This is based upon the likelihood that if you are "like" someone they will, in turn, "like" you. Of course, this makes for a rather interesting scenario if both individuals model each other's voice intonation, body posture, and breathing. I'd love to be there to see it—the perfect set-up for an identity crisis if I've ever heard of one!

As professionals, we must effectively separate business and personal rapport, and since what we're trying to do is become a responsible business partner to VITO, we must focus our attention on building business rapport. If it happens that our efforts lead to a strong personal rapport, that's great! But the sequence should always be business rapport first, personal rapport second (unless, of course, you happen to be lifelong friends with a VITO whom you are now approaching with a business opportunity).

Here is what you must *always do* if you want to build effective business rapport.

1. Make the Best First Impression Possible

We've heard it said often, and it's very true, "You only get one chance to make a first impression." But what "they" haven't told us, and what we've learned the hard way at times, is that there are actually two parts of a first impression:

1. What VITO hears, sees, and/or feels during the first few seconds of your interaction with him or her.
2. What VITO hears, sees and or feels during the last few seconds of your interaction with him or her.

Your best bet is to be as prepared as possible. What topics will you be discussing? What questions should you be asking? What outcomes do both parties expect? To help you end your first impression on a high note, try to find out something about VITO's world, such as recent accomplishments or other assignments or positions they've had. With this information in hand, you'll be able to say: "When we get together next, I'd love for you to tell me what your greatest challenges were when you . . ."

2. Consistently Exceed Expectations

Credibility is a cornerstone of strong, lasting business rapport. The fastest way to build credibility is to simply do what you say you'll do and be willing to go the extra mile beyond that. When you exceed VITO's expectations, sooner or later VITO (and, yes, you) will get the message that there is only one way to operate:

> *In order to succeed with VITO, you must exceed for VITO.*

3. Make Yourself an Appreciating Asset

Like any other great investment, you must increase in value over time without the need to have VITO make a greater investment in you. You must continue to bring new ideas, greater information, and enhanced services to the table—and whatever you bring, "it" and "you" must increase in perceived and real value. The key words are *perceived and real value*. Get in the habit of focusing on how to do this. Make sure that whatever you come up with is sincere and appropriate for this VITO. We'll be discussing some very specific ways to do this in later chapters.

4. Position Yourself as Someone Who Is Indispensable

This goes hand in hand with becoming an appreciating asset. You need to be someone who can't be replaced by your competition. Others may have more knowledge or skill or expertise, but you and only you will be called upon time and time again if you have unique offerings.

5. Make Your Self-Improvement Apparent

Never let yourself become intellectually, emotionally, or physically stagnant. Why have VITOs risen to positions of importance and influence? Because they are on a constant self-improvement journey. Progress and growth are what make businesses and people increase in value. You, too, must constantly seek ways to increase your personal and business value. I suggest you read the sorts of industry and trade-specific books and periodicals that VITOs read and find other ways to expand your knowledge and demonstrate that you, too, are upwardly mobile.

6. Always, Always, Always Be Upbeat

Everyone appreciates a winning attitude and VITO is no exception. Of course, life is not always as good or as happy as you would like it to be, but if you maintain an uplifting mood, attitude, and opinions, then VITO will see and appreciate that you are the kind of person who knows how to make the best of every situation. Enthusiasm and a positive outlook will take you a long way!

7. Dress for Success

Personal image is an important part of building business rapport. Every successful person likes to look the part. Success has an aura all its own, and you can take on that aura with the tasteful way you dress. Have you ever put on an outfit that made you feel like a million bucks? If you have, then you need to own that outfit! But beware:

> *Don't use dressing for success as an obstacle*
> *or something to hide behind.*
> *Don't be an empty suit!*

8. Speak with an Appropriate Vocabulary

The proper use and understanding of words can provide us with the tools we need to make the best possible first impression and build excellent business rapport. We must therefore constantly expand our use and understanding of words to make our verbal communication as epic as possible. The easiest way to do this is to have a small pocket or electronic dictionary at your side whenever you read a business book or journal. When you spot a word that's unfamiliar to you, take the time to look it up and learn its meaning at that moment. Repeat it several times, use it in a sentence, and then as soon as possible make it a part of your own conversations.

9. Become a Useful Team Player

Every one of VITO's teams has room for another player, and the player they will want the most is a "giver." "Takers" are considered liabilities who are avoided or, once discovered, eliminated from the team. You must be looked upon as an asset, not a liability. When VITO sees you coming or hears that you're on the phone, your presence must elicit a response like: "Oh! It's Tony" not: "Oh, it's Tony." Of course, the difference between these two phrases is the intonation and excitement placed upon the word "oh." Business rapport is established and grows on the basis that a contribution is being made without the other person asking for the contribution. That's what team work is all about.

10. Listen Intently

That means listening with undivided attention, focus, and understanding. It means listening with rapt attention. Let me tell you how I first learned about the importance of this. After a tour in the Navy, I began to lose my hearing. Over the years, my hearing got progressively worse. I actually taught myself how to read lips! You know, reading lips is interesting: you really have to concentrate. Your eyes have to be glued to the lips of the person you're talking to, and your mind has to be very focused. You can't daydream. You have to watch every single movement.

Now, back when I was selling large computer systems, I had an interesting experience. I had a number of very important sales meetings with the president of a good-sized company, and I was always right out on the edge of my chair, watching him like a hawk. I'd get as close as I could without getting into the president's personal space. If a distraction took place—if the secretary walked into the office, for instance—I couldn't let the secretary take my attention away. I couldn't afford to miss a single word of what the president had to say.

Throughout those meetings, my eyes and my full attention *belonged* to the president of that company. And I got that sale. I sold his company a fairly large computer system. And you can bet I felt good about it. In part as a reward, I got myself two powerful new hearing aids, almost invisible.

As it happened, that president was the very first business contact I met with after I got my hearing aids.

It was great! I could hear everything! I didn't have to lean forward in my chair anymore! I asked the president, "VITO, how's the installation going?" And as VITO started to tell me, guess what happened? I didn't have to look at VITO's lips anymore! Why, I could look around the room! When there was a noise I could to turn to see what it was! When the secretary walked in, I could smile and nod hello!

All of a sudden, the president stopped right in the middle of his sentence. I turned and looked at him. He looked me right in the eye and said, "Tony, please take your hearing aids out."

I said, "Why on earth would I want to do that?" And he said, "Tony, I feel you're not listening to me. I felt really special before you had those hearing aids. You used to watch every move I made. Please take them out." And I did.

Right then and there I learned one of the most important lessons in my sales career: When you're with a prospect, you listen to them as if you're hard of hearing! Listen to them as though you must read their lips. Give them your undivided attention. Show them you are interested in understanding how they feel. Listen with empathy.

Whenever a VITO makes a complaint, they are really saying they want a business relationship to work. This gives you the opportunity to:

- Show how good you and your company really are
- Learn how to perform even better, thereby lessening any future complaints
- Gain ideas on how to make your future solutions fit the precise needs of your marketplace
- Make your existing business relationships stronger and more loyal

11. Forget about Closing

Now, if this isn't a departure from standard sales advice, nothing is! You read right. I want you to commit yourself to *never meeting with VITO with the intention of closing a deal.* News flash: VITOs don't like "being closed." Think about it. You probably don't like it either. You are not *closing* doors, but *opening* them. You are working to develop an ongoing business relationship for which you will always be willing to take ultimate responsibility. Remove the word "closing" from your vocabulary. Just go out and open relationships and business opportunities. When you get VITO's first order, it's the beginning, not the end.

When you come right down to it, most of all this seems like good, common "people" sense doesn't it? Let me then leave you with this one thought:

> *Building rapport is not about manipulating or controlling people.*
> *It's about controlling the effect you have on people.*

Excerpted from *Selling to VITO: The Very Important Top Officer* by Anthony Parinello, pp. 14–26, copyright © 1999. Used by permission. *Selling to VITO* has been re-written and re-released as *Getting to VITO*, (John Wiley & Sons, 2005).

Corporate sellers have to understand how their message impacts the many diverse individuals operating within a unique corporate culture. One of the best sales tools is a well-crafted presentation that tells the facts in stories that sell. Joe McBride operates a successful word-of-mouth marketing business, and is also a past master speech crafter, with plenty of high-level recognition, within the Toastmaster organization.

THE MYTH OF 7, 38, 55

JOE MCBRIDE

A sales and marketing text book we used in a college business class referenced the work of Dr. Albert Mehrabian of UCLA, published in a book called *Silent Messages* (Wadsworth Publishing, 1971). In the class, we applied Dr. Mehrabian's data to a myriad of situations, including the selling situation. Using his concept, we began saying that "success in selling is 7 percent verbal, 38 percent vocal, and 55 percent nonverbal." The importance of this statement is that it gets us to consider the importance of nonverbal language in our selling conversations. To help illustrate the importance of your total communication, let's review Stu Evey's carefully crafted words, which helped secure massive funding that kept ESPN alive during its early start-up. In his case, words and vocal delivery, and his facial expressions sold his audience.

Stu Evey was nervous. In July 1980, he squarely faced the biggest challenge of his life: Convincing the Getty Oil board of directors, a conservative bunch of bankers and oil men, to provide more research and development money for the fledgling ESPN.

Stu was not new to challenges, and the men he stood in front of respected him. He was vice president of the Diversified Operations Division of Getty Oil Company. He started his career with Getty in 1958 as a management trainee, and had succeeded with one project after another as he rose through the corporate ranks. For 22 years, Stu had handled bigger and bigger projects for Getty, and the board members knew he had a track record of producing moneymaking projects.

This time, however, he was in uncharted territory. On his recommendation, the Getty Board had already committed more than $50 million to a project that had produced no revenue and needed at least another $10 million just to launch.

The project involved a cable television venture called the Entertainment and Sports Programming Network, or ESPN. Today ESPN is an integral part of American culture, but in July 1980, the program was untested and a gamble. Survival of the venture rested squarely on Stu Evey's shoulders.

At that time, cable television reached fewer than 25 percent of American homes, and the only mildly popular venture was Home Box Office (HBO), which also had not proved profitable. Selling this program would be an uphill battle—one sale after another. The first big selling hurdle was to turn the corporate board into raving customers willing to pay for an untested product. The board could pull the plug on the entire operation unless Stu could present a scenario to them in a language they could understand. As recounted by Stu:

That day I commenced my remarks with oil patch vernacular: "Gentlemen, in early 1979, when I first proposed the ESPN project as a possible investment for the Getty Oil Company, I told you our initial exploration investigations showed that we had discovered a reservoir worth tapping. I felt it would be a viable venture."

I tried to smile in a way that wouldn't betray my confidence in what I was about to say. "When you authorized the capital necessary to start this business, I told you that our mission was to find a reservoir. Today, I am pleased to tell you that the reservoir has been discovered." I thought I could see lust in their eyes. They were now hanging on every word. "However . . ." I paused again. "Gentlemen, not only has the reservoir been discovered, it is much, much bigger than I originally envisioned, it is much, much deeper, and I need more drill pipe to reach the objective."

The room erupted into laughter. It had been a slam dunk presentation, one that people still remember as one of those moments in which legends are made. The Board casually flipped through the details of the expanded ESPN "drilling program" and quickly approved the budget requests for the next year.

Four years later, Getty Oil was purchased by Texaco, and Texaco sold ESPN to ABC Television for $225 million. Today ABC is part of Disney, and the value of ESPN has escalated to around $20 billion dollars. In July 1980, this profitable program's survival hung on the words of one man, selling an idea to a conservative board of directors.

The lesson for all salespeople is how Stu Evey sold his idea to the board. He could easily have shown the board reports and barrels of facts, charts, and projection charts prepared by the communication consultants hired to review the project. He could have also given the board information about the value of ESPN's state-of-the-art satellite transponders. But none of those things would have brought to light the clear message these oil men got from his carefully crafted and well-delivered words.

So the next time you face a critical presentation, remember to be multi-lingual. Think how Stu Evey eloquently presented ESPN's situation to the Getty board in a language they clearly understood. Hopefully, you will be as successful as he was in closing your sale.

You might have the perfect product, but if you can't establish rapport in your initial meetings, that perfect product stays on the shelf. James Fischer turned his immense experience consulting with corporations into a specialized analytic model that allows him to conduct a snapshot needs assessment for potential corporate clients. Operating from Boulder, Colorado, he quickly, and through skillfully crafted conversation, builds client rapport by telling the client where their pain hurts the most.

GAINING A UNIQUE INSIGHT INTO YOUR CLIENT COMPANY

JAMES FISCHER

Carl looked up from the luncheon plate in front of him, his face frozen, and asked quietly, "How could anyone possibly know so much about my company? I just met you 20 minutes ago."

It Was a Simple "Blind Introduction"
Three days prior to my meeting with Carl, a mutual friend had arranged for him and me to meet for the first time at a local restaurant. I was given

no information about Carl's company other than a mutual recommendation of one to the other. We all occasionally get these "blind introductions" in the course of our selling careers.

Five minutes into our luncheon I casually asked Carl three simple questions about his company. His equally simple answers unveiled for me an entire tapestry of Carl's firm during the past couple years. I asked permission to share my perspective, and we went immediately to an authentic discussion about his business. During the next 15 to 20 minutes, I shared what I "imagined" were some of his victories, challenges, and issues during the past year.

What You Need to Know to Set Yourself Apart

During my 23-year history of working with 700 small- and medium-sized companies in many industries, I discovered a corporate evaluation model that is activated by three simple questions.

1. How many employees do you have now? (He answered 23.)
2. How many employees did you have last year this time? (He answered 14.)
3. Given that your company is made up of both "builder/confident type" employees and "protector/cautionary type" employees, what would you say is the ratio between the builders and the protectors at your company right now? (He thought about it for a moment and then answered one Builder for every four Protectors.)

Based on Carl's answers, it was apparent that he and his company were going through a tough time. He needed to hear that I both understood and appreciated the challenges he endured in the past year as he managed his company.

Based on his answers, here's what we talked about:

1. I "guessed" he currently was experiencing a tough employee revolt on all fronts. (He sighed, "Yes . . .")
2. We talked about the issues facing him with delegating responsibility and how his workload had doubled as a result of his company's growth. (He once again nodded his head in agreement.)

3. I compassionately suggested that even though his revenue probably went up last year, he was likely making less money. (He agreed.)
4. I further "guessed" that even though he most likely wanted to cut his staff back by five to six people, there were probably better alternatives. (This is when he looked at me with a stare that asked, "How did you know that?")

Build Enormous Rapport and Credibility

Carl was stunned and impressed by my quick and accurate insight into his company. Because I demonstrated understanding, I quickly built enormous rapport, credibility, and influence with this potential client. Customers like Carl appreciate people who understand them and express a genuine interest in their situation. This first step is a crucial key to successfully selling consultative services to busy executives. From that one meeting, Carl and I built a mutually rewarding business relationship where for three years I provided consultative services to his company.

Win Your Customer's Confidence

The secret to my three questions comes from a wider understanding I have about how companies grow. I created a system that analyzes a company's need and shows how my services will provide a solution. Called the Seven Stages of Enterprise Growth, this straightforward approach offers a remarkable insight to a client company. Here are a few key points to the system:

- The Seven Stages of Growth is founded on the company's complexity as determined by the number of full-time employees.
- A company's work environment experiences one of two zones of chaotic transitions while moving from one stage of growth to the next.
  1. *Flood zone.* When the company is flooded with more activity than it can effectively manage
  2. *Wind tunnel.* When what worked for the company is no longer effective.

  With each zone comes unavoidable chaos until the company moves successfully into its next evolutionary stage.

- Each stage of growth places unique demands on the company's leadership. If the steps are not followed, both the company and the leadership suffer.
- The company must balance *confident building* and *cautious protecting* to move through the stages and achieve significant performance. The optimum relationship between confident building and cautious protecting is called the *builder/protector ratio*, for each stage of growth. The builder/protector ratio describes the "mental health" of the company and employees. Generally speaking, two or three building components in the company require one protector to keep progress balanced. Too high a ratio of builders in any given stage of growth will run a company off the cliff and too high a ratio of protectors will suffocate it to death.

If the seller feels the sales conversation is not progressing well, it could be that the message is missing the immediate and most pressing needs of the decision maker. The ideal is to focus your questions and presentations specifically on the way your solutions will address the corporation's most immediate needs. Meet the decision maker's needs head-on and you are more likely to get sufficient rapport and trust to sell longer term corporate solutions.

Three Easy Questions Made All the Difference

Looking back on Carl's company, a salesperson using this knowledge would know that the company just passed through a transition zone between Stage 2 (10–19 employees) and Stage 3 (20–34 employees). This transition challenged the company as it moved from a CEO-centric company to an enterprise-centric company. This transition is one of the hardest for a small company CEO to endure. Carl's company builder/protector ratio of 1 to 4 suggested that his overcautious leadership style was paralyzing the company. He could no longer lead his firm in the same way. Three easy questions made all the difference in understanding my future client's needs.

If you are working with a Stage 1 or Stage 2 company, you are probably selling to the CEO or owner of the enterprise. This type of customer lives in a world of significant pressure, skepticism, and work overload. The principals of his type of company generally won't become a customer until they (1) like you; (2) believe your expertise can help them; and finally (3) trust you. By using these specialized tools, you can quickly acquire a deeper understanding and appreciation of a CEO's unique pressures and challenges, and offer immediate and viable immediate solutions directed at the most pressing priorities of the decision maker.

Attitude determines altitude in selling, and for the corporate sales representative, having an upbeat attitude is essential for the top-dog awards. George Dearing took the high attitude route, and soon found he was winning sales awards. He went on to use his corporate selling expertise to advise other up-and-coming sellers. From his business offices in Texas, George tells us how to survive the doldrums of a long sales cycle by remembering that it's all in how you look at everyday events.

CELEBRATE THE SMALL WINS

GEORGE C. DEARING

A sales cycle of six to nine months from first contact to final signature in the mainframe financial software industry is not uncommon. Selling specialized financial software to *Fortune* 100 companies means interacting with a large cast of characters, including end-users, technical evaluators, outside consultants, recommenders, sponsors, lawyers, and, of course, the final decision makers.

This type of selling is a long and drawn-out—and mostly tedious—exercise. But the rewards of winning a complex sale might be a 20 percent commission on a half-million-dollar deal for the sales representative. It might take a year to close a deal, but the sales representative could earn more than $100,000 on that single contract.

A couple of years out of college, I landed a job with a leading provider of financial and human resources software. I was responsible for providing customer support to a low-cost and not very glamorous product called the "Fixed Asset Accounting and Reporting Module."

In 1980, I was promoted to fixed asset accounting sales support specialist, where my duties included writing lengthy responses to requests for proposals, making system presentations, and answering technical questions regarding the system's capabilities. In essence, my job was to be "a tool in the salesman's toolbox."

At that time, the systems sold for between $15,000 and $30,000, depending on the options chosen. In a multiple-product evaluation, the fixed asset accounting system was never the system driving the evaluation. That role was typically held by either the human resource management or the general ledger reporting systems, with price points in excess of $150,000 to $250,000. *These* were the exciting products.

Because my product represented a small portion of the company's regional revenue, I provided support to the entire west coast of the United States. In December 1980, I was called up to Oakland, California, to demonstrate our fixed-asset system to the Clorox Company. I teamed up with our sales representative, Dan, who consistently was a top company producer. I was frankly amazed that Dan was taking time for us to talk to this company about buying a single upgrade that would result in a mere $10,000 sale.

After my presentation, the controller of Clorox informed us they were comparing our product with that of a competitor the following day, and would then get back to us with any questions. After we left, Dan went on and on about how great the meeting went and started going over a list of things we needed to do in the follow-up process.

"But, Dan," I said. "It is a lousy $10,000 contract."

Dan replied, "George, in a business where it might take six to nine months to win or lose a contract, if you don't celebrate the small wins, you will never get a chance to celebrate the big ones."

Sure enough, the next day the controller called Dan to let him know we had won the contract and asked Dan to put the agreement together. The contract was booked the next week. I thought a lot about Dan's "small win" comment and found myself focusing on celebrating the small wins: a good phone call, receiving positive feedback from a sales rep, even making a meeting on time.

While the sales specialists had as much as four hours to present their systems, I was usually only given ten minutes for my entire presentation. I didn't care. I was determined that if all I got was ten minutes, then it would be the best ten minutes of the prospect's entire day.

My small wins started to turn into a steady flow of small contracts. I continued to focus on the small wins, and soon my days were filled with events to celebrate: a great conference call with a fixed-asset clerk, a good e-mail, a to-do item successfully completed.

That's when I started to understand what Dan meant. By celebrating the small wins, I subconsciously was causing myself to focus on the details that others would let slip by as unimportant. I was also creating a self-image of confidence and competence—and a winning attitude. I learned that regardless of the product's inherent importance, the sales professional needs to attend to all the details with enthusiasm and treat all people with dignity.

The buzz continued: "George can help win you big deals. Get George in front of your client even if they aren't looking at fixed assets." My reputation grew in the company to a point where I was flown around the entire U.S. to do my ten-minute presentation. The sales representatives started bringing me not only to present the fixed asset system, but also to do the important application architecture overview at the beginning of the overall presentation (and in front of the customer's top executives).

A year later, the VP of sales from one of my competitors called me. He wanted me to sell their version of the fixed-asset system for his company. While other representatives would be selling the high-ticket systems for $150,000 or more, I'd be selling the fixed-asset system for $20,000 to $30,000. Thinking of Dan's "small win" philosophy, I took that job.

I continued celebrating small wins: A meeting with a chief recommender, the legal department approving contract wording, a payment received. At the end of the year, I was the number two producer in the entire company and 200 percent over quota, even when compared dollar-for-dollar with representatives selling systems ten times more expensive. I won the company's "Rookie of the Year" award, and earned four times more money then I had earned three years before.

Celebrating those small wins added up to big success as I learned how to sell to big corporations—just like selling to important people—with respect for myself and for the others around me. While celebrating my award that night, I asked the VP of sales how he had heard about me, prior to recruiting me for my position.

"You were recommended by one of our VPs, Alex, who is being reassigned to head up the company's South America operations."

"How did Alex know about me?" I asked.

"He was the sales rep you beat out three years ago in Oakland," replied the VP.

The Buyer's Perspective

The buyer's gospel: "buyer beware."
—ANONYMOUS

Selling has a lot to do with—OK, everything to do with— finding out what the customer wants, is able to pay for, and then making the deal (assuming you can provide the product/service). If it was really that simple, though, there wouldn't be a demand for salespeople; buyers could get all they need from a machine. But, in fact, many buyers head off to go shopping for a product or service with only a vague sense of what might satisfy their needs. Turning a buyer's vagueness into clear solutions is the job of the salesperson. The Master of Sales never forgets that the buyer is looking for the best solution, delivered in an effective and pleasurable manner.

Buyers are multifaceted, and when they shop, they weigh the many pros and cons of a potential purchase. Some of these they will share with the seller, while many other thoughts they will keep to themselves. Learning and adapting to the issues and whims of the buyer while moving the sale forward to a conclusion is a complex and intricate task . . . and it's the responsibility of the sales professional to ensure it happens.

Brian Roach, who sells computer technology, wrote us about a great concept that he calls the *sales clock*. He described it this way:

> *It's a great day. You answered a call from a new prospect, met with their team to discuss your product, and . . . they asked you for a proposal. Soon after delivering your proposal you started your wait for their decision. The sales clock ticks as you wait on the fate of your proposal. It may tick a long time before hearing back from the customer, and as the seller, you don't know if you are being "stiffed" or if the customer is swamped with other pressing priorities. Whatever the reason, waiting out the sales clock can be stressful. The last thing you want is for your own stress to create a negative impact on your prospect.*

Brain Roach reminded us that "It's all about the customer," in the sense that the customer is the ultimate buyer, but the seller also has to earn a commission, meet monthly targets, and ensure proper work scheduling. Brian's sales clock reminds us to always look at both the customer's perspective as well as the seller's demands with each sales scenario.

Attentive listening can help you, the seller, determine if the buyer is putting you off or merely attending to pressing internal demands. Personality profiling also helps by giving you the knowledge about how to craft your sales and reporting program to the style of communication most comfortable to the client. All customers like to be communicated with in a manner that is most familiar to them, and knowing their personality profiles helps the seller customize a sales approach for each unique individual. One form of customer communication is the product presentation, which has a strong influence in a successful sale.

Andy Bounds, from Liverpool, England, is a sales communication expert who reminds us that the ". . . prospect is really interested in the total opposite of most commonly delivered product presentations. The prospect really only cares about his or her own present and future, whereas most presentations focus on the seller's past and product features." Andy reminds us to talk about what the product will do for the customer rather than its features. His favorite phrase is, "Customers don't care what you do; they care about what they're left with AFTER you've done it." He uses the word "after" to keep the product presentation focused on the customer's needs, and recommends the following customer-oriented questions:

- "What are you looking to achieve after our work together?"
- "What would success look like to you as a result of this project?"
- "Looking back a year from now, what will need to happen for you to think things have gone brilliantly?"

Nothing works perfectly every time, and being able to read the customer's buying signals is crucial to making necessary course corrections that meet the customer's top-of-mind concerns. The state of the selling art allows masterful salespeople to combine a little science with human relation strategies to create a wonderful buying experience for the consumer, while still maximizing the seller's commission. Most of the time, timing is everything, which is why we wanted to take the time to share several concepts, strategies, and techniques to help you land the hesitant customer in front of you (whose hesitation may have nothing to do with your product).

If you want your selling experience to result in more referred buyers, then creating a memorable buying experience for each customer is the objective. The seller's prayer might be, "Let my buyer leave happy, and with fond memories." James Cruickshank, an experienced and well-traveled marketing consultant from England, shares a true tale of a customer who left one rather unusual retail place happy and with fond memories.

SALES IN THE DESERT

JAMES CRUICKSHANK

The shops in Santa Fe were every bit as elegant as those in New York, London, and Paris. Like most shoppers on the tourist route, my wife and I were "browsing" on our visit to Santa Fe, but as so many had experienced before, we were gradually being overwhelmed by the sheer volume of goods, plethora of shops (mostly all the same), and complete indifference of some retailers we encountered. Something was missing, and it took me a while to realize just what that "something" was: essentially, there was no engagement between those who wished to make a sale and us, the potential customers.

We were, therefore, susceptible when the concierge in our hotel referred us to the Babbitt's Trading Post, somewhere out of town. His referral promised something different and alerted me to the possibility that "word of mouth" was alive, well, and active in this part of the United States. So it was that my wife, Pandora, and I found ourselves heading north on Highway 84 in search of the recommended Babbitt's Authentic Indian Goods Cottonwood Trading Post.

Seven miles west of the main highway we found the dirt track that was to take us to our destination. A collection of single-story buildings came in to view, and clearly we were entering a Native American Reservation.

The sign we passed on the way did nothing to instill confidence—stating *"No tourists allowed after 5:00 P.M."*

I parked the car in the deserted homestead and switched off the engine. The wind in the cottonwood trees was the only sound that broke the stillness of the air. Two dogs greeted us in a most friendly manner as we crossed the wooden veranda and entered what appeared to be a private dwelling.

Inside soft music played and a fragrance filled the air. A worker paused long enough from painting hand-carved ornaments to advise us that the owner, Judith Babbitt, would be with us in a moment. Expecting a high-pitched sales approach I braced myself for the inevitable and then, as if by magic, Judith appeared. I relaxed. Her languid manner and knowledgeable conversation immediately put me at ease, and I hardly noticed that Pandora had started to "browse."

Judith was enthusiastic about us, and wanted to know where we came from, what we did, and how long we were visiting the area. In the background, I noticed that Pandora had now begun to "select" various items, and still there was no sign from Judith that selling was on her mind.

"All our visitors come here via word of mouth," she cheerfully explained, and was clearly happy with this arrangement. By now the visit had taken on the atmosphere of an experience, rather than just a shopping trip. We certainly enjoyed spending time with our newfound acquaintance, and all too soon it was time to leave. As Judith bade us farewell it seemed almost immaterial that we had, in fact, spent over $400. This had not been in the plan at all.

Before leaving, I just had to ask "How come the two dogs were so apparently friendly towards us when we, total strangers, arrived?"

"That's because they always receive a biscuit when customers appear," said Judith. "This way they associate the arrival of visitors with a treat." Dogs as visitor hosts? Certainly a novel and imaginative approach to greeting retail customers.

As we drove back to the main highway and headed north to Taos, I reflected on this brief encounter in the desert. There had been three visitors to the Babbitt Trading Post that day, including Pandora and me. All had spent money, a 100 percent success rate that would have been the envy of most high-end street stores.

Our experience of shopping in the desert highlighted just how woefully inadequate most retailers are when it comes to understanding their target market, their customers, and their sales technique(s). From our initial meeting with Judith, it became perfectly clear that:

- She knew her target market extremely well. (Marketing)
- She had extreme confidence in how her products would be received by her visitors—i.e., us. (*Product Knowledge*)
- She had allowed herself sufficient time to spend with us in order to establish a relationship and thereby achieve the desired result. (*Rapport and Trust Building*)
- She knew exactly where her business came from. (*Referrals*)
- She understood the psychology of when to move the sales process along—and when not to do so. (*Closing Communication Technique*)

The trading post was not easily accessible, and relied entirely on word of mouth to attract customers. To most retail experts, this would be a high-risk strategy, but Judith managed to provide us with a whole new buying "experience" that was not only enjoyable, but also left us feeling that we had made the right choice. Her customer care was second to none, leaving us (the client) feeling pleased with our purchases, which we realized later were exceptional value for money.

At a time when most retailers are finding the going tough, it takes courage to market goods from an isolated trading post in the middle of the San Ildefonso desert. And enlisting the help of two canine sales assistants frankly takes the—er—biscuit! It's so simple, but not easy. Make the customer feel valued and comfortable, provide them with a wonderful experience, and they will invite others to walk in your door. In fact, they might even write a story for a book, all about your store!

Few buyers are able to zero in on exactly what they want, and they often communicate in a secret code. "I'm just looking" might really mean, "Please gently open a conversation with me." Bill Buckley is a serious businessman who now operates a national franchise organization that specializes in communicating through the written word. His career started in the corporate sales arena within a challenging environment. He shares his experience at cracking the buyer's code and suggests, "If the buyer signals move ahead, you'd better move on."

FIRST READ THE BUYING SIGNALS ... THEN SELL BY FORMULA

BILL BUCKLEY

Almost nothing gets sold without a salesperson, and all salespeople sell through a process of human interaction. A successful result from this selling process is a detailed exchange with another person. The process includes artfully weaving one's knowledge about the product/service/idea to the buyer's needs through a skillful presentation that leads efficiently from one selling stage to the next—right through to conclusion of the sale. The buyers usually add a degree of difficulty to the selling process by signaling their readiness to move forward to the next stage, but they often do it in a secret coded communication. The seller's job is to recognize and interpret the customer's signals and move on to the next phase at the right moment. If a seller does not recognize the customer's readiness to move on to the next phase, he might continue negotiating when the customer is ready to close. Frustrated, the customer may close the dialogue and leave.

Master Sellers Crack the Code

Common buying signals are: positive facial signs, affirmative nodding, questions, friendly body language, buyer recognizing the product's value, or transitional language from resistance to acceptance. On the negative side, the buyer might vocalize real or imagined objections to the use of the product or service. Instead of being acutely aware of their feelings about a product, a buyer might mask his indecisiveness about buying the item with a stated objection such as, "The price is too high" or "I need to think about it" or "It's the wrong color." Experienced sales professionals know that even a strong objection might be a buyer's coded signal for specific information necessary to overcome a final concern before announcing their buy decision.

I experienced a unique buying-signal situation in Maine during the 1990s. Its workers' compensation policies were rated the worst in the nation. Overly-generous legal settlements and bogus claims were placed by workers suffering from obesity, smoking, drug and alcohol abuse, and poor work habits and attitudes. Inadequate remedies and inept worker health practices added to a state of crisis that led to excessive injuries, illnesses, and high absenteeism.

As a new product representative, my job was simple. I got appointments with the safety directors of various prospects, and then had to sell to this person sufficiently for them to arrange an audience with the president. At this subsequent meeting, I gave a slide presentation, and usually walked out with a signed contract ranging from $5,000 to $300,000, depending on the size of the company. It was a simple formula!

Big targets of ours were large, well-known shoe manufacturing companies like Dexter and Bass. One company eluded our effort to land them, and as a new sales rep, I was equally determined to get an appointment with them. I followed the program and the safety director arranged an audience with the president and senior management team. A half hour early, I set up a screen, aimed the projector, and prepared the handouts.

Promptly at 9 A.M., ten officers and production supervisors marched in and took their places around the huge wooden boardroom table. Patiently they sat waiting for the president to enter. We fidgeted with the equipment to control our stress and joked nervously about nothing. Suddenly, the president entered. At 75 years of age, direct, brisk, efficient, and in charge, he immediately convened the meeting. Definitely of the old school, he made no small talk here.

After introducing his staff, he peered directly at me and said, "Tell us about your program and how it can help us."

"Thank you for allowing us to come to speak to you today," I began . . .

He interrupted. "Have you done this program in any other shoe company," he asked? My boss responded that we had worked for Dexter Shoe.

"Dexter Shoe!" the president replied. "You mean to tell me you have worked for Dexter Shoe? Were you hired by Harold Alfond at Dexter Shoe?" Harold was part owner of the Red Sox and was considered one of the richest men in New England.

"Yes," responded my boss.

"No, what I mean is did you speak directly to Harold about this program?

"Yes," my boss responded again. "As a matter of fact, we have been working for Dexter for about five years and I was just up to their plant last Thursday and bumped into Harold."

At this point, the president leaned back in his chair and folded his arms and said, "That's all I need to know. Anybody else have any questions?" No one spoke. The president continued, "OK, what do you need from us to get this program going?"

"I think if we could have a few minutes with your safety director after this meeting, and do a brief tour of your plant, we'll develop some numbers and prepare a proposal for you," I quickly responded.

"You got it," he said.

At this point, we packed our equipment, completely forsaking our usual 45-minute slide presentation. We shook hands with everyone and left the corporate boardroom to meet with the safety director.

We got back in the car and headed back to our office . . . and I knew we had just sold a $70,000 contract in less than two minutes, without the need to do a 45-minute sales presentation. My boss was still not convinced that we got the contract until later when the deal was signed.

Here's what happened. Initially, the shoe company president was skeptical we could do the job. We offered a testimonial from another shoe company that was well-known and respected in the industry. The testimonial about Dexter Shoe made the sale for us during the first two minutes of the meeting. The company president signaled his intention to buy by referring us to the safety director to work up the details. The shoe company president invited his staff to present questions or observations. No one spoke, not wishing to "throw themselves in front of the train."

Had we gone ahead with our full-blown presentation, we would have generated lots of questions. The risk is that one of those questions could have derailed the entire sale. When a customer says yes, either verbally or nonverbally, it is time to accept that the deal is done.

When you read that your buyer is ready to buy, leave as soon as possible, even if you haven't finished your formula. If you continue to sell, you can easily lose the sale just by "over-selling" *and wasting time of busy people.* When the buyer signals yes, it is time to congratulate the buyer and quickly move on to the next stage in the process.

———

It is no secret that some consumers buy differently than others. Some people love to shop, while others are just the opposite. Dawn Lyons is a sales expert who specializes in personality profiling. Dr. Ivan Misner is a recognized expert in word-of-mouth referral marketing. Dawn and Dr. Misner teach us that buyers like to be treated in the manner to which they are most accustomed.

———

KNOWING YOUR GEMS LEADS
TO MASTERFUL SELLING

DAWN LYONS AND DR. IVAN MISNER

What makes a consumer say "yes" to a purchase? Is it the product? The service? Is it you, the salesperson? People buy "stuff" worth tens of thousands of dollars a year. But, why should they buy from you?

To better understand buyers' motives, let's start by focusing on people skills. If we understand people better, we can understand why they buy, when they buy, who they buy from, and what they like to buy.

The study of personality types has long been of interest to psychologists, and one model that has stood the test of time was initially described by Dr. William Moulton Marston in 1928. His early work with personality/behavioral types led to the DISC behavior profiling system, which outlines how a specific behavioral style can predict reactions to different selling and social situations. This system is still widely used today in a variety of situations, one of which is sales training.

Dani Johnson is an internationally-known speaker and sales trainer whose clients regularly achieve high incomes. She modified the DISC system to one called GEMS, which enables her to easily differentiate a valuable contribution made by four distinct personality profiles. A self-made millionaire at the age of 23, Dani has certainly proven that she understands people's buying motives.

Your approach to prospects is so critical that we recommend you get GEMS training yourself. Dani Johnson holds her "First Steps to Success" program around the world, and the Referral Institute offers an eight-hour program that incorporates GEMS training with referral marketing.

Here's a brief peek at each GEM in Dani Johnson's system:

- *Rubies* are risk takers, go-getters, and like challenges. They like to win, be right, and are fast paced. They need control, authority, and thrive on commission. Their bottom-line approach helps them make quick buying decisions. Sellers, be prepared!

- *Sapphires* are stimulating, enthusiastic, and on-the-go people. They like fun, being the center of attention, and receiving tons of recognition. Enjoying people, influencing others' decisions, and being popular is their style. Skip the details with them, just make the buying process easy, fun, and spontaneous.
- *Pearls* are patient, relational, and incredibly harmonious. The quality time they spend with others is seen as supportive. Their relationships are longstanding and oriented to helping the team. Don't push them from their low-key approach, or your sales style will overwhelm and scare them away.
- *Emeralds* are effective, thorough, and detail-oriented. Their behavior of following rules, collecting data, and completing tasks pushes them toward excellence. These are the detail people who need to carefully conduct their research before making a buying decision.

Know thy Customer . . . and Adapt Quickly

Masterful sellers learn to quickly asses the type of GEM their prospect is as they walk into their appointment (more often, they have a pretty good idea even before getting to the meeting). Prospect or client research can be done over the phone, whether by using an intake form or by getting more information from your referral source. Knowing your GEM is critical to the success of each appointment.

It definitely helped Glenn Antoine, president of eSystems Design Inc. The following is his GEMS testimonial:

> *Two days following our GEMS training, I met with a potential client who was very stressful and in no mood for a sales pitch. It suddenly hit me. I was meeting with a Pearl—a person who prefers harmony, rather than discord.*
>
> *I dropped my agenda and inquired how I could help. After listening to the many stresses he had had that day and the previous week, I noticed a significant mood change. An hour later he was smiling, more relaxed, and open to my pitch. I gave a very brief description of our vision of the project. Lastly, I explained that I would leave information*

for his team to review, so they could deal with their more immediate challenges. My friendly follow-up call the next morning resulted in our selling them a new project.

My immediate return on the GEMS training was a $40,000 sale! During the coming years, this client will easily generate in excess of $100,000 in revenue for eSystems Design.

Wow, change your game plan mid-stream when it is apparent that your GEM needs different treatment, and see what happens. Glenn completely gave up his agenda to focus on helping his Pearl client. All he really did was back off and listen, leaving his material and follow-up for the next day.

Digging Deeper

To sell like a pro, we must understand *why* people buy, *when* they buy, *who* they buy from, and *what* they like to buy. Here are some examples of the *why*, *when*, *who*, and *what* for each GEM.

RUBIES

Why: They buy because they have to have it or just want it.
When: They buy on the spot . . . typically before you can even finish your presentation.
Who: They buy from great salespeople who give a great first impression.
What: They buy whatever they spontaneously want, or the best, or the most expensive.

SAPPHIRES

Why: They buy because it's new and cool to have, and they want it.
When: They buy spontaneously, or when it's easy and they have the money.
Who: They buy from fun salespeople who aren't negative or rude.
What: They buy new, exciting stuff; they are shopaholics and will always find the sales.

PEARLS

Why: They buy because it is a necessity or it offers functionality.

When: They buy after a lot of thinking and ensuring it is right for them.

Who: They buy from people they trust, people who do not push or rush them.

What: They buy things for other people, or necessities for themselves . . . nothing overboard; it must be within reason dollarwise.

EMERALDS

Why: They buy because it is the right choice; it is a correct and practical selection.

When: They buy after researching all the alternatives so they know it's the proper selection.

Who: They buy from people with integrity who do what they say and follow up.

What: They buy practical, above-average quality items that are efficient and long lasting . . . things that make sense by adding value to their lives.

Make It Real

Glenn's "pearl" trusted him after he listened patiently for almost an hour. By leaving materials to review, he wasn't acting pushy. He called the next day to see how the rest of the (hectic) day had gone. This approach resulted in a long-term contract worth tens of thousands of dollars, and all because he understood the GEMS.

Focus on Your GEMS to Help Prospects Respond

Every sales appointment is like going into a jewelry store. There are lots of GEMS around, and you just have to identify what type he or she is and polish them just the right way . . . the way that brings forth the most luster.

Learn what a Ruby, a Sapphire, a Pearl, and an Emerald client expects from you the seller and you will enjoy buyers who feel compelled to buy *from you* and refer *to you*!

Selling is a challenging enterprise of providing solutions to buyer problems, many of which may not be fully understood or even considered as a problem by the buyer. Cindy Mount, from Toronto, Canada, is a word-of-mouth marketing expert who gained her early career experience in human relations and project management. She shows us how to qualify the buyer, sort through all the details, and find just the right solution.

QUALIFYING THE BUYER IS A FOCUSING PROCESS

CINDY MOUNT

The marketplace churns out a plethora of nearly similar products. Some buyers are discriminating in their preferred choices, but most others are confused over their choices. The stressed seller sits right in the middle between the manufacturer and consumer and has the job of discovering the buyer's special interests, ability, and desire to buy her product and what barriers might impede that consumer from owning what she is selling.

Qualifying a prospect is a complex human interaction between consumer and seller, which is dependent on sufficient rapport being established so the two can explore working a deal together. The customer barriers to overcome are many and varied. They may include personal preferences, features, function, payment ability, sideline decision makers, acts of God, timing, personal health issues, and a million other potentialities. Qualifying the prospect is a process of discovering and eliminating all hesitancies that might impede the sale. It's not easy and requires extraordinary talent at interviewing, so that the prospective buyer doesn't feel like he or she is being interrogated—it's more of a sales conversation.

Often, the prospective customer won't know what she wants as much as what is causing her discomfort. When and if the seller can hear (get in touch with) the pain, she is more able to present an effective product or service as an appropriate solution. A stressed and novice seller might rush in with her best solution (whatever she is selling) before the real problem is fully understood.

Hoping to demonstrate her competence and make a commission, our novice merely illustrates an unwillingness to patiently listen to and assess the customer's real interests, which will put off a potential customer. Qualifying the buyer is a form of research that pulls together information necessary for the buyer to decide if the seller's product truly meets her needs. The qualifying interview is so important to effective sales that we wanted to offer a few more tips to help you improve your interviewing skills.

Encourage Others to Talk

Most prospects want to be encouraged to talk, and if done artfully, it will create an impression that you are a great conversationalist, when all you did was to listen. A few simple techniques to get people talking are detailed below:

- *Ask open-ended questions.* When you get an answer, ask another open ended question that directly flows from the preceding answer. "Are you here just to look or do you have a specific product in mind?" Answer: "I am just looking." Next question: "Have you been looking for a while?"
- *Use connecting words and sounds* to help people move from one topic to another, such as "hmm," "uh huh," "I see," or "do you think." These connectors assure the speaker that you heard the last comments and are open to hearing what comes next.
- *Paraphrase*, or parrot back to the speaker, what he just said. This reassures the speaker that you truly did hear his statements and caught their meaning.
- *Lead with emotional/cognitive directives.* If you get a brain flash about where the conversation might be going, say, "So it sounds as though you feel (summarize the feeling) and if so, then it suggests that you think (take an educated guess about what the next logical thoughts or steps would be for the speaker)"
- Let the speaker guide the discussion until you have a clear idea of the meaning.

Your job initially is to listen with the purpose of understanding the other's attitudes, circumstances, and desires, and then assess if your product is appropriate to her needs.

Following are some dos and don'ts for qualifying your prospect:

Dos	Don'ts
Be interested (nonjudgmental) in their views.	Be interesting (it's about them, not you).
Give the person your undivided attention.	Look around the room as if looking for escape.
Be curious and genuinely interested in the other person.	Push your views or product too early.
Start thinking, "How can I help this person now or later?" Be genuine and the answers will come.	Miss vital clues by thinking only, "How can I get them to buy from me."
Practice listening alertly and attentively.	Slip into old habits of pushing your solution.
Respond verbally and nonverbally with eye contact and facial expression.	Mentally rehearse what you will say, ignoring their body language.
Go with the speaker's flow of discussion.	Change the topic away from the speaker's interests.
Offer your total attention to the speaker.	Stand near distractions such as a buffet table or bar, or allow others to distract you.
Tune into the body language of the speaker.	Let their appearance cause you to pre-judge them.
Stay rested because attentive listening takes focused energy.	Get so drained and tired that you are not able to attend to this very important customer task.

As you are better able to understand the full pain, interests, and situation of your client, she will trust you more and consciously or subconsciously make you a part of her problem-solving team. As your discussion and opinions become part of her team picture, the sale is inevitable.

Let's see . . . should I sell to people who are perfectly satisfied with their current model, or should I get in front of those who are ready to buy right now? It seems like a ludicrous question, but targeting your clientele goes beyond merely identifying your most likely customers. Craig Elias, MBA, from Calgary, Canada, understands big time. His business, InnerSell, teaches us to include sales strategies for (1) those not quite ready to buy and (2) those satisfied with their status quo.

BE FIRST WITH MOTIVATED BUYERS

CRAIG ELIAS

Timing is essential to closing. The adage "timing is everything" is especially important in sales.

Buying Modes

Almost every individual has in his mind a product or service he would like to obtain in the near to distant future. People are buyers, and all buyers are always in one of three *buying modes*:

1. *Status Quo.* A potential buyer perceives the product or service he currently uses meets his needs.
2. *Searching for Alternatives.* A buyer realizes what he has no longer meets his needs and is actively searching for alternatives.

3. *Window of Dissatisfaction.* The buyer realizes that what he has no longer meets his needs, but at this point he isn't searching for alternatives.

Buying Modes and Prices

The buying mode of a buyer has a strong influence on the price a buyer is willing to pay for your product. Buyers pay for the value they think equates to the difference between your solution and their next buying mode.

The buyer's perception of value shifts as he moves from one buying mode to another. For example, when a buyer is in the Status Quo mode, the difference between what he already has and your solution is too high for him to buy from you.

But when the buyer realizes his current solution no longer meets his needs, he moves into a Window of Dissatisfaction. Now, because the value of difference between what he currently has (which no longer works satisfactorily) and what you provide decreases, he becomes a *motivated buyer.*

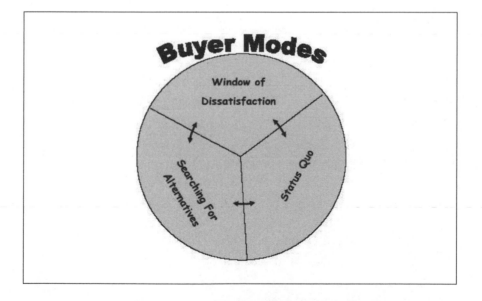

Master sellers adjust their selling effort according to the buying mode of the buyer. The seller is *five times more likely to make a sale* if he is the first person in front of a buyer who is in a *Window of Dissatisfaction.* This person is a motivated buyer. The priority for the master seller is to identify and be first with motivated buyers who are in a window of dissatisfaction. These customers are willing to decide more quickly about buying more products at a higher profit margin, just for the opportunity of owning your product. Acting quickly with these motivated customers bonds the buyers to your solution. Once they happily obtain and use your solution, they revert to a status quo, which neutralizes your competition. They will remain committed to your solution and quite possibly be a raving fan as long as their status quo is maintained.

The REAL Value of Timing

Being first with motivated buyers (in the Window of Dissatisfaction) gets you a core group of loyal buyers who represent 80 percent of your profits. These buyers provide great testimonials for you and offer the most treasured object in sales—referral clients.

When you are the first to connect with buyers in the Window of Dissatisfaction, the perceived value of your product is heightened. This value translates into a greater profit margin. With higher profits, you are able to assign more of your selling resources to the buyer and therefore offer the client better service. Now you are creating a spiral of met expectations, which continues to add success to your relationship with this client.

Connect with Dissatisfied Prospects

There are three simple ways to be the first sales professional to connect with a potential buyer in the Window of Dissatisfaction:
1. Becoming a buyer's emotional favorite
2. Getting referred by another buyer
3. Creating a window of dissatisfaction

Becoming the Emotional Favorite

A buyer's emotional favorite is the salesperson the buyer knows, likes, trusts, and most importantly, *wants to see succeed.* The buyer believes this seller has earned and deserves his business. The buyer will connect an emotional aspect to the seller when he shifts from his own status quo to a window of dissatisfaction. Being the go-to person for the buyer is a favored position for the seller.

Getting More Referrals

Increase your closing ratio by getting referred to potential buyers. Referred buyers don't feel as at risk from doing business with an unknown but referred vendor, because the referrer passes along some of his credibility to the referred seller. Use these three occasions to ask a buyer for referrals:

1. *Won sales.* Immediately after you have won a sale, ask for referrals because the buyer is most satisfied with your product and with YOU.

2. *Lost sales.* Losing a sale doesn't mean the buyer wouldn't refer you. Impress the buyer with your professionalism and responsiveness, and most will want to help you with a referral. (Some prospects may feel guilty for not buying from you, and offer a referral instead . . . but a referral is still a referral.)

3. *Before a sale.* Once you are the buyer's emotional favorite, you can also ask for referrals *even before you make a sale.* This is especially applicable if the closing cycle is long and you are staying in close contact with the waiting buyer. Many sales professionals join special referral marketing groups (such as BNI) to obtain third-party referrals.

Creating a Window of Dissatisfaction

It is possible to shift a buyer's *buying mode* from status quo mode (buyer believes that his current solution meets or exceeds his expectations) to window of dissatisfaction. This is done by raising the buyer's expectation of how his current solution should perform. This can be accomplished in one of three ways:

1. *The sales professional.* Teach the buyer about how to be more successful through use of your product.

2. *The solution.* Teach the buyer how your solution will help him catch up to, or stay ahead of, his competition.

3. *The company.* Educate the buyer on how your company is a better corporate citizen and therefore, a more desirable business partner for the long run.

What to Do in Each Buying Mode

Your first daily priority is to get in front of buyers in windows of dissatisfaction. Spend the first 50 percent of your selling time with the first-in-line opportunities. Your only objective is to sell, sell, and sell. Don't get distracted by other opportunities that might promise a greater return. Focus on becoming the buyer's new status quo and closing these sales.

Second, focus on those buyers actively engaged in searching for alternatives. Spend the next 25 percent of your selling time on opportunities that promise to close in the near future. If you are not first in line, become the buyer's emotional favorite. Become the seller who earns and deserves the buyer's future business (or referrals). Gaining this favored position may take time, but eventually you will deserve all the referred rewards that show up.

Your last priority is those buyers who are in the status quo mode. Use the last 25 percent of your selling time working to

- raise the buyer's expectations about use of his current product/vendor, and
- become the buyer's emotional favorite so he calls you first when dissatisfied with his current supplier.

Masters of Sales know that timing in sales is seldom an accident. It's the result of finding, creating, and maximizing selling opportunities with customers in their respective buying modes. Masters of Sales create an environment that encourages their customers to come to them *first* when a solution is required to a problem or need. If the buyer is a corporate buyer or otherwise busy person, the value of being a go-to seller becomes paramount. If you are first in line and have the best product or solution, your selling position is clearly favored.

Customers always react to the seller's attitude and behavior. It shouldn't be surprising to learn that buyers respond well to sellers who demonstrate a respectful and caring demeanor with the customer at all times. All the buyer really wants is to be respected, understood, and helped with his buying needs. Don Boisvert, a marketing franchise owner in Massachusetts, reminds us of the simple human relationship principles that must be followed whenever dealing with the public, especially in sales.

WHAT THE CUSTOMER WANTS FROM THE SELLER: SOME TIPS OF THE TRADE

DON BOISVERT

The brand-new salesperson knows very well that customers mean income. However, many of those just starting their careers have not yet gained an understanding of how to consistently turn a prospect into a *customer.*

The following tips serve to remind sales professionals—whether neophyte or seasoned pro—that both our attitude and behavior are carefully reviewed by our potential buyers, and can make the difference between success and failure.

Seek Some Knowledge of Your Customer's Company
To acquire a new customer or to keep a current customer, show that you are knowledgeable about your customer's company.

Tim was a fine detailer, the owner of a prosperous vehicle cleaning and polishing business. To increase his profits, he wanted to expand his business to include detailing private and corporate jets. He researched the jets, even touring a couple of them as if he were a prospective buyer. Then a friend arranged his introduction to the COO of a nearby charter company. Tim did not need to know the details of the COO's company; he did need to have in-depth knowledge about the jets in the company's fleet. He knew things about the company's jets that the COO did not know. During the meeting, Tim offered a complimentary service for one of the company jets. And, yes, he did land the contract.

Knowledge Is an Integral Part of Your Reputation

Be the exceptional expert. Your customer expects you to know more about your product/service than he does.

Susan's company had specific payroll requirements. The sales representative of a nationally known payroll company assured her that his firm was the "Cadillac" in the industry and could handle these issues with ease, winning the sale. However, the services offered did not fit with Susan's specific requirements. She became deeply disappointed with their quality of service and, citing breach of contract, terminated the relationship. Needless to say, she did not have good things to say about the company or the sales rep.

Be Likeable

Within the first seven seconds of meeting a salesperson, a prospective customer is already making decisions about him and his products/services. Customers do business with people they like. Repeat business is almost always a result of a long-term positive business relationship. The following suggestions can help make—and keep—a great first impression:

- *Be on time.* Arrive at least five minutes early and then walk through the door at the precise time.
- *Smile.* Smile frequently: Show that you enjoy what you do, and show your customers that you enjoy their company.
- *Offer a solid handshake.* Let it be solid, but not crushing. Look into the person's eyes, smile, and hold his or her attention as you shake hands. (Note: Be aware of the many cultural differences in shaking hands.)

- *Respect everyone.* Be courteous. Do not discuss politics, religion, or sex unless they have a direct relationship to your product/service (even a mention of your favorite sports team may turn people away!).
- *Say "thank you."* Thank the person for his or her time and follow up with a unique thank-you card that speaks to your prospective customer.
- *Follow through.* Forward additional materials, schedule a follow-up session, or call the customer within the time frames specified.

Listen Twice as Much as You Speak

Give your undivided attention to the customer. Leave your personal problems and causes at the door.

> *At a gathering, a new acquaintance spent almost an hour with Ron. Apart from asking one or two questions, Ron did not think he had spoken for more than a minute or two during the entire period. As they were breaking, the new acquaintance announced, "Hey, everyone, Ron is one of the best conversationalists I've ever spoken to."*

Listen for the Need, Not Just to What the Person Is Saying

Conceptualize the customer's needs as he/she is speaking.

> *Peter sells cleaning solutions and waxes to institutions. The head custodian of a local school showed off his hallways, telling Peter how proud he is to be able to have clean and highly polished floors. No sale here, right? Wrong! Peter learned in the conversation that the durability of the products being used was poor, necessitating frequent stripping and applications, and involving staff time and expenditures. Peter was able to provide more durable products. Though they were slightly more expensive on a unit basis, they ultimately saved on labor and cost. The head custodian became a repeat customer of Peter's.*

Show Your Willingness to Help—Regardless of the Payoff

Justin is a mortgage officer. One prospect was saying that he had an alternative that was cheaper than Justin's. Justin replied that he thought he had the best products at the least expense but that, if indeed the customer had access to a similar product at lower cost, then he should use them. However, Justin also made an incredible offer. He said, "Get the printed disclosure statements and the offering. Let me review and interpret it for you. If it is a better deal, I will be pleased to recommend it to you. If there is something in the small print of which you should be aware, I will let you know, as a complimentary service."

Justin clarified what the customer was looking for and what options were important to him. In reviewing the customer's "cheaper option," he was able to point out additional charges and penalties that were written into the fine print. The customer decided that Justin's product, and the additional service and flexibility, was just what he really needed . . . and he also recommended Justin to his friends and associates.

Your professional image will be heightened by building a reputation for being helpful, with no guarantee of a sale.

Be a Proud Representative of Your Product/Service

Speak with belief and confidence about what you do and what your product or service will provide. Demonstrate excitement and passion about your career and your abilities.

Customers buy as much with the heart as they do with the mind. When you represent yourself as being confident (rather than boastful), as being knowledgeable (rather than arrogant), and loving what you do (rather than being disdainful of your competitors), your customer will be more prepared to do business with you.

Customers get caught up—and even infected—with your excitement for the product or service.

Sometimes the Simplest Actions Can Bring Big Returns

During her meeting, Cathy's client kept telling her about his three golden retrievers. His children were now grown and out of the house, and the dogs had become his surrogate children. Following her appointment, Cathy sent her customer a thank-you greeting card featuring a pair of golden retrievers on the face of it. Not only did the customer appreciate the card, he now keeps it displayed on his desk—a constant reminder of Cathy who, through efforts such as this, has become his favorite sales representative.

The client always knows when you have gone that extra mile on his behalf. He will remember you!

Finally…

Assume that You Are Going to Close the Sale

Yes, presume that the customer really *does* want what you have to offer at the prices you have quoted. Have confidence in yourself and in your abilities. Assure your customers: "I can and will deliver quality products and services, not just with this order but on an ongoing basis." Then deliver on that promise!

Sales Systems

*The only way to discover the limits of the possible is to go
beyond them into the impossible.*

—ARTHUR C. CLARKE

There are many forms of sales technologies or systems used to facilitate a successful sales transaction. Sales techniques can be social systems, highly mechanical computer based systems, or even a standardized format of interactions followed with great dedication.

The amazing thing is that most colleges and universities around the world don't teach sales techniques! This skill simply is not part of the core curriculum of courses that are taught in virtually every school. As a matter of fact, colleges and universities give bachelor's degrees in marketing to people who don't have a clue how to close a sale. Not a clue. That's why there is such a big industry (outside of universities) in teaching people how to sell.

College professors prefer to teach what we call "sterile marketing." They educate their neophyte students in how to create and manage multi-million-dollar advertising campaigns (like that is something they are actually going to do right out of college)! They almost never focus on teaching students any comprehensive sales techniques. Heaven forbid that they actually get their hands dirty and "sell" something. Probably one of the biggest reasons for this is that most college professors have never sold anything in their entire life. (OK, Dr. Misner is an adjunct college professor, but he also started out his career in sales.)

This section of the book is about sales systems. Yes, there are systems that one can employ to learn how to "sell" better. They are good systems, and they are being taught around the world . . . just not in most colleges or universities. In fact, there are scores of sales systems—too many for one book. Therefore, we are offering you just a few key points, each of which, if utilized, has the capacity to accelerate your sales success. Progressing to a mastery level means learning and integrating the basic systems, and then going beyond what is ordinary to the *extraordinary.*

———•·•———

This first contribution is a true story. Although the story isn't directly about sales per se, its message is all about something that is very important to any successful sales person: Don't reinvent the wheel. Instead, learn from other people's experiences. Ivan and Elisabeth Misner are partners, both in BNI, the largest referral marketing organization in the world, and in life.

———•·•———

WHY MAKE ALL THE MISTAKES,
WHEN WE CAN LEARN FROM OTHERS?

DR. IVAN MISNER WITH ELISABETH MISNER

There are "tried–and–true" sales techniques that are so simplistic that it seems they cannot be really effective. Many times, we try to re-evaluate, improve upon, and complicate them. An experience I had once while on vacation reminds me of how we try to make some things harder than they really are.

I was in Hawaii enjoying the surf when, unbeknownst to me, the water became thick with Portuguese Man O'War jellyfish. Suddenly I felt a stinging sensation across my chest. I wiped my chest with my right wrist and arm and lifted my arm up out of the water. I saw the tentacles dripping off my arm and followed them with my eyes to the body of the Man O'War jellyfish about eight feet away. With mounting alarm, I shook the tentacles off my wrist back into the water and quickly swam out of the surf to the shore.

I ran up to the first hotel employee I saw, a cabana boy, who was serving drinks to a sunning couple just off the pool deck and urgently exclaimed, "I think I've just been hit in the chest by a Man O'War jellyfish! What should I do??"

"Are you feeling any pressure in your chest?" he wanted to know.

"No, none at all," I replied anxiously.

"OK, OK, here's what you need to do. Go on over to the market off the lobby and ask for some vinegar and meat tenderizer. You're going to want to spray the vinegar onto your chest and then shake the meat tenderizer onto the same spot and rub it all around. You'll be fine," he assured me.

Well, I must say that I was less than impressed with this bizarre advice. He was entirely too calm and that was entirely too easy to be a real solution—not to mention that it was just plain strange. I figured he was doing a version of "let's goof on the tourist," so I moved on to ask someone else for help. Strangely enough, I asked two more hotel employees what to do about my injury, and got the exact same answer: vinegar and meat tenderizer!

179

I reluctantly trucked down the hall to the store just knowing that they were all back there laughing at the goofy tourist who was actually going to do a self-imposed "meat rub" on his chest. I was sure they had some barbecue grill going for when I returned to the lobby all slathered up with vinegar and meat tenderizer.

I entered the small market off the lobby and started my search for char-grilled products when I started feeling short of breath. Suddenly, very quickly and forcefully, I began to experience a crushing weight on my chest. Was I having a heart attack? Great! I'm having a coronary after wasting so much time talking to members of the hotel staff, who were trying to get me to rub meat tenderizer on my chest. I walked out of the store and staggered to the front desk, which by now was very busy with new guests checking in to the hotel. I made eye contact with the hotel manager and almost immediately, dropped to the ground, clutching my chest, barely able to gasp, "Man O'War!"

What happened next was a total blur. I seem to remember a small child yelling and pointing at me as I lay there in my bathing suit, gasping for breath.

"Look mommy, there's a man on the floor." The mother said something about staying away from people who do drugs. I looked over and tried to say no, not drugs—jellyfish! But all that came out was gibberish.

The paramedics rushed to the scene. Finally, I was going to get the medical attention I needed. After determining what had happened, the paramedic opened his lifesaving kit, and I knew he was about to pull out a defibrillator. I made my peace with God and I braced myself for the big jolt. Instead, he pulled out—yes, you guessed it—vinegar in a spray bottle and some Adolf's meat tenderizer! He then proceeded to spray the vinegar, sprinkle the meat tenderizer on my chest, and thoroughly rub the mixture around. Within seconds, literally seconds, the excruciating pain began to subside. Within a couple minutes it was almost completely gone.

What I thought was a big "barbeque joke" on the tourist turned out to be a well-known cure for some jellyfish strikes. You see, the meat tenderizer contains the enzyme papain, which breaks down the toxin proteins and neutralizes them. It sounds too simple to be really effective, but it is, in fact, one of the best things to do in that situation.

Thinking back on it, I am amazed at how many people gave me the solution before I had to learn the hard way. Sure, who's going to believe a cabana boy? I mean, what does he know, right? And the hotel employee—OK, maybe there's the start of a pattern here but, I have a doctoral degree—I'm "smart," and these guys have just got to be kidding me . . . Right? And then the hotel manager as well . . . OK, I admit it, at that point there's just no excuse. I should have figured out these guys knew what they were talking about, and I did not.

I made one of the biggest mistakes that people in business (and especially in sales) make—I didn't listen to the people who have experience. I assumed that I just had to know better . . . and the truth is, I didn't know better.

There is nothing like experience. It beats education every day of the week. The only thing better is a combination of education and experience . . . or a willingness to learn from other people's experience. There are many basic sales techniques that any good salesperson knows to be effective. They don't try to look for something more complicated or involved, because they know from their own experience, as well as the experience of others, what works in sales and what doesn't work in sales.

Throughout this book you may read things that seem too simple to be effective or may see ideas that you've heard before. Don't dismiss them. Embrace them. Masters of Sales learn from other people's success. So, go get that vinegar and meat tenderizer, and learn from other Masters that sometimes the simplest ideas can have the biggest impact.

It is a fact that more than 50 percent of all businesses fail within three years of starting. This is a devastatingly large number of start-up companies, and their failure relates to lack of selling. Sales drive a business. You can have the best product on the market, but it won't sell itself. The next contribution is a great example of what can go wrong if a business doesn't focus on sales. As a professional financial consultant and marketing expert in Ohio, Geof Scanlon has seen his share of business start-ups and failures.

———•—•——

DEATH OF A NON-SALESMAN: A CAUTIONARY TALE

GEOF SCANLON

After 30 years of service as a vice president at an international *Fortune* 100 company, Bill R. got the axe. His corner office on the 30th floor, big staff, and great perks were all gone with the flutter of a pink slip and a corporate restructuring.

Bill wasn't worried. He figured he had the financial expertise, the business savvy, and the contacts to go it alone. He'd do things his way, be his own boss in a financial planning business for high net worth individuals. "*Should have done it years ago,*" he thought. It would be fun—a slam dunk!

He said his good-byes, and found office space on the Kentucky side of the Ohio River just across from the scenic Cincinnati skyline. He hired a staff, bought computers, cell phones, and some business casual attire. He was on his way. At the kickoff party, ex-coworkers, business associates, and friends congratulated him on bouncing back. *What a beautiful office, Bill. You'll do great, Bill. I'll call you!*

Monday morning, Bill was the first one in the office. The Dow was up 40 points. All staff accounted for. Computers humming. Bill started making some calls. No one was in. Bill went to lunch—alone. On his return, his voicemail said he had three messages. *Yeah baby, here we go!* People wanted to talk to him! Right. People from the Yellow Pages, the local chamber of commerce, and the United Way rep all urgently wanted to talk to him.

For months, Bill struggled. He was a member of the chamber of commerce, Optimists, Rotary Club, and other groups. He knew tons of people, had good business relationships and contacts. But he had no business.

What was he doing wrong? Eventually, Bill realized he had to close the office. End of a dream. What could he have done to ensure a different outcome? He could have *learned to sell.*

Bill told me this true story after he had closed. In spite of his credentials, education, business contacts, friends, and his breadth of experience in the financial world, Bill had never learned to sell.

Referrals? Yes. Networking? Yes. Relationships? Yes, again. But, Bill had not relied solely upon these peripheral sales assets. Somewhere along the way, he needed to have *mastered* the art of selling. And whether you're starting your own business or just want to achieve success in your current business role, *you* need to know how to sell, too. Here are eight tips for a good start.

1. *Commit to the notion that you can and will become an excellent salesperson.* Make it a daily affirmation in your mind's eye. Visualize yourself as an excellent sales person.

2. *Visually picture and define a salesperson that is consistent with your own personality.* Never mind the visual cliché of the fast-talking, plaid-wearing sales guy with the white shoes and belt. Envision yourself as a sales professional who brings a product or service value-wrapped brightly with character and integrity. Imagine yourself as the seller who allows the prospect to buy.

3. *Study everything you can get your hands on about sales.* Books, CDs, videos, DVDs—they're all available free at your library.

4. *Create a short list of sales goals you can attain over the next two years.* Design rewards, from conservative to exotic, for achieving each one.

5. *Confront anything that might be holding you back.* Are you afraid of rejection? Are you a procrastinator? Do you have time management issues? Are your priorities skewed? We all suffer from these maladies, and we all have to work through them.

6. *Be honest with yourself.* Are you really in the right business for the right reason? Could your passion and talent lie elsewhere? If you carry massive emotion and energy into learning about and working in sales, you can win big.

7. *Commit to the mastery of the sales process.* Make prudent, intelligent commitments. Take action. Get on the right path and stay on it. See *Mastery: The Keys to Success and Long-Term Fulfillment* by George Leonard (Plume, 1992).

8. See tip 1. (Commit to being an excellent sales professional!)

Get serious about your career. Quit listening to everyone telling you what you *can't* do. Focus on where you want to go and figure out how you intend to get there. Don't tell yourself how hard it's *going* to be when you zero in on the target. Don't engage in procrastinating self-talk like, "Gee, the market is down," or "I'll jump on this right after the holidays," or "I'll start on it at 8 A.M. on January 1st!"

Want to learn to sell? Then how about campaigning for your favorite politician in the next election? Go door-to-door and host neighborhood meetings. How about getting involved in fundraising for United Way, the American Heart Association, or Muscular Dystrophy? Or even more drastic, raise several teenagers (not recommended for the faint of heart).

Create a daily strategy to execute your plan. Determine how many referral sources, networking events, prospecting phone calls, and how many hours a day you'll need to devote to selling. See Chapter 19 of *Business by Referral: A Sure-Fire Way to Generate New Business* by Ivan R. Misner and Robert Davis (Bard Press, 1998). It'll help you forecast sales from your referrals.

Sell every day, honorably, and with integrity. Measure your progress. When you fall, get up and try again. Just keep moving forward! Yes, you'll have disappointments, but you'll also enjoy your success more. Most importantly, be consistent in what you do. If you quit, you're toast! And for goodness' sake, don't forget poor Bill from the beginning of this piece. Nothing happens until YOU make it happen. All the techniques, strategies, and sales tools in the world won't help until you decide to learn the selling technologies—and then *master* them!

———•◦•———

The Sandler Sales training program has trained thousands of business professionals around the world to become better salespeople, including Sam Schwartz from Northern Virginia. It must have paid off because Sam Schwartz now has an international marketing business with operations in four countries. Sam openly shares how he learned selling through adherence to a simple, replicable, structured sales system.

THE SANDLER SYSTEM: FROM PRACTICE TO THEORY

SAM SCHWARTZ

I was the east coast publisher for an annual arts guide that survived on ad sales. I had no sales experience, and my selling results were equally dismal. With total frustration, I wished for a "magic sales pill" to aid in my sales disease. I hated to admit it, but I needed help.

My solution was to sign up for a sales training program at the "Sandler Institute for Sales." Quickly, I realized that my coach, Ken Smith, was right. He told me that I would not be able to master the whole system at once. So, I decided to focus on three simple concepts to learn and use until I mastered them: I chose to learn more about (1) a self-confident attitude, (2) the "sales submarine," and (3) the "upfront contract."

Concept One: Maintain an "I Don't Need the Sale" Attitude

The first and biggest lesson I learned was to make an attitude adjustment. I had to pretend that "I was independently wealthy and I did not need the next sale." This required practice and self-reassurance because my reality didn't match this attitude. However, after a few months of practice, I developed a more self-assured attitude, and my results changed. I was closing more business deals.

The hardest part was to convince myself to willingly give up a sale when I really needed it. I took to heart the old phrase, "Fake it until you make it." There is truth in this simple concept.

I also kept repeating one of David Sandler's comments: "You cannot lose what you don't have." Learning and then internalizing this attitude increased my sense of power and control over the selling process. I became more relaxed and was able to let go of the self-imposed pressure to "close" (or die trying).

The "close at all cost" attitude kills many deals because customers sense your desperation; they fight you harder as they sense your increased desperation. We've all seen a desperate salesperson pushing a sale. Most of them ultimately fail.

Masterful salespeople always appear confident and calm. Good sellers never need to push a sale; instead they allow the buyer to buy. If you believe your product or services will truly help your prospects, then you must emotionally allow them to own it.

I still remember the day I met with the managing director of a Bentley, Mercedes Benz, and Rolls Royce dealership. It took two years of prospecting phone calls to get this meeting and it held potential for a great commission.

I arrived early. I sat in my car and imagined delivering a signed contract to my partner. How great that felt! I repeated the image in my mind again and again, until I could taste the success and feel it in my bones. It was a great feeling. My mind propaganda carried me right through the meeting. I successfully closed the deal. If I had entered the meeting possessed with negative thoughts about my sales goals, the time making prospecting calls, etc., the results of that meeting would most likely have been disappointing.

When you feel down and desperate before a sale, take a minute and think about your last success story. Put yourself in that moment and internalize the emotions. Then go into the meeting with that success moment having a strong influence inside you. If you have a particular goal in mind, take a moment and visualize the reality of reaching that goal and rewarding yourself, then go into your sales meeting.

Concept Two: The Sales Submarine

Central to the Sandler sales training program is a submarine analogy, in which you should not move from one stage (compartment) to the next before making sure that you have completed all the tasks associated with your current stage. You must go through the different compartments of the sales process step-by-step. If you transition each stage properly, the prospect will feel comfortable with your sales approach and be more willing to complete the deal.

Concept Three: The Upfront Contract

The first time I heard the term "Upfront Contract," I had an image of a 200-page legal document full of legaleze. But, an Upfront Contract is a simple understanding between two people regarding (1) what will happen during the meeting (the process), (2) the discussion topics (the agenda), and (3) the desired and acceptable outcome of the meeting. In other words, it is a simple and transparent agreement about what will transpire during the meeting, which decreases potential for meeting-mystification.

The idea is to allow all the meeting parties to influence how the meeting will be conducted prior to beginning. This collaborative involvement allows everyone to "own" the meeting. A good upfront contract should cover when and where the meeting is to take place, the length of the meeting, the agenda items, and the mutually desirable and acceptable outcome for the meeting. Any potential changes must be covered by a mutually agreed upon (second) contract that effectively amends the first.

I use this tool automatically when planning all my meetings, not just my sales meetings. I ensure that mutual objectives and time constraints for the meeting are established by inviting the other party's input. Later, if the meeting gets off course, I refer to our agreed-upon guidelines to refocus the discussion onto the agenda.

This simple process saves me time and earns me money. When arriving at a new meeting, I generally refer to our agreed-upon half-hour of undisturbed time in my first sentences. If I discover the client only scheduled ten minutes for me, I then offer the client an opportunity to reschedule or to give me the time needed. Most often, when reminded of our understanding, he allocates the full undisturbed half-hour.

This technique works with prospects, employees, family, and friends. People appreciate having clarity about what's going to happen and what is expected of them. This is especially important in a selling scenario.

As David Sandler says, "Having any system is better than none." The Sandler System did more than change my outlook on professional sales. The program also helped me develop and grow as an individual.

 *You have the appointment. You're sitting in front of the prospect. Now what? What do you say? What do you do? Just as important—what don't you say or do? David Donnelly, from Edmonton, Canada, has a unique twist on giving the product presentation to the prospective client. His insight, gained from years in professional sales and teaching others to sell through his sales training company, provides key points to consider, and from which all successful salespeople could benefit.*

GET INVITED TO PRESENT

DAVID DONNELLY

The conquering salesman proudly produces a flashy binder, flipchart, or PowerPoint . . . and your stomach drops. As his dreaded presentation drones on, your thoughts shift to more important items, like the kids' school, pesky in-laws—anything but his self-serving display. Your interest is waning; soon it may vanish. This sales presentation was doomed before it began.

We've all been on the receiving end yet, too often, are tempted to believe our own presentation is the exception to the rule.

It's Not to Them What It Is to You

Presentations rarely create sales. Getting overexcited and starting a sales call with a big presentation usually deflates the prospect's attention and interest. I call this *Premature Gesticulation* (or PG). A client will stop talking, stop sharing information, and worse, disengage from a salesperson overcome with PG, because the presentation introduces information that is superfluous to the prospect's early considerations and interests. In effect, the buyer has not had a chance to warm up to the seller or the product. Unfortunately, many salespeople force their presentation on unsuspecting prospects at the first opportunity—and kill the sale.

Don't assume your standard presentation will address what's important to a prospect. Once, when I was buying a new mini-van, I asked the salesperson about cargo space. He defaulted into a rote speech about the benefits of movable seats and cargo and configuration, about ease of movement. Blah, blah, blah . . . He didn't ask why I wanted to know about cargo space. If he had, he would have learned that all I wanted to know was whether all of our bicycles would fit into the back when I had all three boys in the van. He lost his sale because he couldn't control himself and let me tell him why cargo space was important to me.

A salesperson overcome with PG appears to be more concerned about pushing the sale than in doing the sales job professionally, step by step.

Don't Present Too Early

Be careful about not launching your presentation immediately upon hearing the first problem indicator. Yes, you might have a sincere desire to help your prospect, but launching your presentation too early creates a hair-trigger response from the prospect. He shoots away from you as fast as a speeding bullet.

Sales training programs—and dating advice experts—all say to "get the prospect talking." So let a client talk about his needs, wants, and aspirations. The more he talks, the more important his needs become in his mind.

Buried deep below the expression of need is an emotional buy-in that, when tapped, will motivate the prospect to action. Adopt a quiet but encouraging attitude to help your prospect discover his core buy-in emotion.

Get Emotional Buy-In

It's also important to remember that the mere mention of a problem does not necessarily mean a person is motivated to fix it. He may not have the money; he may not think it worth the time and effort; or he may not have the necessary authority. If all a prospect does to provoke your presentation is to mention a problem, then you are skipping essential steps, and that will kill the sale. Don't do what is easiest (relying solely on the company's presentation and your finely honed presentation skills). Instead, say something like "Tell me more about that," and let the prospect lead the discussion into areas of his interest.

As a person talks about a problem in greater depth, the problem becomes a pain. If well prompted, your buyer will talk himself into asking you to present your product in the hope it will ease his pain. Be a good listener and ask the right questions. You will learn good timing.

Your prospect may clearly indicate that he wants his needs addressed. But you also need to know he has the ability to make a purchasing decision. Once your prospect expresses both his need and his authority then, and only then, should you offer your presentation.

Don't Ask "Are You the Decision Maker?"

Most people won't admit to not having decision-making authority. If your prospect is the decision maker, he'll answer "yes." Unfortunately, if he isn't, he'll probably still answer "yes" for two reasons: because he doesn't want to feel unimportant, and/or because that will be his "out" when you try to confirm a commitment.

To find the right prospect, ask, "Is there anyone who can say 'no' to this?" This will politely get you the answer you need without compromising an initial contact's self-esteem. If they say "no," you're in front of the right person; if they say "yes," they're not getting a presentation today.

Qualifying Precedes the Presentation

The sales presentation should not be used to qualify a buyer. It is an end-of-sales-process tool to address the prospect's clearly articulated needs when he is emotionally ready to buy. In essence, it is the deal clincher.

The canned presentation stops you from listening to your client. It cannot be overemphasized: in the early stages, you want your prospect to talk about his needs. If you look only for an opening to whip out your presentation, you are not listening, you are suffering from PG. You are not questioning deeply enough to respond to his needs. The call becomes less about what the customer wants and more about your need to present.

Present Only After the Qualified Prospect Says "Yes"

A prospect is ready for the full presentation when he begins using strong emotional words to describe his problem. Your goal is to "feel his pain." If he feels pain, and expresses a desire for cure, the presentation is on. Listen for your prospect's language to change from passive to active:

- "I should do something about that" becomes "I have to do that."
- "I could do something about that" becomes "I need to address that."
- "I would do something about that" becomes "I've got to address that."

When the shift from passive to active occurs, you are almost ready to let the prospect discover the cure in your presentation . . . *almost*. You still need a bit more information.

The Green Light

Once the client's problem has been expressed emotionally, and he has confirmed he has the money and that no one else can say no, then you can present your solution. Your final step is to tailor your presentation to the prospect's needs. The full pitch may not be necessary to get the job done. You must decide what parts can be left out and what parts of your presentation need to be accentuated. Even a rehearsed presentation can be customized to a prospect's needs. You are putting to use all the information you collected during the earlier investigatory stage.

Focus on prospecting through artfully questioning potential buyers. Listen carefully to their answers so that you can qualify them. Only qualified prospects with real pain, real money, and real authority are good candidates for your final, custom-tailored presentation. You will save yourself a tremendous amount of time by presenting only to people who are motivated to buy. Stay in control of your urge to present; it's all about selling smarter, not harder.

 Did you ever hear the sales lesson "Sell the sizzle, not the steak?" This cliché says it all: It highlights the need to sell not just the features of your product or service, but also the benefits. Tom Hopkins, through his sales training organization, has trained more than three million sales students on five continents. We can learn a lot about features and benefits from one of the world's best sales trainers.

THE MOST EFFECTIVE PRODUCT DEMONSTRATION PROCESS EVER!

TOM HOPKINS AND PAT LEIBY

As with most things in life, there are many ways to accomplish a single task. Wise salespeople are constantly on the lookout for better ways to make a point or present their products. We teach a proven-effective procedure for product presentations or demonstrations that is sure to work for you.

It begins with preparation. Thinking about the client you will present to next, break down your product demonstration into segments highlighting each individual feature of your product or service that you know will benefit this client.

The second step is to present each of those features in the following manner, and only in the following manner.

First, you state the FACT. Then, you show the BENEFIT. Once the benefit is given, you must create URGENCY. And ask for FEEDBACK.

Facts and benefits create the sale. Urgency and feedback make it happen now. The first two—fact and benefit—are pretty easy if you are a professional who truly knows your product.

Urgency for each feature is something that the salesperson must create. It's not there until you make it so. It's not being pushy or trying to force your customer into a quick decision. Creating urgency requires effort and creativity to assure that your potential client feels a genuine need to make a purchase today and now.

In my seminars, we create urgency by offering special investments on products that are only valid the day of the seminar. It's the today-and-today-only method of developing urgency. Retail outlets use sales or offers where they indicate quantities are limited to create a sense of urgency in their shoppers. Investment counselors show charts and graphs of growth potential based on today's market figures. If the client wants to earn those kinds of returns, he should start his program today.

The fourth step of asking for feedback serves two purposes: (1) it provides a way to monitor your progress, and (2) helps you see if your potential client is ready for the next logical step.

To give you a better idea of how the process works, here are a couple of examples. Read them, study them, and customize the system to work for your product and your customers.

Here's an example for the automobile industry:

Fact: "This powerful V8 engine is the largest stock gasoline engine made in the United States."

This fact is obvious. You can simply lift the hood and show it. Even if the facts aren't that visual—anti-lock brakes or a roadside assistance plan, for example—one of your product brochures will list these facts and more. The point is that facts are easy to come by.

Benefit: "This engine will allow you to pull your boat with ease and it's a standard feature with this model."

To discover the appropriate benefit, just put yourself in your customer's mind and ask "what's in it for me?" In this case, the customer is concerned about the ease of pulling a boat from the house out to the lake. Power is obviously what's in it for him. Gas mileage, acceleration, braking, and turning ease could also be important benefits. After achieving trust and need, facts and benefits may do the selling, but urgency and feedback will do it now.

Urgency: "This particular engine will not be an option on next year's truck and even with the smaller engine there will be a higher sticker price on the new model. So, next year you'd be paying more for the same model, but with less power."

Without using any high pressure or being pushy, the salesperson has merely pointed out the significant advantage to making a purchase right now over procrastinating until later. Buying now is clearly in the customer's best interest according to the customer's own definition of need.

Feedback: "Because next year's model will look and ride exactly the same, which one do you think would fit your needs and pocketbook the best?"

The answer is rather obvious, isn't it? With these four steps, the potential client should realize that, too, and be prepared to move to the next step in the system, which would be to discuss the money aspects of the sale.

Let's see how this works with something as simple as a DVD system:

Fact: "This particular unit is a state-of-the-art DVD system."

Benefit: "It is the highest quality DVD available at this time and will give you better picture and sound reproduction than anything else on the market."

Urgency: "I have just two of these units in stock right now. One was returned because it was a gift and the person receiving it already had one. The package has been opened, but the unit has never been used. However, because it's been opened, I can give it to you at a lower amount with the same guarantee."

Feedback: "Although the unit is new and has never been used, or even plugged in, the carton was still opened. Technically, we can't sell it as new. Is having that carton opened something you can live with, if it would save you money?"

Use the preceding examples to spur some thought as to how the process will work with your product or service. Creating urgency might require a little thought on your part, but it can be done. Asking for feedback is critical. If you don't generate feedback, you may never discover the concerns until it is too late to effectively address them.

When you get positive feedback throughout your presentation or demonstration, your close becomes much easier because your customer would be contradicting himself by refusing to go ahead. Your customer is not an opponent to be overcome, but a partner to be helped. Even negative feedback is valuable because it lets you know where your customer stands on a particular issue or feature.

Product demonstration is basic. It's simple, but it's not as easy as falling off a log. You have to do your homework, study, and practice the techniques. You also need to research your client's real needs, wants, and concerns. Beyond that, you have to apply your own creative resources to put the entire system together in terms that provide the unique solution to your client's unique situation.

When you use the system properly, the "math" will astound you.

Fact + Benefits + Urgency + Feedback = Sold Today, Sold Now

Repeat this mantra over and over, "I will never give a product demonstration again without presenting the features in this manner:

- State the facts,
- Show the benefits,
- Create urgency and ask for feedback."

It will make a world of difference in increasing the number of people you serve, improving your closing ratio, and allowing you to do it in less time. It's a sales professional's dream come true.

———•••———

 Use it or abuse it, suggestive selling can be very powerful and helpful when used with the customer's best interests in mind. Steve Bell, from Regina, Canada, is a selling dynamo who fully understands the power of suggestive selling. As a professional salesman having the customer's best interests in mind, he slams down a full sales ticket with plenty of extra profit margin, and the customer buys him a steak dinner in gratitude.

———•••———

SALES DYNAMO THROUGH SUGGESTIVE SELLING

STEVE BELL

Years ago I discovered the value of suggestive selling first-hand while working with a large electronics chain. The company had a reputation for providing poor customer service, yet I was the number-one salesperson month after month and built a loyal base of repeat customers. Co-workers and managers alike wanted to know the secrets to my success. Looking back, I believe the only thing that really set me apart from my colleagues is that I had embraced a proven sales strategy called suggestive selling and utilized it over and over again.

Here are three simple steps to suggestive selling that work for me every time:

1. *Two ears, one mouth.* Use these attributes proportionately by talking less and listening more.
2. *Sometimes listening isn't enough.* Ask relevant questions to reveal the customer's needs. Remember, they may not know what they need but instead are driven by a vague desire. A skilled professional is able to anticipate needs and suggest complimentary products/services.
3. *Fill the customer's specific needs.* Based on the customer's answers, summarize to make sure you've interpreted their responses correctly. Once you're armed with the right information to fill their specific needs, you can offer to sell them the full package . . . not just what they ask for initially.

My favorite experience using suggestive selling techniques began with a customer who entered my store near the end of the day to purchase inexpensive computer speakers for his 52-inch TV. I asked him a few questions about the TV to understand what he might be looking for, and my last questions sounded something like this . . .

"You have a nice TV, but do you want substandard sound? May I show you something that might be better suited to your large new TV?"

He answered, "Yes," which gave me permission to continue asking questions. I discovered how much time was spent watching TV, what components he had, and what other components or accessories he was looking to add or upgrade in the future. This allowed me to suggest products and services that filled the needs he had outlined by his answers.

Originally, this customer entered the store to purchase computer speakers. He left with an amplifier, five-disc DVD player, Sony Play Station, extra remotes, stand, games, and high-end wiring for all of the components. The sale ticket was over two feet long and had concluded with the sale of an extended warranty on his entire purchase. The sale was concluded, but the customer service was not. I made arrangements for delivery and personalized installation by me, which carried us well past regular store closing hours. The customer was very grateful and pleased with the purchase—even offering a steak dinner as a thank you. In the end, I sold two and a half times more than my co-workers had all day.

Fortunately, I learned early on that customers expect to be sold the complete package or experience. Customers expect that YOU, the professional, understand what they need and are prepared to fill the need. For example, if a customer buys a remote control car, they most likely want to be sold the batteries needed to operate it. They want to buy it now, in the moment, not after they get home and read "Batteries not included."

Suggestive selling can be applied to a sale in virtually any industry, from electronics to air travel. My wife and I recently purchased a new SUV. We realized after the sale was complete that the salesperson had not asked if we wanted undercoating or an extended warranty. Realizing that we would have purchased these add-ons had they been offered left us feeling very unsatisfied with the sales experience. We were not completely satisfied because we did not receive everything that we needed. The salesperson was not looking past the moment, and failed to adequately assess our needs. The result was missed sales opportunity and an unhappy customer.

Suggestive selling is a very effective sales technique. You have to be patient with your customers, ask simple questions, and listen to the answers. This allows you to suggest items customers may desire that are related to their needs. Some people call this "up-selling," but I think it is really a key to providing great customer service. Some additional tips are to be sincere, listen carefully to what the customer has to say, resist the temptation to make a quick sale, and be honest when a sale isn't in the customer's best interest. It's OK to let a sale go once in a while when it's the right thing to do.

Suggestive selling is a bargain for the customer and adds significantly to the company's profit margin. Try to incorporate these suggestive selling techniques into your sales strategy. Continually work on your sales process. Knowledge is power when fueled by action. Become attentive to your customer's needs, and commit to providing great service. Not only will you have happy customers, you will be the top sales dog in your company.

People hate being sold to, but they love to buy. The six points in this next contribution will help you formulate a sales process that will enable you to leverage your time and efforts by working with referral partners. Christel Wintels is a sales and marketing expert from Hamilton, Canada, with two decades of experience. She teaches us how to train referral "partners" to guide buyers to you. (Oh, yeah—you've also got to do the same for them!)

SIX STEPS ALL THE RICHER:
SELLING BY HELPING PEOPLE BUY

CHRISTEL WINTELS

It's the dream of every salesperson: getting others to make positive buying decisions without our presence. This is selling through word of mouth. Word-of-mouth buying is based on win-win relationships of people wanting to help others they know and then leveraging these helping relationships to profitability.

A word-of-mouth buying system demands that we know the right people. We need to know people who are well-connected and have the right message about us (the seller) and our business. The objective is to pass our message along to others within their respective networks *without the message changing.* When our message hits a person who wants our product (right people at the right time), a buying process is initiated between one of my contacts' contact and me. This is one-on-one word-of-mouth selling for me, the seller, and word-of-mouth buying for the consumer. It all works through a business network structure.

Following are six simple steps to initiate word-of-mouth buying and start our journey to greater sales and riches.

Step 1: Who Do I Want to Sell To?

We must be able to specify who buys our product or service. We begin by finding common elements to our typical customer group. What does she look like? What do we have in common? Why do we want to sell to her in particular? Do we have experience with this particular type of person or company? Have we had success with her? Is she fun to work with? Does she appreciate us? Any combination of answers will help to define our buyer group, or our ultimate target market.

Precisely defining the target market is actually harder than it seems at first glance. "Who do you want to sell to?" often elicits the reply, "Anybody with the money to buy." But in our word-of-mouth buying system, we sell at arm's length to people who want to buy from us but are not known to us. Traditionally, we would sell to primary individuals wanting our products—our prospects. In this new method, our network contacts line up potential buyers and funnel them into a pipeline of customers heading straight to us. To start this line-up, we must accurately define our ultimate customers in terms of (a) what they might look like, (b) where they are found, (c) which of our contacts can find them, and (d) what message will the prospect respond to most readily.

Step 2: Why Should People Buy from Me?

All businesses have competitors who appear to do what we do faster, cheaper, easier, or more conveniently. It's our job to differentiate ourselves from competitors and make sure our primary referral contacts know about our uniqueness.

Tough questions need solid answers:

- What differentiates me from the competition?
- Why did I choose this particular business?
- What do I like best about my business?
- What can I do better than anyone else?
- Why choose me over the competition?

Our uniqueness gives the potential buyer reasons to be impressed by our personal niche and a "hook" that enables her to make a positive buying decision in our favor.

Step 3: What's My Sales Message?

Our uniqueness is formed in part from what others say about us, and this is influenced by our answers in Steps 1 and 2. If people relay a positive sales message given successfully to the right people at the right time (sending a time-critical message to a motivated buyer), the buying process is as quick and simple as saying, "They want what I have, all obstacles are overcome, I am well recommended, and we can make a deal."

For example, you are a printer and a friend of yours (who knows you and your printing business well) is speaking to a friend of his. His friend says, "My boss just told me that I have to get estimates for all our printed forms. It's going to take me hours. I have no idea where to start."

Your friend says, "This is your lucky day. My friend owns a terrific printing company and it happens to specialize in printed forms. I know his work is excellent. I'll ask him to give you a call this afternoon, and he can give you a professional estimate. How does that sound?"

And he gets this reply: "That would be great. It would save me all kinds of time. I'll watch for his call."

Here's what happened in our example:

1. The potential buyer had to express a need (printed forms).
2. His friend knew he could help him ("I know a printer who can help").
3. The recommendation came with a personal endorsement ("He does excellent work").
4. The buyer had to agree to a contact that would be initiated by the referral partner.

It sounds simple, but a word-of-mouth message with those four elements can be deceiving. To design and activate a word-of-mouth buying system takes dedication and intentionally designed action. It is a system, after all, but one that produces billions of dollars in referred business.

Step 4: Where Do I Find the People to Pass Along My Message?

The people who are most interested in our success are those who care about us, those we've helped, and those who benefit from our success . . . and they are found within our support network. They could be family, friends, associates, or mentors. They want to see us succeed for no other reason than the fact that they love or care for us, or are grateful because we have helped them significantly. Teach your family and friends how to recognize a sales opportunity for you. What are the words they should listen for, and when they hear them, what should they say?

Step 5: How Can They Help Me?

Your network contacts help increase your sales in any number of ways, including passing along a testimonial or endorsement you received to people they know. Prepare a few key questions your network can use with people they know that will screen for potential people interested in your products. If they suspect a person fits the bill, they can qualify the "suspect" by sharing your testimonial and then gauging the response.

Our friend the printer could get many referrals simply by asking his contacts to ask *their* contacts if they are happy with their current printer. Those that are not can be immediately referred to our friend; those that are happy might still be perfectly happy to take his card from someone they know to save for future use.

Step 6: When (and How) Can I Help Them?

The driving force behind a successful word-of-mouth buying program is helping other people in return or, better yet, helping prior to being helped. It's a good idea for our printer to ask his friends and associates to speak favorably about his printing business to the people in their networks, but what's in it for them? The printer must be prepared to drive business to his referral partners just as he is asking that they drive business toward him.

Our printer agrees to send business to his contacts. He agrees to learn their key questions to ask related to their business, how to recognize a need, and what to say to close the prospect.

It's really about reciprocity. There is enough business for everyone, and what goes around comes around. If you're willing to help others gain greater sales through positive and profitable word of mouth, then folks will be more than happy to do the same for you.

We were recently reading reviews of one of Donald Trump's books at Amazon.com reviews, submitted by many different people. One reviewer blasted Mr. Trump's ideas, saying he offered "typical nuanced clichés." Another reviewer said that Trump uses a "compendium of over-used bromides," and yet another said, "Donald Trump's advice is worthless." OK, Donald Trump is a bombastic showman. He is a risk taker and a deal maker. He is also a billionaire. If you are a billionaire, then your opinion about his sales ideas may be worth challenging "The Donald." If you're not, you might want to pay attention to what he has to say. Donald Trump is, without a doubt, an icon who is a true Master of Sales. Tim Houston, a word-of-mouth selling consultant from New York City, offers his perspective on how "The Donald's" selling style matches best advice from research. (Note: this contribution is optional for billionaire readers.)

HOW DONALD TRUMP MADE $1 MILLION IN AN HOUR

TIMOTHY M. HOUSTON

The name Donald Trump evokes a spectrum of images: Images of luxurious real estate, lavish world-class hotels, jubilee golf courses, resorts, and casinos readily come to mind. Donald Trump also symbolizes the star of the hit television show *The Apprentice* in which young, hopeful businesspeople compete against one another for a chance to work for one of America's most famous billionaires.

Love him or hate him, people are inevitably drawn to him—including 140,000 people (myself included) who paid from $49 to as much as $500 to hear Donald J. Trump speak for one hour at a Real Estate Wealth Expo event in New York.

For months, New York City and the surrounding area were plastered with electronic and print ads promoting the two-day seminar on real estate investment. Trump was paid $1 million to speak at the event—that's about $16,000 per minute! This was not a secret; in fact, it was a featured headline in the ads promoting the event. This exorbitant amount helped to attract the public, and 125 exhibitors who each paid more than $5,000 per booth, according to the *Chicago Tribune*. That's another $625,000 attracted to the event.

A couple of questions spring to mind. First, what motivates people to spend large sums of money to see one person speak for one hour? Perhaps more pointedly, one might ask, "How can I achieve similar results?"

Rober Cialdini, Ph.D., in his groundbreaking book *Influence: The Psychology of Persuasion* (Collins, 2006), describes six techniques used by those seeking to influence us. Donald Trump influenced me and thousands of others to spend our money to hear him speak for 60 minutes and support most anything he attaches his name to. How does he do it? Through his constant message of refusing to accept anything less than success.

1. Reciprocity

Sociologists find *reciprocity* in every human society, to the point that it is now a law of human nature. If we are given something, we feel obligated to give something in return. Trump and other celebrities are perceived as avid philanthropists by the sums of money they donate and the time they give to favorite causes and events. In this case, Trump "gave" one hour of his time to attend to "ordinary people," who normally would never be able to hear his message at an affordable price. He gave us a message, and we readily gave him our money in return.

> *The law of reciprocity says that if Masters of Sales give their clients something perceived as valuable (a promotional item, free consultation, a discounted rate, etc.), those same people will often feel obligated to return the favor by buying your service, referring people to you, or offering some other gift of value to you.*

2. Commitment and Consistency

Trump masterfully manages the media by conveying a consistent and committed message. Whether he's pitching pizza for Pizza Hut, a credit card for Visa, his books, his hit-TV show, or one of his billion-dollar projects, his message is consistently powerful in its consistency. He conveys a strong belief in the product, whether it's one of his buildings or his own persona. His image, words, and deeds represent a total commitment to the best in life, and this image is conferred onto the product he is pitching. Advertisers know that anything he touches turns to "sold." The person whose beliefs, words, and deeds don't match is considered indecisive, confused, two-faced, or even mentally ill. On the other hand, a high degree of confidence is normally associated with personal and intellectual strength. Trump displays confidence and strength, and therefore is influential.

> *Masters of Sales know that personal commitment and consistency pull people in their direction. They display belief in their product/ service and constant commitment to helping their clients.*

3. Social Proof

The Real Estate Wealth Expo was a great exercise of *social proof.* The concept of social proof is that people will do something if others are doing the same thing and are achieving results from their actions. The two-day Expo paraded speaker after speaker giving strategies on how to make money in real estate. To solidify that claim, the expo produced the biggest, most well-known names in real estate to draw the crowd and to validate the messages presented by other speakers. "If Donald Trump can make billions of dollars in real estate, so can you" was the implication. Trump was the epitome of social proof at the Expo.

> *Masters of Sales use social proof to attract motivated buyers. Third-party testimonials, statistics, and case stories are presented during a sales process to convert the prospect into a buyer.*

4. Liking

People are drawn to other likable people. Trump has a public image that people like and are attracted to. He is unusual, but we like him for who he is and what he represents. His years of self-branding resulted in much criticism and ridicule among the same media who now love to promote him. He now earns millions of dollars partially because people like him. It was an easy buyer's decision to pay money just to be in the same room as he was, surrounded by thousands of others who like him.

Masters of Sales understand that people do business with those that they like and trust. Masters of Sales must be likable to their clients, and in turn, they must like their clients. Everything they do in business markets their likeability and trust, and influences their ability to get new customers and close sales.

5. Authority

Trump is viewed as an authority on, well . . . everything. By deliberate design, Trump cultivated his authority in real estate, and then in his other areas of endeavor. Through being perceived as an authority by his public, he pulls customers to him and intimidates his competition. At this event, Donald Trump was the most notable speaker among the many other big names, including Anthony Robbins and Robert Kiyosaki. "I want information on how to get rich," said Ethelia McKay, an anesthetist from Elmont, New York, quoted by UPI "and Donald Trump is definitely the man to get it from." She, like the majority of attendees, came to hear and see the man called "Trump," who was promoted as "the authority" on real estate.

Masters of Sales are the authority in their respective fields. They know (or are perceived to know) their product or services better than anyone else. They constantly reinforce their authority directly through advertising and marketing strategies and indirectly through personal and more subtle intonation in their sales presentations. This technique, done masterfully, is more about educating the clients than hard-selling them.

6. Scarcity

The technique of scarcity is masterfully handled by Trump, who promotes his own personal scarcity of time and personal access. Illustrative of this is showing him commuting around New York by personal helicopter and featuring his senior advisors on his TV show. The Expo sponsors also used scarcity to their advantage by opening off-site satellite venues for the overflow crowd to participate in Trump's event through closed circuit TV. These folks paid between $49 and $99 for this opportunity. As Cialdini writes, "Not only do we want the same item more when its scarce, we want it most when we are in competition for it."

Masterful sellers know how to increase their profit margin by presenting the product so it is perceived as having a high value and being in limited supply.

At the conclusion of the New York event, Trump signed a $15-million deal with sponsors to speak for one hour at ten of their seminars across the United States in the following year. The president, Bill Zanker, says, "In the 25-year history of The Learning Annex, there's never been a bigger draw than Donald Trump. He's worth every dollar we're paying him and then some!" Earning $1.5 million per hour, Trump has truly shown why he is indeed, a Master of Sales.

———•—

Organization, procrastination, planning, time management, and falling squirrels are all things that salespeople need to deal with. Well, the "falling squirrels" thing may not apply (on the other hand, you might be surprised at how it might apply). Elaine Betts is a professional organizer (a new profession created out of needs imposed by our increasingly hectic world) who teaches us great techniques and managing systems to help close a sale. Her original career in pharmaceutical research provided her with organizational and methodical skills that are now put to use helping us less-organized sales-people close sales.

———•◦•———

SELF-MANAGEMENT IS KEY TO GETTING THE SALE

ELAINE BETTS

John's goal was to expand his business by 70 percent in a given time. But as a solo operator, he had to attend to administration and a host of other details, leaving little time for his favorite activity (and strongest skill)—sales. He wanted to hire administrative staff to handle his day-to-day office chores so he could sell to prospects and customers.

The solution was logical, but in John's case it had a downside. Most of the company's operational information resided only in John's head. He had no procedures or systems that could be used universally by his new staff. Master salesman John had a management problem: himself. Without organization, growing his business would create a nightmare for anyone he hired. Fortunately, he knew he had a problem, so he called in a professional organizer (me) to help.

Salesperson, Know Thyself

I'll get back to John in a few moments. First, let's talk about you. How organized are you? Be very candid with yourself about this. Why? You cannot be a master without being masterfully organized. "Organization helps your credibility," observes sales professional Gary, another client. "It doesn't matter how nice a person you are. You are what your prospects see, and they see what walks through the door. Organization helps the psychology of the sale."

As a professional organizer, I've observed over the years that people tend to fall into certain categories of disorganization. Knowing your own category is a first step to improvement. See if you find yourself in any of these categories.

- *Totally overwhelmed.* You're swamped. Business is expanding faster than you can handle.
- *Distracted.* You can't focus on one thing for very long before going off on a tangent. You start something else before finishing a task completely.
- *Clueless.* You've never lived an organized day in your life, either because everything has always been done for you, or because you have never been taught organizing skills.
- *Perfectionist.* Every detail must be just right—but it never is, so you rarely complete anything. (Variation: You analyze a situation or problem forever without reaching any resolution.)
- *Emotionally involved.* You have to keep every piece of paper or item that enters your life, because each one reminds you of an event, person, or place.
- *Later gator.* You don't know what to do with something, so you just put it down to deal with later. Your stack of stuff has no home and is shuffled from one place to the next, where it can't be easily found or used.
- *On-the-ball.* You're a totally organized, smooth-working machine that fits so much into a day everyone wonders how you do it.

Unless you are consistently in the On-the-Ball category, you lack a system that works for you—and you would benefit from basic organizing skills. Getting and staying organized is a skill that everyone can learn—if he or she is willing and has a suitable teacher.

Organization Tips

If you run out of time trying to fit everything in, here are seven tips to help you get organized and stay in control.

1. PLAN TO PLAN. Planning will save you valuable time. Always add planning time into your schedule. "When you have a plan you can be more persuasive with customers because you have thought more about them," advises Gary.

Another of my sales clients, Ron, suggests having a plan for no-show appointments. "Don't get mad," he says. "Plan to have business cards and brochures and stop off at a few other places and introduce yourself. The same goes for a cancelled appointment—decide that you are still going to work. Don't just get in a position where circumstances push you."

2. MAKE A LIST. Your plan isn't complete without a prioritized to-do list. It is easy to get thrown off course in an emergency situation—you forget what you were doing and what needed to be achieved. A list helps you get back on track.

3. BEWARE OF FALLING SQUIRRELS. Prime example: A squirrel once fell down my chimney! Bizarre, I know. It obviously wasn't something I had planned for, yet was not something I could ignore. The squirrel had to be dealt with immediately. It took two hours out of my schedule. When it was resolved, however, my list helped me to refocus and reprioritize. The lesson: Prepare for unexpected problems and chance opportunities. A squirrel probably won't fall down your chimney, but what if a major sales lead falls into your lap? Are you organized in such a way that you could catch that lead before it scurries away, without jeopardizing your other commitments?

4. OBEY YOUR BODY CLOCK. Everyone has different energy levels at different times of the day. Are you a morning person or a night owl? By knowing when you have high energy, you can use it to your advantage. Do the things that take the most energy when you have the most energy to do them. Whether it is sales calls, or writing up sales reports, make sure it is done when you have the most energy. It sounds like common sense, but many people ignore these natural rhythms. Listen to yours.

5. ASK FOR HELP. You're expected to be the "expert" at whatever you are selling—but you can't know it all. So ask for help when appropriate. Know your strengths and weaknesses. Asking someone else to take over a task at which they're more proficient can save valuable time and free you to focus on what you do best. For example, this might be a good time to call your tech expert into the sales presentation.

6. MASTER YOUR SOFTWARE. Do you use a computer program to keep track of your contacts, appointments, and other information, such as ACT, XL, or Outlook? If so, do they actually save you time? Or, do you find yourself stumbling over functions you're not sure how to use? Computers and software can be great tools, but they are also great time eaters. Don't waste time trying to win over the machine. Take a class, or ask someone to help you solve the tech problem. Learn to effectively use your sales tools—or don't use them at all.

7. DON'T PROCRASTINATE. He who waits tempts fate, or "you snooze you lose." Pick up the phone now, and make those calls or set new appointments. Having said that, however, we all have things we don't like doing. One solution: Schedule a regular time for getting the "baddies" out of the way.

Organization Fosters Success

Being organized can save you valuable time, money, stressful moments, and heartache. When you are organized, there is an awareness and energy about you that people notice. Organization gives you power. If you want to be noticed and have the competitive edge, be organized.

"Organization affects your credibility," says Pat. He writes everything down in a log that goes back years. That way when he speaks with someone he can pull up all the details. If there is a problem, he can remind the customer what was said on a particular date from his log. "Nobody ever questions me anymore," he adds. "They know I can pull the rabbit out of the bag."

A business can literally succeed or fail by not being organized. Remember John? He wanted to expand by 70 percent, but his business was missing organized systems and procedures that could be used by his new administrative staff while he was making sales.

Had he hired a staff before setting up those processes, he would have created chaos. To use an automotive metaphor, he would have built a fast car that had no steering or brakes! You wouldn't want to ride in such a car . . . and you would not want to work for such a company.

So, John worked with me for several months to get his business organized to handle the expansion. He didn't grow by 70 percent, but by *108 percent*, and he was quickly looking to take on another two staff members. By solving his management problem—his own lack of organization—he got more sales than he had ever dared to dream of getting!

The Virtual Salesperson

Online Selling Technologies

Truth is what stands the test of experience.
—ALBERT EINSTEIN

The planet is changing. Cold places are hotter, and hot places are cooler. Moon walking is old hat and La-Z-Boy armchair generals direct the world's wars on CNN after dinner. Grade school kids do homework wirelessly, researching data banks that were accessible only to the most serious of academics a mere decade ago, and buyers can know more about a product than the sellers. The world is truly changing, and at a very rapid pace indeed.

All professions are influenced by rapid rates of technological change, and the professional salesperson is no exception. A sales pro with three decades of experience might say, "I remember when . . ." What he might be remembering is his utter delight in getting his first portable dictation unit that could fit in a product case. This new technology saved many hours by allowing him to dictate sales orders while on the road. Imagine the salesman's thrill at getting his first fax machine, so the sales orders or requests for proposals could be sent instantaneously to the fax machine waiting at the other end. (My first fax machine cost $3,500 and was a salesman's demo.)

We've lived through the innovative technologies that promised to make the salesperson's job easier and more efficient. Many of you may still remember lusting after a leather-bound, three-ringed Day-Timer® where you could stash all your business cards, leads, appointments, and even a sandwich to eat on the road. Now in the electronic age, new selling technologies are created at an accelerated pace, and just learning to use the newest time-saving devices could take a lifetime.

New sales technologies are ripping apart the classic cliché "Necessity is the mother of invention." Now our "inventions are the mother of necessity," and we need new technologies to handle the older technologies. It's an endless loop. For example, first we got the PC computer, and then we learned to hook it to the internet. Now, internet selling is the newest frontier, demanding new inventive selling strategies and e-mail selling, and then comes the spam. Well, need we say more?

Internet selling in earnest is less than a decade old, and the savvy professional sellers are taking this technology to its next level. In fact, internet technology is literally becoming a member of the sales team.

A book on masterful selling would be remiss if it did not offer at least a glimpse into this state of the art. At the rate this technology is growing, the second edition of *Masters of Sales* will, from necessity, need to devote more space to this ever-growing sales tool. In fact, given this sales technology, it's conceivable that sales as we know it today will not exist in the near future.

While others may have introduced internet selling, the founder of eBay is an undisputed leader in the new field of selling through web sites. Connie Hinton and Mavis Lamb are marketing pros who love the high-tech, as well as the high-touch, marketing and sales approaches. From their offices in Seattle, they share their excitement about selling/buying through eBay.

THE BETTER MOUSETRAP: HOW EBAY CHANGED THE WAY WE BUY AND SELL

CONNIE HINTON AND MAVIS LAMB

It all started with one guy who wanted to help his girlfriend find some collectibles, or did it . . .? It's one of those urban legends that sounded too good to be true. Did eBay founder, Peter Omidyar, really start his online selling site to help his girlfriend find, sell, and trade her collection of PEZ™ dispensers? It sounds great—a bit romantic, a bit practical, a bit of an overnight success—but it turns out it was all hype created by eBay's PR department. So what really happened? While its origination may not be as romantic as the PR story, eBay has nonetheless had an amazing impact on consumer buying behaviors. eBay has changed the way people buy and sell—forever.

Started in 1995, eBay was originally more of a glorified online garage sale, where people could buy and sell odd items and collectibles. But by 1998, eBay was catching on, and after going public, the company started to significantly change the face of consumerism. The internet (and eBay in particular) has created a new generation of savvy shoppers who want lots of information, the best products, and at the best prices. Early online shopping took a lot of time. There was no easy way to search the countless online stores and sites, and the buyer had no way to assess the seller's credibility and reputation. Price shopping was hit-and-miss.

eBay created a better tool for the consumer market. Whether buyer or seller, eBay provided a better mousetrap to get what buyers wanted, and a rush of customers swarmed through eBay's virtual "doors," giving folks a first stop for their shopping. The site remains one of the most effective and profitable places for sellers to share their wares.

One of the reasons for eBay's success is that it addresses and adapts to individual buying styles. For those who are "in a hurry and just need to buy it," eBay's "Buy-It-Now" function allows consumers to search for the item they want to purchase and pay the stated price. For example, Mavis needed to purchase customized auto taillights as a gift for her nephew. He supplied all the product information. With no time to waste, she logged onto the site, looked up the part, and in a few clicks made the purchase for the "Buy It Now" price and arranged to have it shipped directly to her nephew's address. The whole transaction took just a few minutes.

For those who enjoy the thrill of competition through a competitive bidding process and want good value, the eBay auction process is available. Connie decided to give the online bid process a try. NASCAR micro machines were her product of choice. The bid close coincided with a dinner out, so she completed her winning bid on her handheld computer just as dinner was served. It was the most fun she'd had shopping in quite some time!

A third option appeals to research-oriented buyers. These people need all the facts and options before making a buying decision. They can research the products online, get the best price available, and even check the seller's reputation . . . all on the eBay site. This is made possible through the feedback function, which is automatically requested at the end of each transaction and allows consumers to rate their experience, the product, and the seller. The rating result is then available for everyone to see! Try finding *that* information posted at your favorite retail walk-in store.

While some online shopping sites still practically require you to be a programmer to maneuver through the site and find the product area you are looking for, eBay makes the search and shopping experience simple and straightforward. Its user-friendly interface assists in finding the part of the "store" you want—from the hottest "must have" video game system to the most obscure collectible—even William Shatner's kidney stone!

The impact eBay has made on the world of buying and selling is amazing. This phenomenal buying/selling technology is a mere decade old and just hitting its stride. Our language of selling is changing, and with the language change, comes a new buying culture.

Have _you_ "checked eBay?"

First impressions, creating just the right look, and keeping the viewing audience engaged in the process are not exclusive to movie producers or sales professionals. Indeed, this process is critical to every activity designed to present the best picture to a public, and the selling web site is no exception. Steven Van Yoder uses his extensive experience in journalism to help his clients become "slightly famous" through creative use of PR and media campaigns. His view of selling web sites turns our previously-held concepts about masterful selling inside out.

SELLING IN THE AGE OF THE VIRTUAL CUSTOMER

STEVEN VAN YODER

In this age of the virtual customer, you must incorporate the online world into your overall sales program. The internet has made it perfectly possible to land a major client you've never met in person, and it has created new consumer expectations.

Before the advent of online buying, sellers created a first impression by the clothes they wore, their overall demeanor, and attitude and the look of their place of business. In the internet age, first impressions are formed with the click of a mouse.

Buyers now demand that sellers have online visibility that looks and feels professional. Circumstances of the internet age have reversed the buyer/seller roles. The prospect now makes cold calls on the seller, who must make a strong initial online impression while also mastering all the other stages of the selling process.

Role of Search Engines in Buying Decisions

Search engines play a growing role in helping your customers find, evaluate, and decide whether you should be on their short list of prospective preferred sellers. A recent study by internet research firms Marketing Sherpa and Enquiro, entitled *The Role of Search in Business to Business Buying Decisions*, demonstrated that search engines are a dominant force driving most business buying decisions. A key finding indicated that 93.2 percent of respondents rely on online research to influence their buying decisions!

Test the importance of search engines by doing a Google search for your product or service, using common words and phrases used by your customers when thinking about your product. For example, a tile worker from Denver might search for "custom tile work" or "custom tile work Colorado." Or, try typing in the generic words "business networking," and see what pops up!

Did your business come up in the results? If your business was buried beneath a huge list of competitors, your online presence is not as effective as someone else's, who may get the business simply because of his or her site ranking compared to yours. Becoming "search engine optimized" is a new selling art and science that demands attention if you want your site to sell for you.

There are many tricks to optimizing your site for search engines, not the least of which is to update your site's content regularly. Don't let your web site languish in obscurity. Search engines prefer web sites that are well-maintained and have original content that is frequently updated. Your web site is like a store's display window that must be changed and updated periodically.

The Virtual First Impression

Buyers researching your product or service through the web will be influenced by the first impression of your web site. If your web site is like a messy, ill-prepared showroom window, the customer is likely to move on to the next showroom display. It's important to have all sales staff, including your internet selling web site, creating a positive first impression, because this is very important to the buyer.

Does your web site load quickly? Do your graphics display a positive image? Does your site have valuable content? You never get a second chance to make a good impression, and your virtual first impression often means the difference between a shot at your prospect's business and being shut out.

Earning Online Credibility

Establishing a reputation as a knowledgeable seller is important, and your web site will help accomplish this objective. A study by the U.S. Department of Commerce, National Telecommunications and Information Administration, September 2004, states: "Searching for product/service information is the second most popular online activity after e-mail or instant messaging. In 2003, 76.5 percent of internet users ages 15 and over indicated they researched products online."

Start by making your web site a resource for your industry. Discover what information is most sought after by your target customers, and use your site to generously provide useful and relevant information, through articles, links, downloadable files, and customer resources. Be creative and generous and give, give, give! Your prospects will appreciate easy-to-find content that helps them determine that you are qualified to solve their problems.

Tip: Every time you answer a business question by phone, e-mail, or face-to-face, ask yourself if that answer can be transformed into useful information content for your site. Posting relevant up-to-date information about your product or industry will help position you as a knowledgeable seller and leader.

Join "Niche" Communities

Identify online "niche" communities that relate to your passion, business interest, or industry. Participate, share, and contribute with the objective of becoming well-known within your new online community. Soon, other viewers who happen to be in your preferred customer target market will seek you out as their preferred vendor.

Become a resource that others want to listen to, learn from, and emulate. Position yourself as an online center of influence:

- Share inside knowledge with your target market.
- Participate, listen, contemplate, and offer thoughtful responses.
- Be willing to voice an opinion.
- Assume leadership positions in your industry.

Web sites and online discussion lists allow the seller to gain access to communities of prospects, while at the same time creating for them a virtual selling platform. When this happens, your web site becomes a vital sales tool, and you are using hard technology to significantly leverage your sales results. Like all technologies, there is a right way and a wrong way to use the device, so begin now to master the use of selling through your web site.

If we truly buy into a new concept, sooner or later we will have to commit to turning the concept into a real-life operation. Online selling web sites don't have decades of experience behind them, but already Bob Scheinfeld has a winning formula for what works and what doesn't. He grew up in a wealthy family, amassed wealth, lost it, and spent years learning how to regain his "ultimate lifestyle"; he now freely shares what he learned with others.

A MAGIC FORMULA FOR SELLING ON THE INTERNET

ROBERT SCHEINFELD

Throughout my career, I've sold products and services face-to-face, by phone, through direct mail and print advertising, and on the internet. My favorite by far is the internet, so allow me to share with you several concepts related to a very effective model I developed for selling high ticket items on the internet.

My internet selling program works very well for selling items I priced from as low as $400, and as high as $28,000. The upper price limit for my internet selling model hasn't been reached, but economies of scale recommend that a price point of less than $400 per item would not have enough of a profit margin for a good return.

This selling model rests on four foundational pillars:

1. A mind-set for designing web sites.
2. A methodical sales strategy that complements the site design.
3. A careful process to optimize one's strategy for increased sales results.
4. Using multimedia to turbo charge the program for leveraged results.

The Million-Dollar Mind-Set

I use the acronym TOT to describe the mind-set behind my model:

T = The
O = One
T = Thing

Internet users are notoriously "click happy." Like bored kids surfing 250 satellite TV channels, the internet offers over-choice. Internet surfers will give your site just a few seconds to grab their attention. If you don't succeed, they're gone from your web site and on to another.

To capture attention, a TOT web site is designed to sell only one product or service at a time. So, if you have five high-ticket products or services to sell, you'd need five separate TOT sites, each with their own unique web site address (URLs). A catalog business like Sharper Image or

Amazon.com, for example, will link people from their main catalog site to a separate TOT site for each of their higher ticket items.

The design of a TOT site aims at getting the viewer to do only one thing—allowing him to make only one decision. The entire site is simple; it encourages the visitors to take one step at a time—in a direction preferred by the seller. The step might be to log on to the inner section as a member, buying the product right now, clicking here to see more, etc.

Once they click/step where you aim them, they must be guided to another page where they're once again motivated to do one thing only. You then keep them moving down a slope of "one thing only" decisions until the final decision is to buy your product, or to contact you for more information if your goal is lead generation.

We are merely applying sound selling practices to our web seller. For example, professional sellers do the same thing during their initial prospect meetings: they establish a connection with the prospect, control the prospect's focus, and then guide the prospect to a most appropriate end to the transaction. Similarly, the TOT site guides the potential buyer using the method detailed above.

Methodical Selling Strategies

My TOT sites are often based on the concept of a free course or a guided tour. A *free course* is when I actually teach the viewer something valuable as part of the sales process. A *guided tour* exists if my objective is to show them how something works, and how owning it will provide the viewer/ prospect tremendous benefit.

All of my TOT sites focus on getting viewers enrolled in either the course or the tour. That's it. No other choices are allowed. Nothing is visible on the site unless it supports enrollment in either my course or tour. My site encourages them to enroll through use of a strong headline or teasing text that entices them to enroll. All I require in return for the free course or tour is their name and e-mail address. Once this is submitted, they are immediately enrolled.

If your course or tour has five segments to it, your design would lead the viewer to move from one segment to the next, until they are funneled to the final segment. Each of the segments is designed to educate, inspire and—most importantly—*filter* your visitors. Only those most qualified prospective viewers (those whose profiles most closely match your preferred customer) would actually finish and see the final segment—your sales pitch.

Now you are ready to invite them to buy your product or service. If you did your job well, the visitor is already pre-disposed toward you and you don't have to push very hard or use sales games to close the sale or generate a qualified lead. An elegant sales letter will do the job. It's a soft close.

Optimizing Your Results

The TOT web site model performs effectively because:

1. It's different. Most people don't use it, or if they do offer a free course, it's done by e-mail, which isn't as effective.
2. The feel of a tour or course versus a "sales pitch" is decidedly different.
3. The educational and inspirational offering of your site builds greater rapport and trust, and facilitates the sale of higher ticket items with less human involvement.
4. You capture the name, e-mail address, and phone (if you choose) of the visitor so you can follow up with them.

There's one other major advantage to the model, which is to divide your sales process into manageable components:

- The main page of the web site
- The educational segments
- The final segment (which does the selling)

By breaking the whole into smaller pieces, you can study the number of visits to each page of your web site, thereby evaluating the effectiveness of each segment. Every web site has the capacity to collect and organize statistical information that indicates what your visitors do when they visit each of your pages.

Using Multimedia to Turbo Charge the Program for Leveraged Results

New internet technologies have opened up incredible opportunities for online sales presentations by using multimedia print, audio, and video. Now we can isolate the best practices of our sales staff, trainers, or company spokesperson, and replicate these best presentations live (or nearly live) online.

For example, if your best salesperson has a killer PowerPoint™ presentation, you can mimic this in a TOT site. If they're at their best using a pitch book with photos, graphs, or illustrations and scribbling on a yellow pad, you can also replicate this on your web site. Virtually anything that can be done live can be re-created online at your TOT web site using new multimedia tools. The results are astonishing, and the sales leverage achieved is literally out of this world.

Handling Objections

A little tact and wise management may often evade
resistance, and carry a point, where direct force
might be in vain.
—AUTHOR UNKNOWN

"Objection, Your Honor," says the trial lawyer when he feels the opposing counsel's statements are not supportive of his case. Objections exist everywhere in life, and are certainly prevalent in the sales arena. Buyer objections can easily derail a sale unless the seller understands what's meant by the stated objection and can uncover the unstated ones.

Sometimes a buyer's objection is a roundabout, vague communication that requires a guessing game of 100 questions to elicit the right information. Other times the objection might be more direct: "It's not the right color, good bye!" The fun objections are those designed to test the seller's skill.

"Can I help you?" asks the salesperson.

"No thanks, I'm just looking." While the buyer might say he doesn't want to be helped, his real message probably is, "I object to having my privacy intruded upon when I am not certain what I want, how much I want to pay, or even if you have it, and so leave me alone . . . now. But if you can establish a friendly rapport with me and make me smile, I might talk to you, but I am not going to help you get started."

This dance-around-objection to buying is an everyday part of the selling scenario, so we'd better make sure to show you how the Masters of Sales handle objections. The masterful seller is thrilled when he hears a sales objection, because now he can zero in to close the sale. The professional knows that contained within the objection is information pointing to the buyer's real interest and ability to buy. There are scores of reasons why a buyer might object to a sale, but each buyer has his own unique cluster of objections. The job of the seller is to determine which features, price, function, benefit, size, or model will best dig through all the objections, to the point where the prospect says "yes." All of this information is found within the objections phase of the buying/selling process.

Karl Heckman's company specialized in restoration of expensive English and European shotguns. As he puts it, "Concerned about spending $10,000 to restore a $5,000 firearm, clients often ask if the gun is worth the cost." Karl responds with a ten-minute, practiced (yet casual) conversation that wins the business nearly every time. His dialogue artfully shifts the client's perspective from the initial concern about price to the truly anticipated result of a wonderful experience in the field.

> *I address the price issue honestly and then gently direct the client's attention to the beneficial value derived from a properly-performed service job on his gun, which would give predictable and expected field results. I paint a verbal picture of the product's true value, which is so realistic that our clients eagerly anticipate owning*

the gun. The client ends up dismissing his own price objective in favor of the picture I painted for him of using the gun in the field. I believe this is the highest form of service: Helping the client more fully understand what he truly wants.

The masterful seller is an artist and storyteller, and knows that word pictures help people see clearly. Stories sell, but facts only tell.

Masterful sellers welcome this phase as a way to pinpoint what truly makes the buyer happy. This phase becomes a process of eliminating everything the buyer doesn't want, shifting the focus to what is truly desired. This becomes a very creative phase of turning the proverbial "no" into a buying "yes," all the while making the buyer feel like a VIP. It starts by not taking objections personally, instead using them as a road map to successful selling.

It turns out that resistance is very useful as a control device, and also a motivating factor for achieving progress. Kevin Eikenberry operates from the American Midwest, taking his transformational messages to people and organizations that wish to achieve their full potential. He teaches us that changes made when encountering resistance often lead to discovery and innovation, which master sellers consider as positive. BRING ON THE OBJECTIONS!

FIVE WAYS TO TURN RESISTANCE INTO OPPORTUNITY

KEVIN EIKENBERRY

Resistance isn't something we usually cherish or enjoy encountering, but as sales professionals, we experience it in many ways:

- People are resistant to new ideas.
- People resist changes in work flow patterns.
- People resist disagreeable feedback and react defensively.
- People resist revised policying if they can't understand its value.
- People resist buying our products.

Leaders, supervisors, and salespeople agree that resistance can be a big problem. Many sales professionals consider resistance to their selling effort as the most objectionable part of selling. But the masters learn to accept and use resistance as a lever to success.

Examining Resistance

The reason resistance might be avoided, or even feared, is because people haven't stopped to think clearly about its functionality. Imagine a meeting where everyone agrees and there is no dissension or difference of opinion. At first glance this might be seen as nirvana. Imagine the bliss: We are in agreement! No heated discussions! No frowns! No stress! And while stress might be minimized because of the absence of resistance, progress and change may also be minimized.

Resistance can be an incubator for innovation, and progress. Resistance to the status quo or sameness brings forth a desire for new products or ways of doing things. Just as professional bodybuilders use resistance training to strengthen their muscles, manufacturers use customer resistance to old product lines as their motivation to invent new products and solutions. Resistance isn't a bad thing; it is just a fact of life.

Resistance in sales helps the masterful seller provide the buyer with the best possible solution to his or her needs. Resistance in sales is not a problem; rather, it is a precursor to pinpointing a most accurate solution for the buyer.

Learning to Love Resistance

The following steps are used by masterful sellers to employ resistance in their sales program and will help you overcome—and even learn to love—resistance.

EXPECT RESISTANCE. It doesn't matter how brilliant your idea, useful your product, or helpful your service would be to the client. Someone will "push back" or resist your proposal or presentation somewhere between the start and end of the interaction. Recognizing this reality allows you to plan your communications to divert, answer, or alleviate expected concerns. The seller must redirect her communication when the client begins resisting the sales proposal. The buyer's objection becomes a starting point for a series of planned questions artfully crafted to work through the encountered resistance.

DON'T TAKE IT PERSONALLY. Resistance is a natural occurrence in the thought process of buyers. Their resistance isn't a personal attack on you. Instead they are thinking (out loud) about the implications of owning your service or product, and generally how buying from you will affect them. Masterful salespeople understand that an objection means the client is thinking about the pros and cons of actually owning the product.

IMPLIED COMMITMENT. This is the first step toward *committing* to owning the product. Masters use this form of resistance as leverage to move the communication forward toward a closed deal, or a satisfactorily concluded transaction.

AVOID DEFENSIVENESS. A prospect dumps on you all the problems associated with your product or service, and why it won't work for him. If you experience your temper rising, your face flushing, or your tone of voice becoming shrill, you are responding defensively. Your defensive response merely strengthens the customer's initial concerns. Guard against responding defensively by reminding yourself that their resistance is not a rejection of you personally.

USE RESISTANCE TO GET STRONGER. A buyer's resistance is often a part of his own process for accepting change. When a buyer objects vocally, he might just be arguing with himself. You can help his internal debate if you keep an open mind and ear to what's being said. If resistance repeatedly shows up, this is your clue to create a smoothing effect to divert similar concerns in the future, all of which makes you a stronger seller.

ACKNOWLEDGE AND PROBE RESISTANCE. A powerful strategy for handling resistance is to let your customer be heard. Draw out your client by asking probing questions appropriate to the level of relationship you have with that person. Get his permission to ask him questions, such as "Do you mind if I ask you a couple of questions about your views?" Don't challenge his responses, but rather seek to fully understand his viewpoint. His opinion is his own and exists for you to respect. Your first job is to understand his concerns and second to provide him with information that accurately satisfies those concerns.

Client objections usually spring from a lack of information about your product/service. You must demonstrate that you respect your client's views if you want him to share his concerns with you in the first place. Once the client knows that you respect him and his ideas, you are much more likely to discover barriers to the sale, and then create detours or bridges leading toward a closed sale.

Resistance can be your friend. Masterful sellers use a buyer's resistance to guide their sales communication toward a successful conclusion. Remember: Resistance training creates soreness, but it also makes you stronger.

———•◦•———

The very nature of the term "objection" is negative and cause for some people to get their backs up. Lantz Powell has an extensive sales background in the southeast United States and offers the view that objections are not good or bad; they are just a natural part of the selling/buying process. Masterful treatment of a prospect's objections will retain the integrity of and respect for all parties in the selling scenario.

———•◦•———

LESSON ON CLOSING AFTER THE "NO"

LANTZ POWELL

One of my more disagreeable memories of being a high school student was the school fundraising drive, raffle, or some other all-important event that required us to knock on neighborhood doors asking (selling, in this instance) for support. Sadly, knocking on doors and seeming to beg for money was not my forte, and I hated doing it.

Interestingly, my father was a salesman who knocked on doors all day long as a profession, and he thought he could teach his son something about selling. I remember many evening discussions, during which he gave me advice on various approaches I could take. Then one day, on a school holiday, he invited me to ride with him on his sales calls.

Like most children, I was anxious to see what my father really did in his job. That evening's discussion focused on the three presentations he was planning for the following day. He showed me the list of ten contacts he would be visiting and how he would modify one of his presentations for each prospective contact. The next morning at breakfast he said, "If you watch and listen, maybe you will help me make a sale." Before leaving for the day, he organized his schedule for the stops, and reviewed with me his goal for each customer call.

On the route, I was amazed at his knowledge and the professional way that he presented to each of his prospects, all the time watching the reaction of those listening. Since I heard his presentation several times, I knew it was canned, but looking each prospect straight in the eyes, he showed each person tremendous respect by delivering each of his presentations as if it were totally fresh and new. His ability to pay close attention to the contact amazed me. He listened to their words, but also appeared to even communicate with them via body language. For example, many times he would start writing out an order when he saw a prospect's head nod or a spark in their eye appear.

Sometimes his presentation was rejected. When that happened, he was polite and would push the product from a different angle while he watched his prospect's reaction. I realized he was attempting one more time to make a sale. But when he saw it was over, he stopped. He would then get on to some neutral subject and begin to leave. He would shake the prospect's hand and thank him for allowing him time to make his presentation, and turn to leave . . . but he never left.

He would walk a few steps to the door and then would stop and, as the TV detective Columbo would always do, turn around to ask one more question.

"Mr. Thompson, can I ask you something?"

"Sure."

"Well, I prepared this presentation to the best of my ability. What did I do wrong? Did I leave something out?"

"I don't think you did do anything wrong."

"Seriously, is the price too high? If it is, I need to let my boss know."

"No, the price is acceptable."

"Then was it something else?"

By this time he had turned and waited for the prospect's body language to allow him to stay. About half of the time the customer indicated that he had a reservation and my Dad opened a conversation about how to overcome the prospect's concerns. Often the buyer's hurdle was with delivery, price, or terms. Resulting from his turnaround conversation, my Dad ended up with about 50 percent of the sales that had originally been turned down.

I watched this happen several times, and as we drove home at the end of the day, I asked him about his Columbo approach. I couldn't figure out why he pursued the sale by asking his prospect if he made a mistake in his sales call.

He replied, "Because people don't think for themselves. You have to urge them to think about what you are selling. Many people say 'no' so they don't have to process the purchase—to think about how to justify it. You need to help them start thinking about it. You have to walk them through the process. But you have to do it in a way that makes them feel your respect for them."

I then understood that his Columbo approach to overcoming objections helped to disarm the prospect, so the real issues related to the sale could surface and be addressed. Once back home, my Dad went over with me the insights he had learned from each of his prospects. When all was done, he wrote a postcard to each person he visited, putting in a comment about their meeting. He either thanked them for their order or their time.

I learned a valuable lesson about handling objections from my Dad. When your sales presentation runs into a roadblock or if you fail to sell someone on the first attempt, don't be afraid to ask why. Often, the buyer is not ready on first thought to move into a buying mode, but if given a second chance, he may offer up his concerns about owning the product today, which will enable you to help him overcome his concerns—and maybe even help him buy.

———•·•———

Buyers are notorious for expressing objections, responding with surprise questions or, in some other manner, distracting the seller's focus. This requires quick thinking, posturing, and strategic decision making by the seller, whose objective is to effectively move through a well-designed process. Harvey Mackay is another icon in the sales training and business consulting field, with more than 10 million books sold on these and related topics. His own Mackay envelope business has grown to a $100 million company, which partially explains the reason for hearing his advice on using the right questions to move the sale forward and avoid a full stop.

———•·•———

ELEVEN QUESTIONS TO ASK YOUR PROSPECT

HARVEY MACKAY

1. Do you have exactly two minutes to discuss a product that can save you money and boost your productivity?

As you say this, take off your watch and set it on your prospect's desk. Exactly one minute and 50 seconds into your pitch—even if it's mid-sentence—stop, and say, "My time is up. There's one thing I want you to know about us and that's this: We keep our word. I'd be happy to continue if you'd like. Otherwise, thank you for your time. I know you're busy. Here's my card." And get up to leave. You'll be surprised how many times you're stopped before you hit the door, and how many orders you'll eventually wind up getting.

The most important relationship you can build with a customer is trust. This will take you a long way toward gaining it.

2. Can you tell me what our competition is doing better than we are?

There are only three answers to this question that go to the merits of the product: price, quality, and delivery. If you can do better on any of these, go for it. Ask for a "sample order," a tiny slice of the business to prove you can beat the competition on its terms. If the answer is still no, then you know you haven't uncovered the real reason yet.

This is when you get, "We've been doing business with them for years." "It's the boss's brother-in-law's account." "We've never had a complaint." "I'm not the one who makes the decision on this." All of them are variations on the same theme: inertia. Go back to the office, make a written proposal, guaranteeing your terms and comparing them with the competition's, and hang in there. Eventually, you'll get a piece of that business.

3. I know something about your product already, of course, but could you tell me what you regard as its most attractive features and best selling points?

Another variation on the last question. You're looking for clues that will help you learn what it is you need to do to help your prospect enhance his product line.

4. Is there any improvement you'd like to see in your current product?

Obviously, another thrust in the same direction as the last: How can you help your prospect do a better job? If you have something in your line that can do the trick, here's the time to trot it out. If you don't have something, maybe you should.

5. Would you let us send you a free sample if you'll use it for 30 days and let me come back and find out what you think of it?
Costly, but effective. They've been doing it for years with consumer products. If you're not doing it yet, it's time to try it.

6. Even though you're not going to give me the order today, knowing what your concerns are about our product, would it be all right if I called on you again when we are able to meet those concerns?
It's tough to say no to that one.

7. I'd be happy to recommend your product to some of my own customers. Would that be all right with you?
What could be better than having a supplier who is also an unpaid salesperson for your product? If you can deliver a customer to your prospect, even if you yourself are that customer, you're bound to increase your own odds of doing business there.

8. Can you tell me of someone who might be able to use this product?
This is the one question every insurance salesperson is trained to ask. Referrals are the heart and soul of prospecting.

9. Could I give you the names of a number of people whom you know who are using our product?
The reverse side of the last question. Instead of asking for referrals, you're giving them, except when you give them they're called references. They work because they establish credibility and reliability, the all-important trust factors in any relationship.

10. Would you tell me what I can do to be of service to you in any way whatsoever?

This is the ultimate open-ended question designed to invite your prospect to test your ability to meet whatever needs he might have. If you can get him or her to make a request, and you can deliver on that request, you've got the business.

And one more for the road . . .

11. Say, is that a picture of your family? My, what a good looking . . .

OK, I couldn't resist. I'm still a peddler at heart.

Mackay's Moral

Good salespeople don't just supply products. They are constantly looking for ways to help their customers improve their own products.

Reprinted with permission from nationally syndicated columnist Harvey Mackay, author of the *New York Times* bestsellers, *Pushing the Envelope* (Ballantine Books, 2000) and *Swim with the Sharks without Being Eaten Alive* (Collins, 2005).

———•◦•———

Having been a business consultant for nearly two decades Denise Beeson, from California, specializes in new business development for start-ups and young, high-tech companies in the United States and abroad. Denise offers practical and well-selected techniques for handling a customer's objections properly. She finds that objections are often not communicated clearly, leaving the seller with the complex task of pulling relevant information from the prospective buyer. Many times the simplest things, practiced until done masterfully, will get the best results.

HANDLING OBJECTIONS THE EASY WAY

DENISE BEESON

How could the customer possibly *not* buy after we spent so much time and energy on the sale? How dare they ask more questions?! The reason is simple: Objections are usually presented because the prospective buyer needs more information or is mentally processing the seller's information in relation to her needs. Professional sellers prepare themselves with the best responses for the two most universal objections, which are price and quality/functionality (i.e., the product or service is either "too expensive" or even too inexpensive, or the product "doesn't work" for me or my organization).

Experienced professional salespeople see the "objection" as a further opportunity to "sell," because the buyer is masking her request for more information with an objection. Alternatively, her objection might really be a discussion in her own mind about the pros and cons of owning the article or using the service being offered. An objection usually allows the seller more time to create a positive influence on the buyer's decision, which is best done through use of the following three types of questions.

Reflective questioning is a technique that restates the objection back to the customer in the form of a question. "The price is too high" can be restated back to the customer "The price is too high?" Remember the buyer is simply seeking more information about the selling price, and the salesperson is seeking more information from the buyer's point of view about price. Sellers using reflective questions will verify that they heard the buyer's comment about price, while in a polite manner asking the buyer to add further details about their view of price and value. Unless you understand why the buyer is not satisfied with the price, it will be impossible to adequately handle the objection. A reflective question serves to politely ask the buyer for a more detailed explanation about her price concerns.

The 5 W's—who, what, why, when, and where—will provide more information about a buyer's objection. When using these questions, less is more. All of us have experienced a rising temperature as a salesperson overjustifies the price or value of the product. Sellers don't want to sound defensive or make their buyers feel stupid and can avoid these negative emotions by responding, "What did you expect to pay?" when the buyer says the "price is too high." A variation of this question might be, "What does your budget allow?" Another example, "The delivery date is too long," can easily be handled by asking, "When would you like it delivered?" We are only limited by our creativity in using these simple questions.

"Oh" questioning is my favorite. Psychologists frequently use "Oh?" or "Oh!" in their client interviews, and so should sellers. Depending on her voice inflection, a seller can indicate that she truly heard the words and even emotion of the buyer, and in doing so convey enough trust to the buyer to share more information about his objection. However, do be cautious with the use of "Oh" questioning, as you don't want to sound patronizing. You must be able to convey genuine interest in what the buyer is feeling. Used skillfully, "Oh" questioning will gently coach the buyer to share his reasons for not yet being comfortable with the sale.

Skillfully handling objections provides the seller tremendous opportunity to move a buyer towards a successful sales transaction. The three simple questioning techniques discussed above help the seller discover information that leads toward buyer satisfaction . . . and closed deals.

———•·•———

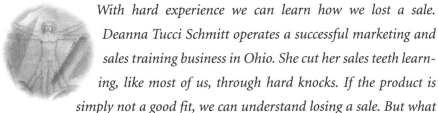

With hard experience we can learn how we lost a sale. Deanna Tucci Schmitt operates a successful marketing and sales training business in Ohio. She cut her sales teeth learning, like most of us, through hard knocks. If the product is simply not a good fit, we can understand losing a sale. But what happens when our product is a perfect match, the customer says yes, and still

the sale goes south? Deanna shares one of her sales lessons learned—the hard way.

MUG YOUR COMPETITION IN THE HALL

DEANNA TUCCI SCHMITT

As a young businesswoman, I sold for a payroll services firm. Sixty percent of the businesses that purchased services from me already used a competitor's service. Often we could offer a higher level of service at a better price than the competing service. This type of customer accounted for a good portion of my personal sales. When I closed a deal—meaning I had a signature on the dotted line and a deposit check in hand—I gleefully packed my briefcase and did a mental high-five as I headed back to the office. I literally had a done deal, right? Well, not always.

Here's what sometimes happened next: My new customer would call the competitor to cancel their service, whereupon he would be asked, "Why are you leaving us?" They explained that they had found more service for a better price. You know what happened next. Invariably, the current service provider would match my pricing and service level, and before I knew it, I'd just lost a new customer before we had a chance to even run a first payroll for them.

As I searched for a way to combat this hidden type of objection, I found a most memorable sales technique that I still use today. It is a technique that Jay Levinson teaches (on a *Guerrilla Marketing* audio tape), called "Mug Your Competition in the Hall." The basic idea is to go over this hidden objection with the new client before it happens. In the excitement of closing a deal, an amateur salesperson won't take this diversionary step for fear of spoiling the deliciously satisfying mood that fills the room immediately after signing a deal.

The savvy salesperson knows from experience that her new customer is likely to call his old vendor and cancel the service right after you leave with your contract. Here's what the pros do: Before the sales transaction is signed, the sales professional stops her closing process and paints an impending scenario for her customer.

"We need to discuss one more item. When some of my other clients who were using XYZ Payroll Company called them to let them know they were leaving, the XYZ Company matched my new lower price." The sales person's next statement is critical: "HOW WILL THAT MAKE YOU FEEL IF THEY DO THAT TO YOU?"

At this point, you will literally see an emotional response as the customer says, "Well, that will tick me off if they do that!" Don't stop here. Ask them *why?* Their answer will also help them formulate their personal reason to get rid of the old vendor in favor of you as their new preferred vendor.

The salesperson's objective is to get the client to realize and verbalize the following: "If they can lower my price now—why didn't they give me that price all along?" Most often your new client will feel betrayed by the old vendor, if the old vendor attempts to keep the business by cutting price just to match your new contracted service. The idea is to get the customer to feel pain associated with their old vendor.

Taking it further, you might even suggest a script that can be used by your new customer: "To keep my business, I believe you could have been more proactive in maintaining a competitive price while improving your services. I did not experience this and consequently you have for now, lost our business." Later, when your customer actually makes the call to leave the competitor, he has already played the scene in his mind, and will almost always repeat at least the words, "Why didn't you offer that price to me all along?" By now it's too late for XYZ Company, *they've been "mugged in the hall."*

More recently, we applied this technique to overcome the objections raised about taking our professional training courses. One of our courses is a 12-week graduate level course teaching word-of-mouth referral marketing strategies. The tuition for this course is approximately $800, which elicits these objections: "It's too much time" or "It costs too much."

We overcome these objections with a slight variation on the "mug them in the hall" technique. We invite our prospective students to attend our preview seminar, which is designed to offer a real-life simulation of the full program. Before the end of this seminar, we "mug their objections in the hall." Graduates from our previous courses attend the preview and give testimonials about how the course increased and enhanced their business. These same graduates also admit that they, too, had serious concerns about the time commitment and cost of the course. Hearing these third-party testimonials motivates many of our prospective students to register for the course on the spot.

The "mug them in the hall" technique is merely a rehearsal of what might (and probably will) happen in the future. Talking openly about a potential objection before it is thought about consciously by the prospect minimizes the power of that objection.

Starving artists, starving musicians . . . both need money to practice their art, which, of course, means selling. Ezra Palmer-Persen is an accomplished musician from the San Francisco area who also operates a successful karaoke business. His first-hand experience at having his own selling pitches rejected qualifies him to offer recommendations for managing emotionally turbo-charged objections.

OVERCOMING OBJECTIONS:
A CHECKLIST FOR SUCCESS

EZRA PALMER-PERSEN

Bob, I like what you have but I'm afraid it just costs too much. I just can't justify it in my budget. I'm going to have to say no.

If you were in that situation selling to a potential customer, or prospect, how would you respond to that statement? When a prospect says "no," he is expressing a form of an objection to what you're doing. Objections can range from disagreeing, doubting, appearing negative, or even getting argumentative during your sales presentation. The question is, how can your response help to close the sale?

Your ability to respond to objections in a way that can turn a "no" into a "yes" on a consistent basis will make the difference between average results and achieving your highest possible sales goals.

Unfortunately, when a prospect says "no," an average salesperson will usually be overcome by the negative emotions of fear, inadequacy, defensiveness, and even anger, allowing these feelings to take over the moment. When this happens, the average salesperson is unable to listen to what the prospect is really saying and then respond effectively.

On the other hand, great salespeople can turn a "no" into a "yes" on a consistent basis because they welcome and anticipate objections. They know that a "no" is a natural part of the sales process. For example, in the car industry, new salespeople are taught that all customers are liars, meaning that when a customer says, "No thanks, I am just looking," he doesn't really mean that—he is really saying, "I want to own, but . . ."

The masterful seller also understands that an objection might not be a negative expression about the product. Instead the prospect might not feel well that day, or be rushed with other priorities or merely have an extremely stressed day. In reality there could be genuine interest in the product, but the timing is bad for even considering the purchase.

So how do you start to successfully handle objections? If you ever find yourself hesitating or are unsure of what to say when a prospect objects to what you have to offer, use the following checklist to help you quickly, enthusiastically, and with conviction successfully turn a "no" into a "yes."

- First of all, you've got to love what you're doing, or what you're doing has got to be getting you closer to what you love! It's nice if you're in a business that you absolutely enjoy, but if what you're doing will provide the means to realize your passion, then that will also work.

- You must be fully qualified to sell your product or service with integrity and honesty, and have as much product knowledge as possible so you can create a sales presentation that resonates with the prospect.
- Know your prospect's business and what he needs. Whether you're giving the presentation on the first call, or if you have a qualified referral, your job is quickly to develop a professional relationship of openness and trust with your prospect so your prospect will be open to offering sincere objections.

If you've done all that, your prospect may still object, perhaps with hidden messages.

- If a prospect tells you he is too busy, use his "busy" objection to say how your product or service can save time.
- If your product or service is deemed too expensive, find a way to point out how it's going to save (or make) your prospect money.

To be effective in finding the hidden messages, use the following format:

1. Listen to the objection
2. Acknowledge it
3. Ask a question

To demonstrate this, let's go back to salesman Bob discussed at the beginning. He has been told by his prospect ("Dave") that his service is too expensive. Bob might respond to the objection by saying, "I understand, Dave. However, would you be open to talking about your budget a little to see if there is a way I could actually save you some money (or make you more money)?" *Or,* "May I ask exactly what is it about my program that seems too expensive?"

Another example might be an objection about time. Years ago when I was selling word processing and database software, prospects would say, "You know this all sounds great, but we just don't have the time to train the staff to use it!"

My response was, "Well, I understand what you're saying. It does take time to get everyone using a computer instead of a typewriter. But if I may ask, what happens now when someone makes a mistake typing a document or entering information in your records?"

They would usually answer, "Well, they do it all over again or use white out," to which I would respond, "Well, would you give me a chance to show you how you can quickly spell check a document or prevent the wrong information from being entered in your database, saving a lot of time in the long run, *and* produce more professional results once everyone is trained?"

Tip: You will keep the process going if you follow this simple format:
- Hear an objection.
- Acknowledge your prospect.
- Then ask a question.
- Keep asking questions until the objection is over.

And don't forget to listen! You may find in this process that your prospect may be masking the real objection, which is either intellectual or emotional.

INTELLECTUAL OBJECTION. In this case, you merely need to find out what the prospect needs in order to say "yes." For example: The prospect may say, "This won't work. I'll need it right away." Your response should be, "Thank you for telling me that. When do you need it?" You will only have to assure them that you can deliver by that deadline (assuming you can).

EMOTIONAL OBJECTION. This requires an understanding of what the prospect is feeling and what's causing the feeling. If possible, find a benefit of your product or service that addresses it. For example, I have a karaoke business. When I market my karaoke shows, sometimes the host wants to have a different form of entertainment that is fun and exciting, but is afraid to sing. He might say, "Ezra, what you are doing is great but it just won't work for us." I may respond with. "Thank you for telling me. I understand that this is definitely not for everyone. Could you tell me why you think so?"

They will usually say that they don't sing or are afraid of singing. I will then ask, "Do you know if anyone is coming to the event that does like to sing?" If they say yes, then I often can show them that even though they're afraid, they and everyone else will enjoy the show because others coming to the event will love to sing, and will really appreciate and remember them for having this kind of entertainment.

Do not ever say anything negative! This is just good common sense. Simply ask yourself. How do you respond when a salesperson says something negative or has a negative attitude when they are presenting something to you? Does this inspire you to want to work with them?

And last but not least: To be successful with this format and to ensure that you will be able to respond quickly to your prospect, do something that master sales trainer Blair Singer recommends. It's the technique of a timed drill. Make an extensive list of all the possible objections that relate to your product or service. Role-play with someone over and over again with the above format until you can respond quickly and correctly no matter what you're thinking or feeling.

If you learn the principles above and practice them faithfully, you will be more successful and you will be one of those truly happy people: you either love what you're doing, or are close to getting exactly what you love!

Relationship Selling

All the Rage . . . or Just a Fad?

---

*Relationships of trust depend on our willingness to
look not only to our own interests, but
also the interests of others.*
—PETER FARGUHARSON

A parallel exists between the psychological counselor and the sales professional. Each has to discover the inner problems, desires, and motives of the counseled client or the prospective buyer. To achieve this objective, each professional engages the same attentive listening, empathic understanding, and rational emotive inquiry to get their respective jobs done. As each professional and his respective client tighten their emotional bond, the element of trust enters the relationship. It is at this point that answers to the buyer's pain or desire begin to appear, and it's up to the professional to engage his client in accepting the recommended solution.

Previously, we alluded to the sales scenario as one wherein the client's problem, challenge, or pain is relieved—or even eliminated—by an appropriate product or service provided by the seller. If buyers shop for the purpose of solving a personal problem or challenge, then the seller has the big responsibility of finding the right solution (product/service) to meet the need. Buyers are inherently skeptical about accepting the first solution offered or a solution from someone they can't trust. Of course, buying a quart of milk requires a different level of personal rapport and connection between buyer and seller than does, for example, the purchase of a million-dollar yacht. An established relationship helps to maintain and manage the buyer's concerns as she transits through the shopping and buying decision process.

"Recently, I presented a $300,000 38-foot new sailboat to an eager customer, who upon follow-up seemed to lose his initial interest. A day after I accepted my own discouraged conclusion, I got a call from a sailmaker asking for technical specifications on this new boat on behalf of my customer. He still was interested! I guess I still had a relationship!" says Dave Woreland. An experienced Canadian yacht broker, he has an interesting perspective on relationship selling:

> *The real time to build the relationship is after the deal has been signed and before the product is delivered. With our products, there is a time delay between buying and delivery, which causes customer anxiety. If there are unavoidable delays, hearing me tell the brutal reality in plain unemotional logical words helps the customer manage their emotions and increases their respect for me. Masterful yacht brokers are masters at managing customer emotions. Our clients are typically self-assured business professionals, but when yacht lifestyle shopping, can become very hesitant. It is up to us to help them manage their own emotions.*

Selling is a slippery sport. Those sellers who can establish a close connection with the buyer clearly have a competitive edge because the relationship helps bond the buyer to the seller. Nancy Morgan sold cars for a while and then was laid off because the car dealership was in a downturn. Her sales manager told her, "You are too nice for this business." A week later, one of her recent customers took her to lunch and confided, "The reason I bought the car from you instead of your competition was because I like you the best. The other dealer offered the same car—even at slightly less price—but both my wife and I enjoyed you the most." Nancy actually sold a lot of cars, but used relationship selling with her customers—always looking out for the customer's best interests. The masters use every tool, including their personality, to get the edge.

The current buzzword for this is "relationship selling." This term is actually a bit misleading because so many types of relationships exist. Not only are there many types of relationships, but there are varying degrees of a relationship.

One way to understand variable relationship selling is through the perspective of the VCP model, wherein the selling relationship is divided into three distinct phases: (1) visibility, (2) credibility, and (3) profitability. The VCP model of relationship selling explains that selling can take place at each level, with the more sustained repeat sales occurring at the third level of profitability. Some sales will take place between a seller and customer who have minimal or even no visibility within their relationship. The example would be selling at a big box store. Increased visibility and credibility as a seller are earned by offering repeated quality service, which over time leads toward a profitable relationship, wherein buyers want to do repeat business with the seller. True profitability comes from sustained and loyal customers. In these relationships, value is given both ways—to the seller and the buyer.

Relationship selling is meeting a client's needs to the point where the client realizes an increased sense of respect, trust, and personal affinity toward the seller. If this is done consistently over time, the ingredients for friendships may exist between the seller and buyer, even if the sale is a quart of milk at the corner grocery store.

Each seller has a different way to connect with buyers, and the same methods will not necessarily work for every seller. As you read through the following stories related to relationship selling, see if you can find your personal style reflected in at least one case study.

———•———

Many people learn how to be really good at their particular job, partially by circumstance and partially by inherent good sense. When early lessons learned are retained and turned into habit, wisdom emerges. Debby Peters is an experienced salesperson who learned her craft in part through the school of hard knocks. She did well in this school, and now trains other up-and-coming salespeople in the Ohio area. Debby wisely realized her desire for a free meal led to great sales.

———•———

WILL WORK FOR FOOD

DEBBY PETERS

Early in my career I was a brand-new recruit for the sales team of a national payroll company. I was the only female among many experienced male sales staff. The guys weren't too excited about having a "girl" crash their *club*. At that point in my new selling career, I really didn't notice because I was still trying to figure out the difference between gross and net! It was 1986. My personal budget was stretched tighter than a drum, and the company had just implemented a new marketing program called "Dine with CPAs."

The sales guys all pooh-poohed this new program, but I embraced it with glee. The program was voluntary, but we were *highly encouraged* to have breakfast or lunch with at least two CPAs per week. The idea was to get the accountants to refer their clients to us. Heck, I wasn't so much worried about referrals; I was more concerned about eating. While two meals was the minimum, I figured I could cut my food expenses considerably if I tried to have ten meal appointments per week. I figured spending the company's money on food meant that there might be enough in my pocket left over for skiing.

There were probably very few weeks where I was able to score a perfect 10, but that was my goal. I seem to remember (20 years later) that my average was six meals per week. Those numbers were good, but another problem loomed on the horizon.

We Didn't Talk Business at a Business Lunch

I remember that most times I took the CPA back to his (in those days, 99 percent of the CPAs were men) office, shook his hand, and thanked him for his time, and then I realized, "We didn't talk business." As I got into my brown Dodge minivan, I became very concerned about what my sales manager would say if he found out that I didn't talk business. Of course, in my mind it would have been very stupid for me to actually broach this subject with my manager, because I might derail my company-paid gravy train. If this happened, my home budget would have to be adjusted to include more groceries and less fun. I continued to fly under the radar, thinking that I'd use this perk for as long as I could make it last.

A funny thing happened, though, as I waded through the feeding trough with my new accountant friends. After several months of *not* talking business but just being pleasant, these very same CPAs began to call me with their referrals. They were referring their clients to me. These were the dream referrals: businesspeople that wanted to buy from me even before I ever got involved. I'd get a phone call from the CPA telling me to call his client. Immediately after the phone call, I'd contact his client. Without me ever having to sell, the CPA's client also became my client. My manager said that I was an overnight success.

Getting to Know the Person Leads to Trust

What I didn't know then, but now know, was that in my ignorance, I was doing something right . . . very right. Instead of forcing an artificially business-focused conversation, I got to know the person sitting across the breakfast table from me. I found out the ages of his kids, where his wife worked, and how they met. He also told me where he went to college and high school, too. I found out the types of clients they liked best and that usually their very first clients became the industry they targeted.

I received an education, too. Since most of the CPAs in my territory were Jewish, I found out about all the holy days, and where to buy good bagels. I even learned some Yiddish, but have forgotten most of it. One lesson, however, has not been forgotten. Because of my company's marketing initiative—the one I considered my feeding trough—the CPAs and I became *friends*. As we developed a rapport and then a relationship, they began to trust me and finally—because of that trust—to refer solid business to me.

During the three years that I worked for the payroll company, I was ranked in the top ten nationally . . . actually never lower than sixth place. Not bad for someone just trying to cut her personal food budget. To this day, I still remember the lessons I learned about chatting with a client to discover areas of mutual interest and, most importantly, finding issues of special interest to the client. Through refinements gained during my maturing phases, I understand that building relationships with one's clients has a long-term (and very profitable) payoff.

—·◆·—

Our typical image of a salesperson suggests a gregarious, extroverted type who likes flashy cars, red ties, and smooth fast talk. If this were universally true, what would shy, retiring Linda Macedonio be doing in sales? She, like others, didn't invent her personality, but still had to sell her professional services if success was to be achieved. Now the owner of a thriving marketing franchise in Massachusetts, Linda teaches multiple ways to get the selling job done.

—·◆·—

SHY PEOPLE CAN SELL, TOO!

LINDA MACEDONIO

Picture in your mind a stereotypical "salesperson." What do you see? An obnoxious used-car salesman? An unwelcome door-to-door rep pushing something you don't need or want? Perhaps you are visualizing an insistent telemarketer interrupting your dinner to "set a free appointment" for a home improvement inspection? You probably characterize these people as more concerned with getting their canned sales pitch correct than about your best interests.

Yuck! No wonder people have such a negative image of salespeople. If you happen to be a professional used-car salesman, this image is a sad problem. But it's an even bigger problem if you are, say, a rather shy bookkeeper, graphic designer, or accountant working for yourself or in a small partnership, because the prospect of selling your own services sends shivers down your spine, or leaves you feeling . . .well . . . slimy. Rest assured, masterful sellers operate at a different level than our stereotypical sellers mentioned above.

As a service provider, "selling" is vital to your livelihood. In fact, every business requires effective sales to survive and thrive. In spite of its negative image, there's nothing inherently wrong with sales. What matters most is how the selling is done.

Quite often people who provide professional services have exquisite training related to their professional qualifications, but virtually no training in sales. Even more problematic, they may completely hate the notion of selling or feel their personality just doesn't fit with "sales."

That's how Lynette felt. After relocating with her husband to another state, Lynette was faced with helping him find clients for their newly-transplanted graphic design business. She was comfortable spending most of her time behind a computer doing the design work and talking with existing clients. But the thought of getting out in a sales role petrified her. How, she wondered in a panic, was she going to drag herself out of her safe, behind-the-desk niche to assertively pursue new business?

Friends steered Lynette and her husband to a networking group that specialized in referral marketing. The group enabled them to meet photographers and other designers, and they began building relationships with these other complementary professions. Soon they found that each of these services was referring prospective customers to the other . . . including to their own graphic design business.

Shy Person's Lesson 1

Lynette had learned an important lesson about succeeding in sales: Get involved in a referral network where you can help new friends and they can help you. Another businesswoman I know, Linda, followed that lesson and discovered a second important insight.

When Linda first started her bookkeeping business, she struggled to find new customers. She tried running an ad in the local paper, which resulted in a few calls and one short-term client. Next, Linda tried direct mail. She sent a letter to 35 certified public accountants whose addresses she got from the local phone book, asking for an appointment to discuss mutual referrals. No reply! So, with a pit in her stomach, she called each one to see if they would meet with her. This resulted in two appointments.

Her persistence paid off. After meeting them, each of those two CPAs agreed to a trial arrangement. They also discussed ways they could help each other. Each of the CPAs referred some clients to her, and she did likewise for them. Her referral marketing generated a tenfold increase in her client base within two years.

Linda's experience reinforced the lesson about cultivating a referral network. Equally important, she discovered that it is easier to sell someone else's services than it is to sell her own. By having confidence and trust in others, and they in her, Linda and her network began to experience the synergy made possible when people work together.

Shy Person's Lesson 2

Linda learned that a referral network can transform your weaknesses into strengths. The discomfort Linda felt about selling herself wasn't a problem when she was selling someone else.

"That all sounds good," you might be thinking, "but what if I'm just too darn shy to even participate in a referral network?" You're not alone. Yet another graphic designer I know, Kara, was OK talking with small groups of two or three people, but petrified about speaking to a larger group.

When she first joined a networking group, she shook uncontrollably, her voice quivered, and she turned beet red when she had to speak! After a few months of getting up each week in front of her group, however, she noticed a dramatic change. Now, three years later, she speaks regularly to groups of more than 50 people. She finds humor really helps, and she also realizes that most people experience the same fear of speaking.

Shy Person's Lesson 3

Kara used the safe environment of her new referral group as a place to build her confidence and public speaking skills. Despite starting as a quivering and quaking speaker, her self-confidence grew . . . along with her sales. She discovered that her new public speaking skills transferred directly to improved sales presentations.

"Sales" is a difficult and demanding discipline, especially for shy individuals. But it is necessary, and may even contribute to surprising personal growth in addition to business success.

The real strength behind a network is the relationships you establish to help sell you as a trusted and high quality service provider. You help them and they will help you because "what goes around really does come around."

Most outside salespeople are at least vaguely aware that networking with people might provide new customers, but the Masters of Sales consistently network through all phases of the sale. John Suarez realized that his own sales career required him to network in a unique fashion; he became the *protégé of a master seller and learned by doing. Under the careful guidance of his mentor in St. Louis, John learned to build relationships with those prospects in his sales pipeline. He learned to strike up a conversation, start a relationship, and then systematically follow up.*

———•◦•———

BASEBALL AND THE ENEMY WITHIN

JOHN SUAREZ

At one point in my early days as an independent career development specialist struggling to find clients, I experienced a moment of blazing clarity. I had to find a selling system that worked for me. *Like it or not (and I didn't), I was in sales.* If my career development business was to become profitable, I had to come to terms with my previous antipathy for selling. I needed a selling process that enabled me to become friends with the enemy.

When the Student Is Ready . . .
Headfirst I dove in, reading books on how to sell, taking the best sales training I could find, and out of the blue, the phone rang. Terry, my brother-in-law, recently left his family's commercial real estate business and launched a solo career in the same field. He wanted me to work for him and help grow his new real estate company.

"I'm looking for someone who is educated but has no preconceived notions of how to do the job," Terry explained. "I want to train someone how to do things my way, without them having to unlearn bad selling habits." Terry was looking for an educated idiot, and I fit the bill perfectly. He was the *most successful salesperson I knew,* and he wanted to teach me to be a master salesperson. His exact words were, "I won't let you fail." With hope and uncertainty, I made the leap. In a matter of weeks, I went from the anti-sales guy to the guy who embraced sales as a necessary component of his career life.

I soon learned that salespeople like Terry network behind the scenes for months or even years to make deals happen. Terry's sales process was amazing in its simplicity. He taught me to create a "hot sheet" listing all the deals in their various stages of development. We often had up to 20 deals under contract at any given time.

Network to Increase Relatedness

Because all minutiae associated with each file involved a person or several people, Terry always had his appointment book by the phone or in his possession to reorganize and reprioritize his daily schedule so efficiently, he rarely had unproductive downtime. He was wired to his system. Occasionally he walked past my office and barked, "Bring me your hot sheet," a request that often left me scurrying to update my disorganized files and notes so I could brief him on the status of my contacts.

By using his detailed client follow-up system, I learned to relate to the most immediate needs of my confirmed customers in a timely manner and send the right messages to my prospective clientele based on the status of their situations. Over time I realized that by using his system, my own clients' appreciation of my professionalism was enhanced. Basically, his system involved networking with each of his clients, sending them the right information at the right time, and in doing so, his relatedness to each client increased.

Terry networked for new clients with the same kind of efficiency. He targeted his network and circulated with selected power brokers who spoke the language of high-stakes commerce and economic development. He was exceptionally good at connecting with the people he targeted at any networking events he attended, always looking to add to the strength of a relationship whether it was in an early formation or later mature stage of development.

Build Relationships Bit by Bit and Wherever

One memorable lesson came about while Terry and his young family were enjoying a beautiful day at the ballpark. The sounds and smells of Busch Stadium made rooting for the St. Louis Cardinals a welcome distraction from the daily grind of the office. Terry purposely but reluctantly left his cell phone in the car to spend an uninterrupted day with his family. It wasn't to be.

While most fans were glued to the baseball game, Terry saw a piece of real estate with endless possibilities. To him, the ballgame was simply a metaphor: *move a deal from base to base and across the plate . . . keep swinging and eventually you will hit a home run . . . sometimes you have to strike out to advance the deal.* For him, baseball and selling were synchronized. A few rows back, Terry spotted someone he barely recognized. "*Where do I know that guy from?*" he asked himself. The question bothered him for a few innings, and finally when the family left to get snacks, Terry seized the opportunity to say a quick, harmless "hello."

Soon the two were chatting amicably. It turns out the other man was CFO of a large organization that owned prime real estate in southern Illinois. Terry had met him briefly at a local chamber function, and the ballpark provided a casual environment to learn if the rumor was true about his company developing one of their prime properties into a new retail center. One thing led to another, and Terry was invited to visit the CFO's office the next week to talk further. He returned to his family and enjoyed the rest of the game, but his mind was already in extra innings.

In November of that year, Terry closed the largest deal of his career on that prime piece of real estate, and it all started because of a networking encounter at the chamber of commerce, followed by enhancing the relationship during a ten-minute conversation at the baseball game. Three years later, Terry had an orange file and a commission worth more than $300,000 to his credit. I learned the secret of building relationships by seizing every realistic opportunity to communicate with people. In some environments, like a baseball game, one's business guard is lowered and a deal can rapidly advance, but only if we change the statement "*I am not going to talk business today*" to "*I will talk up a relationship today.*"

Keeping Everyone in the Information Loop

In my third year of working for Terry, I closed a $1.6 million land sale, resulting in the single largest commission in the company's brief history.

Terry coached me through the entire transaction. He showed me how the selling process worked and encouraged me when it looked like the deal might fall through. Ultimately, I moved my deal through the colored file folders to the final orange closed file. Losing a six-figure commission after eight to ten months of work was one of the risks and realities of the business, but Terry taught me how to keep all the prospective parties happy and in the spiral loop that moves forward. That's what relationship selling is all about. Keeping everyone involved in the deal, secure in your own self-confident belief that the deal can be made despite potential troubles along the way.

Networking and sales are a perfect fit because both are concerned with building long-term relationships. I now prefer to build long-term relationships that can help me sell today and in the future. Baseball players use a baseball glove and bat in the way professional sellers use network connections and long-term relationships. Both are tools necessary to move the game forward. The ballplayer knows that stepping up to the plate might result in a strike out or might result in a home run. The networker knows that stepping up to engage others in conversations might lead nowhere or might advance a sale.

Master sellers are open to serendipitous connections in the most unusual circumstances and always seem to know how to make the numbers work in their favor, even on a day when they happen to be sitting amongst 40,000 baseball spectators.

If relationship selling is in vogue, how come there are still lots of salespeople cold calling after one sale, and then the next, and the next, and so on? With a long background in selling throughout the eastern seaboard, Jerry Schwartz likes to get to the bottom of paradoxes. Jerry's word-of-mouth marketing franchise is thriving, and his product is clearly relationship oriented. He offers his perspective on the not-yet-complete shift to relationship selling. The industry currently has one foot in the single transaction camp and the other in the relationship camp. Clearly, relationship selling is a better fit for our pluralistic society.

THE TRUTH ABOUT RELATIONSHIP SELLING

JERRY SCHWARTZ

I first learned about relationship selling 25 years ago, before it was a buzz-word. My business partner, Bob Greene, was the perfect example of a relationship salesman. Bob made an effort to learn everything about our clients, and I mean everything—both personal and business. I couldn't understand why everyone wanted to help Bob more than me. I tried emulating Bob: I asked our clients lots of questions, but it just wasn't the same.

Dr. Harry Olson, author, speaker, and executive coach, helped me understand the difference between Bob and me. He says: "Relationship selling works best when prospect and seller, in the course of meeting, discover a natural affinity or shared interests between them. This facilitates a common bond *outside* of the business context. The salesperson who can *create an emotional bond* with the customer has the winning edge—hands down. This requires artful skills in relationship-building."

Bob was truly ahead of his time. Today, traditional sellers collide with a modern culture that has significantly altered how customers hear and interpret sales messages and make buying decisions. People are more knowledgeable about products than ever before, and they're what I call "over-choiced"—they have so many options that making choices is very difficult, and once they decide on one product, how does that vendor keep their loyalty?

A business associate of mine, Eric Eisenberg, truly understands this dilemma. "My passion is to help businesspeople connect with other businesspeople," says Eric. "You do not need to look for favors or rewards. If you truly believe in what you are doing—not just doing something to look good—the rewards will find you."

Talented salespeople have great transactional skills that help get a buyer to like them during a sales meeting. However, I can be friendly, knowledgeable, and insightful, and hit your sales buttons, but that doesn't guarantee that you'll have a great relationship with me. A transaction is an interaction that usually occurs once per event. A relationship is a process built and nurtured over time and during multiple positive contacts.

The key to relationship selling is found in the dynamic that occurs between business contacts. Dr. Olson talks about two types of salespeople: The R-type is the *Relater*. These folks think and breathe relationships. They naturally find ways to nurture friendship bonds for the long term. They instinctively know how to get close to people and build trust. Do they always do it right and know all the answers about positive communications and relationship skills? Heavens, no! They do, however, place a high value on strong relationships at the outset, and are prepared to learn from their mistakes as they go along.

The T-type, the *Transactor*, is friendly, extroverted, and caring. Most T-types like people and want to be liked. Their motives are pure, but they think in terms of the more immediate transaction, not the long-term relationship. Their understanding of a relationship is limited to a series of transactions. They assume that if we have good, productive outcomes each time we meet, that's enough to automatically build a good relationship. The Transactor will typically not make contact between meetings, nor think much about customers' other potential needs, or their families, etc. They can successfully sell, but will have to work diligently to get repeat business from previous clients.

Our modern western culture and sales climate favors the Relaters because they add to a client's sense of self-worth and importance. Yet millions of Transactors inhabit the sales profession and still succeed. Are they a dying breed? According to Dr. Olson, Transactors face a triple challenge:

- First, they need to develop a belief in the process of seeding relationship beyond the level of one great transaction after the other.

- Second, they must recognize and draw out the extra human nuances that inhabit all people and are a key to building strong relationships.
- Finally, the T-types have to learn how to use the newer values and norms that create longer-term emotional bonds, even though it's not in their nature to do so.

R-types take relationship skills for granted. It surprises them that T-types sometimes fail to establish great sales and customer service relationships. T-types are often mystified when they lose business, or don't get repeat business in spite of their efforts. Most often, it's not the failure of their transactions. Perhaps they just didn't stay in touch or send that extra networking thank-you card. They had an opportunity to start a relationship, but didn't think about or understand how to sow the seeds. Because they didn't, their clients are likely to move on to the next T-type, or perhaps will be wooed away by an R-type who knows how to emotionally appeal to their needs.

Dr. Olson provides five tips on how to help Transactors succeed at relationship selling:

1. Don't take relationship-seeding skills for granted. Don't assume all nice people know how to form relationships.
2. Focus on the methods and actions that seed a relationship with your contacts. Zero in on personal human nuances outside of the business context. It's here where serious relationships are built.
3. Spend serious time with sales staff discussing how to improve relationships with your customer base. Discuss the general methods and use in-depth case analysis.
4. Identify "best practices" in relationship-seeding skills. Emulate them and mentor your salespeople in those areas.
5. Finally, find ways to help each of your customers outside of the immediate selling arena. By helping others, you are setting in place a "givers gain" dynamic where those individuals will want to help you, and if not them, trust the universe and it will give back somewhere somehow.

What do Bob, Eric, and Dr. Olson have in common? They have built their lives around caring about others and wanting to help. And they truly understand that relationship selling comes from the heart. (And, as you might have guessed, I am a reformed T-Type seller!)

———•—•———

Named by Forbes *and* Inc *magazines as one of the world's most "connected" individuals, and one of the youngest chief marketing officers for a* Fortune 500 *company, Keith Ferrazzi operates out of California and understands that in our increasingly competitive world, the top masters typically do not leave things to chance. Instead, they fully prepare for all contingencies by researching their subjects carefully*

———•—•———

DO YOUR HOMEWORK: REALLY

KEITH FERRAZZI

Before I meet with any new prospect, I make sure I do my homework. And when I say homework, I mean more than checking to see if the company has a web site and reading its posted public information. Your homework needs to include the everyday items such as the major news about the prospect's company, how well the stock is valued, or details about a new product. But what you really want to know is much more personal.

Think of it this way: A good salesperson does research on companies, but a great salesperson does research on people. As my tagline says, "Business is human," and as I say every time I speak, "business relationships are *personal* relationships." No one has ever sold anything to a company. Selling is done with people within the company. I also find that without fail, *all* people care about, above everything else, themselves.

Therefore, I prepare a one-page synopsis on each person I'm going to meet. My synopsis includes what's most important to him: his hobbies, his most remarkable achievements, what he's most passionate about. I want to know his favorite charity or the college he attended. Perhaps his kids are hoping to land internships, he has health issues, or he just wants to cut strokes off his golf game.

Information about the person's company is only included if it also affects him personally, in his daily life. Did the company have a good quarter but his division is on the rocks and his career status questionable? Is there a hiring freeze at the company, and he's very concerned about his overworked team and that other teams are not pulling their weight?

These days, doing such research is easy. Here are a few places to start:

- *The internet.* The Google search engine can easily check a person's affiliations and accomplishments. Annual reports and recent press releases offer clues about the company challenges and opportunities. Social networking tools like LinkedIn or Ryze can show you a self-updated professional profile and potential connections your target has with others.

- *In your backyard.* Contact your friends and friends of friends, telling them you're trying to learn about your prospect and asking if they know him. Even if you can't find anyone who knows your prospect personally, it's still useful to hear what people know about him.

- *Within your prospect's company.* Look for opportunities to speak with people who work a couple levels below your prospect. These people can give you the lay of the land and may mention personal tendencies about your prospect without even thinking about it. Make sure you engage in real conversations with his assistant. Assistants are gatekeepers and they know everything you'd ever want to know.

Your purpose for this research is to find common grounds that are deeper and richer than what might be found in an initial encounter. Even more important your research may turn up areas that your services, talent, or product can offer that have personal importance to your prospect. Your sales mission is to make your prospect more successful, both inside and outside of his company.

Recently, I took part in an annual three-day roundtable discussion sponsored by the Milken Institute's Global Conference in Los Angeles. This event was a forum for the world's top thinkers and CEOs to work on global problems. Participating in the event were 15 executives of companies far bigger than my own.

Because I helped organize the conference (always an advantage), I was invited to participate and knew beforehand who was coming. This helped me in my research on the few people I wanted most to rub shoulders with and meet.

The events were planned with a CEO's tight schedule in mind. There was a brief mixer before the event to allow the participants to mingle and get to know one another. This was followed by a panel discussion on the future challenges of marketing big brands. Then dinner was followed by more meetings. In other words, I had a narrow window of time to establish a foundation for developing one or two relationships with key participants.

Earlier I discovered that one participant, the former CEO of Proctor and Gamble John Pepper, was also a fellow graduate of Yale. I admired him since I was an undergrad at Yale and heard him speak on campus. John Pepper was committed to human rights and wanted to ensure the story about the Underground Railroad was preserved in a museum he was founding in Cincinnati. Pepper knows a lot about marketing large companies and is well known for the leadership and the marketing innovations he brought to Procter & Gamble. I hoped that a relationship with him might shed light on how to market my young company.

Knowing he had attended Yale, I tapped into my alumni network and the Yale University web site for more information. There, I found a treasure trove of old college affiliations and interests. It turned out we had both been in Berkeley College at Yale. That meant he must have known Robin Winks, a warmly admired and much-respected professor for whom I had worked while in college. When I brought up our many common experiences, we hit it off.

By the end of our conversation, John was giving me insightful advice and contacts for my company. He invited me to keep in touch in the coming years, and we have. When Professor Winks passed away just a week later, we shared our memories of him. A few months later, I met a successful businessman from Cincinnati who was bragging about the museum enshrining the Underground Railroad and I made a point of putting him in touch with John Pepper for fundraising. I've probably introduced two or three potential donors to John in the last year. While my relationship with John Pepper may not have created a new sale, it certainly helped me with key information about how to get new sales.

My research revealed that another CEO I wanted to meet had run the New York City Marathon the previous year. I know firsthand how much commitment and sacrifice it takes to train day in and day out to complete a marathon. I had tried—and failed, because my knees started to act up.

When I ran into this CEO, I said, "You know, I don't know how you do it. I like to think I'm in great shape, but the training for a marathon killed me. I had to stop."

Of course, she was surprised. "How the heck did you know I ran a marathon?" she happily quipped.

I explained that I always make a special effort to inquire about the people I'd like to meet. This flattery seems to always work. Instantly, the other person knows that rather than suffering through a strained half hour with a stranger, they're able to connect to someone who shares a common interest, and who has gone out of his way to get to know them better.

The day before, I had gone through Barry's Boot Camp, a tough-as-nails but totally exhilarating exercise regimen in West Hollywood, not far from the conference. I said, "If you want an amazing and different workout sometime, you should consider boot camp." In return, I received some welcome advice for extending my running regimen. Later, she tried boot camp with mc and loved it.

To this day, each time she and I meet, we talk about Barry's Boot Camp and I give her my progress report on my goal of running a marathon. I am a devotee of Barry's Boot Camp and have converted quite a few L.A. guests to his workout. While these visiting executives might not have time to meet or have lunch with me, they often do make one non-business detour—and we have one hardcore workout together.

Your goal when meeting new people is to transform what could be a forgettable encounter into a blossoming friendship. It doesn't matter if you are seeking new information or a sales contact; if you can reach out to selected individuals and truly connect with them, you will be set for a long time. This can only occur by doing really good research or good ol' fashioned homework.

Selling technologies change gradually, and today the competitive edge comes to those who grasp the concept of referral selling. Some of us must learn quickly, while others like Brian Buffini learned at a young age that relationships and selling are symbiotic. Getting referred clients on a sustained basis and seeing those clients begin to refer new clients starts with organizing and using your contact database in a systematic and methodical manner. However, it must continue through the lifetime of the relationship. Brian Buffini's sales training organization is highly respected and has strong brand recognition.

REFERRALS SELL YOU BETTER THAN YOU CAN SELL YOURSELF!

BRIAN BUFFINI AND DAVID LALLY

In the real estate industry, relationships are the cornerstone of a successful business. In fact, if you are in any service business, building relationships is *the* number-one way to increase business.

Growing up in Ireland, my brothers and I worked in the family business every summer. *Buffini & Company Painting and Decorating Contractors* was known for high-quality work. Because of this reputation, the company never had to advertise; it relied totally on referrals. Referred clients knew about our work and already had a positive impression about our work in their mind.

Entering the real estate industry in San Diego, I discovered that the traditional methods of lead-generation (cold-calling, door-knocking, etc.) were not in keeping with my personal philosophy on how to treat people. The turning point for my career came when I realized that appreciative clients would actually help me build my business by referring others to me.

The referral systems I now teach at our Turning Point Retreat™ seminars are proven in the field. I stand behind them because I implemented them in my own office and saw the dramatic impact they had. I became one of the top agents in the nation by developing a sophisticated yet easy-to-use system that generates a predictable number of high-quality, referred leads.

A continuous and predictable stream of referrals doesn't just happen; you must have a system in place. You may say, "I already get referrals." Everyone gets some passive word-of-mouth business, but not everyone knows how to guarantee a consistent stream of referred business. It boils down to a simple equation: waiting vs. finding. We help our clients start to consistently find new business with three concepts related to re-organizing their database:

- *Build.* Gather the names of all those you know, including past clients.
- *Sort.* Prioritize this database and consistently communicate with those who refer you most.
- *Qualify.* Using targeted dialogs, continue to determine who is willing to do business with and refer you.

We also teach the ABC method of organizing the contacts in your database:

- A—most likely to refer you
- B—would refer you, if asked and shown how
- C—might refer you in the future
- D—names to be deleted from your database. It's good to get rid of a headache, so do this up front!

> Our system requires the database to be put into a priority that enhances a referral system to be put into place. A prioritized database allows you to effectively manage your time.

A prospector must sift through rock to find the gold nuggets. Consider your database as the rock ready to be refined. Building your database lays the foundation for what type of gold—or referrals—will result. Whether you currently have 20 or 2,000 people in your database, you always need to add "ore" to produce the right kind of new clients, because not all pieces of ore become your clients. You don't need to market to everyone; you just need to market to your most responsive audience—the pieces of gold.

Add Value to Your Clients

Concentrate on providing first-class value to your best referring clients, and you will have a relationship that will help sustain momentum when the market changes.

Most Realtors® and other service providers "forget" about their customer after the sale is made. They may keep in touch initially, but before long they move on to the next prospect and forget about their last client. I teach a three-pronged communication system designed to stay in contact with clients after the sale is made. This system has these foundational elements:

1. Contact
2. Care
3. Community

Contact involves making calls, sending personal notes, and doing what I call "Pop-Bys" (visiting clients with a small, meaningful gift). While building my business, I demonstrated *care* by regularly visiting clients with items such as movie tickets, restaurant gift certificates, etc. Building *community* came in the form of business-to-business luncheons and client parties. I kept in constant contact with past and present clients, and always focused on providing value. I can steadily increase my business by consistently delivering excellent aftercare service to my previous clients.

It is important to let clients know that you do not spend time prospecting for business. Instead you devote your time to serving their needs. I based this system on the principle of "Give, Ask, & Receive." I focused my efforts on *giving* outstanding service and providing regular items of value to customers. I would always follow-up each conversation with a *request* for referrals and—because I delivered first-class service—the *referrals poured in*. If you are continually delivering top-quality service, clients will want to refer you. So let them!

Say the Right Thing at the Right Time

At the end of every conversation, it is important to remind your client that you appreciate her business and would be happy to give the same service to her friends or family who want to buy or finance a home. I never missed an opportunity to remind people that I worked by referral. I became known for TV detective Colombo's unique way of signing off: "Oh, by the way, I work by referral; who do you know who . . .?"

With the right dialog, we can get people thinking about us without the use of other marketing gimmicks. Implementing a referral system allows us to do business with people we like. Instead of prospecting for new clients, we intentionally provide value to our existing ones. Our system is based on principles that stem from the heart of sales: building relationships.

Closing the Customer

It's in the WOW Factor

Exuberance is better than taste.

—GUSTAVE FLAUBERT

(And both leave a lasting impression.)

—MISNER AND MORGAN

This book is nearing its end. Traditional sales books might be tempted to end with a discussion about closing. Indeed, such a discussion can be both instructive and enjoyable. Don can illustrate this with a story from his days selling cars.

There was an older couple looking to buy a new car. They had been through the full car presentation and were sitting in the sales-man's office considering model, features, and the scariest of all: price. They wanted the car, but it was just a little out of their agreed-upon price range. As they were religious, they asked the salesman to leave while they prayed for an answer to their dilemma. The salesman left and they prayed. Unbeknownst to the couple, the salesman left the office intercom button open and went to the manager's office. When the couple asked God out loud what they should do, the manager, in his most pious and deep, gentle voice, spoke over the intercom, "You've considered all sides, and you really want the car. You are good people who always help others. You deserve the new car. BUY IT!" Though taken aback, they did buy it, and left happy customers!

Sometimes closing on a customer is as simple as asking him, or even *telling* him, to buy the item, as it will truly suit his needs. We all know that it's important to ask a prospect to buy several times to make the deal happen, and most of us use the traditional closing techniques. The trial close, for example, is when we test if a customer is ready to make a buying decision. ("That suit looks great on you!") The assumptive close is useful when you are pretty sure the buyer wants to buy. ("So, I'll see you at the closing meeting tomorrow morning!") We were a little more assertive in car sales, putting a pen on the application and accidentally dropping the pen in the customer's lap, whereupon when they picked up the pen, we said, "Press firmly when signing your name, as there are several carbon copies."

Our more nontraditional sales book has mapped out a consistent theme: The sales industry is midway through a huge paradigm shift in the way people sell and, most importantly, the way buyers buy. In 1992, Don sold cars and predicted that in the next decade, car buyers would buy cars through the internet. Of course, everyone thought he was crazy. Today though, people research cars, make feature choices, and even place orders for cars through the internet change influences all forms of human interaction, even sales.

Traditional selling techniques have included highly persuasive, manipulative, and even tricky selling techniques to get our sales foot in the door and convince people to buy our product or service: "We have a one-day special price today, but you have to sign up right now!" or "There is only one left and the new models are priced higher!" In fact, these old techniques still help move a buyer from a hesitant mode to a buying mode, but there's a newer phenomenon happening in sales that is truly making a difference in closing clients. This strategy converts clients to raving fans if done properly.

The newer approach is a dedicated effort to building a relationship with the client suitable to get the job done. But it's even more. Masters are masters because they put in more effort than others. They "apply an uncommon application of common knowledge about the proven techniques to achieving success in business and life." See *Masters of Success*, Misner and Morgan (Entrepreneur Press, 2004). Moreover, master sellers know that to get a customer to buy from them all that is really needed is to create such an extraordinary positive impression in the buyer that there really is only one option—to buy from them, the master salespeople.

You've got an unhappy client. It can happen easily, given the crush of fast-paced priorities and change. The question is what are you going to do about it? Robin Schuckmann, a writer and business owner in Oregon, specializes in teaching people who sell that it is easier and more profitable to maintain existing clients than to sell new ones. By maintaining positive relationships with existing clients, you add significantly to your profit margin. Do this by going above and beyond what is "expected."

DELIVERING THAT "PERSONAL TOUCH"

ROBIN SCHUCKMANN

Selling software in the high-tech field was very competitive during the early 1990s. Each software sales representative competed for the same clients, in the same field, with a similar product, at about the same price. The way to stand out and keep one's clients from going to the competition was to provide over-the-top service. Mark McDonald started his entrepreneurial career as an account manager for Software Spectrum in Portland, Oregon. He was responsible for closing multiyear, third-party software contracts, and he had just taken over the U.S. Bancorp account.

Taking advantage of a visit by his boss, the regional manager, Mark set up a meeting between his boss and two VIPs at U.S. Bancorp, the head of purchasing and the vice president of contracts and vendor relations. During the meeting, the U.S. Bancorp managers told Mark and his regional manager in no uncertain tones that their company, Spectrum, was U.S. Bancorp's worst vendor. To this point, Software Spectrum had only earned 10 percent of U.S. Bancorp's software business, about $100,000. With these figures in mind and learning of their client's serious dissatisfaction with Spectrum, Mark set a humble goal of increasing the company's market share by an additional 15 percent during the coming year.

Over the next several months Mark did extensive internal research and conducted key personnel interviews to discover what his clients expected from their business relationship. During lunches and various business meetings, he asked lots of questions about their challenges, their goals for the upcoming year, and how they would be evaluated. As he got to know the client better, he always asked how he might be able to help each person with his job.

The information Mark gathered through his research enabled him to be a better team player. He was able to supply useful information from time to time, as well as communicate with each one in the specific manner with which he was most comfortable.

The Golden Rule of Sales: Treat Each Person in the Way that Person Wishes to Be Treated

Mark lived and worked 45 minutes from the U.S. Bancorp's offices. Modern telecommunication would have allowed him to conduct much of his connecting and networking work by phone, fax, e-mail, and internet. Instead, Mark treated every request for a quote, or detailed project information, as though that department head really wanted a personalized delivery and one-on-one discussion of the information. Mark took the time to personally hand deliver every price quote, proposal, product information, program specification, and other important correspondence. With each client contact, he deepened—bit by bit—his level of understanding of the client, thereby increasing his rapport while gaining its trust.

After one particular meeting that lasted about 45 minutes, the client said, "Wow, this was the most productive meeting we've had in a long time!" What Mark realized is that the personal touch he had made over the last several months was totally appreciated by the clients. They had missed this in their previous interactions. Each representative within the company wanted to be treated differently, and Mark took the time to discover how to make each person feel like a top VIP client.

Social Capital Correlates with Selling

Of course, Mark added to his reputation with each personalized visit and slowly restored the reserve of credibility that had been depleted by his predecessor. In fact, he was rebuilding his company's social capital along with his own through his extraordinary personalized service.

Mark also set up quarterly update meetings with all departments involved in purchasing decisions, including representatives from IT, along with sales and purchasing employees and managers. They reviewed the previous quarter's goals and performance, factual product information, and current goals and projects for the upcoming quarter, and Mark found out where they might need special assistance to achieve their internal goals.

It turned out that the U.S. Bancorp employees actually enjoyed attending these quarterly meetings, because they learned more about their own company than they did through their company's internal communication system. Since Mark worked with several similar companies in neighboring states, the employees gained knowledge about the status of their company compared to the other large competing corporations.

Following nine months of consistent face-to-face communication and rapport building, an opportunity arose to have a meeting between Mark, his regional manager, and the original two senior U.S. Bancorp executives.

Their attitudes had markedly changed. They told Mark and his regional manager that it was very uncommon for vendors to recover from the tone of their first meeting. However, Software Spectrum had not only recovered, but had actually become one of the best companies they worked with in the software field and was considered a true business partner.

With the time and energy Mark put into this client-customer relationship, he increased his company market share to 90 percent and increased sales from $100,000 to over $2.2 million with his (now) key client.

If you are even wondering if you should apply a more "personal touch" to your clients, it is likely something you should be doing.

Each year, auto companies spend billions to make slight changes in their product line. Every five to seven years, a new car model is introduced. Consumer electronics are also notorious for introducing product change. Buyers are insatiably hungry for a little WOW factor in their new product. Linda Forte-Spearing, a business writer from Mississauga, Canada, illustrates how adding a small product change can create massive sales, even in an unlikely industry. The truth is, no matter what the industry, all sellers of products or services need to put a WOW factor into their product to satisfy the consumer's need for something new.

WOW YOUR WAY TO INCREASED SALES

LINDA FORTE-SPEARING

L ooking for ways to take your sales to the next level? Whether launching a new product, experiencing a slow season, or trying to reach a new audience, your ultimate sales success may hinge on creative selling, or your ability to create the proverbial *WOW* factor.

Take the confectionary icon PEZ®, for example. Invented in 1927 by Austrian Edward Haas, the (originally peppermint) candies were marketed to Europeans as a breath mint or an alternative to smoking. They were initially housed in small metal pocket tins. The packaging then evolved into a more hygienic container resembling a BIC® lighter.

In 1952, after achieving moderate success in Europe, Haas launched PEZ peppermints in the United States. Unlike the Europeans, however, American adults weren't receptive to the innovative candy dispensers. Within just two years, Edward Haas conceded defeat in the U.S. marketplace and was forced to find an alternative approach to selling his candy. In other words, he needed to come up with a real *WOW!*

Thinking outside of the traditional candy seller's box, Haas added a flip-top cartoon character head to the end of the dispenser. As a result, he ended up creating more of a toy than a dispensing unit, and kids just loved them. Further capitalizing on his new-found *WOW* factor, he switched to fruity flavors to appeal to the palates of his younger clientele.

Today, PEZ is one of the most recognizable commercial names worldwide. In fact, Americans alone consume more than 3 billion PEZ candies a year. More than 70 million PEZ dispensers are produced on a yearly basis, and annual sales in North America are estimated to be between $35 and $45 million. Not impressed by mere statistics? Do a quick Google search on the internet and you'll find hundreds of unofficial PEZ web sites. There are PEZ newsletters, PEZ collector guides, PEZ conventions and— believe it or not—there's even a PEZ museum or two.

From a tangible product perspective, the PEZ story clearly shows the interdependence between sales and marketing. When sales are down, we might have to go back to the "marketing room" to enhance or *WOW* our product offering. Haas repackaged his candy, and then redirected his efforts to the children's market. Funny enough, his *WOW* was so powerful, he inadvertently created a secondary group of buyers . . . adult collectors of the PEZ dispensers. PEZ has an extensive online catalog and ordering system to help meet the needs of its voracious collectors.

It doesn't matter if the product is a tangible candy or the services of an accountant—selling the "sizzle" and not the steak means selling with a high WOW factor. A remarkable sales increase will strain the manufacturing and sales distributions departments, meaning that sales departments and sellers have to be well integrated with the other functional departments of the company. For example, sales were so high that the PEZ facility in Orange, Connecticut, had to start manufacturing 24 hours a day.

When a WOW factor is added to the product, soon you will find it necessary to add further WOW to the first WOW. Buyer complacency can be disastrous to sales. PEZ continues to add new flavors and cartoon characters to their mix. It's estimated that more than 400 different heads have graced the top of the dispenser.

> *A silver rule of selling is that the seller's personal enthusiasm is a most powerful sales tool because it adds a WOW element to the sales scenario.*

If you're selling a professional service, you must be concerned with the *WOW* factor, and it will come from *within* the selling experience. How can you make your potential buyer feel special? Do you have a helpful receptionist to make clients feel more comfortable? Can you offer an assortment of magazines to make waiting time more pleasurable? Do your small customers feel they are as important to you as your larger ones? Whatever it takes, you must find creative ways to sell yourself and keep people coming back for more of what you offer.

In today's global economy, there's one thing you can count on, and that's competition. Somebody out there somewhere is bound to be selling the same widget or service at a similar, even lesser price. You become the master of your sales domain by identifying your *WOW* factor and creating a *WOW* reaction in each buyer. Do this and you too will enjoy PEZ-tacular sales success!

People are asked to do something every day—everywhere. In effect, asking someone to do something is similar to a sales pitch: "Please do this for me." As the top salesperson in the billion-dollar service industry for over eight years, Christine Clifford Beckwith knows how to ask for the sale. Part of her experience came from "selling" her own company from a million dollar per year loss to over $54 million in sales and signing the largest contract within her industry with Procter and Gamble. What makes the difference? It might be in how you "stage" your sales proposal. Stage it right, and it's nearly impossible to say "no" to you.

SEARCHING FOR LARRY GATLIN

CHRISTINE CLIFFORD BECKWITH, CSP

A prospect might reject our proposal for the simplest of reasons: we didn't make our offer sufficiently compelling, missed their hot buttons, or failed to convert the product's unique features into buyer benefits. I happened on this lesson when I was selling Grammy award-winning country singer Larry Gatlin on playing for my charity golf tournament, the *Christine Clifford Celebrity Golf Invitational.* Mr. Gatlin's second passion in life is golf, and each year, hundreds of golfers plead with him to play in their tournaments. I was one of them.

After learning that Larry Gatlin was performing in my home of Minneapolis, I immediately thought of Nido Qubein. Mr. Qubein is an American success story: a highly recognized speaker, consultant, CEO, and general all-around good person. A year earlier, I had met Nido at a National Speaker's Association event he was hosting. Nido had persuaded (sold) Mr. Gatlin on appearing at his event for free.

Ever the believer in the power of networking, I called Nido, who then called Mr. Gatlin and introduced me. Within a few minutes, I was on a firm phone connection with Mr. Gatlin, ready to begin my sales pitch. (Later, I learned from Larry Gatlin, "When Nido says, 'Take this call,' I take the call.' This confirmed my understanding that networking and sales are strongly linked.)

However, at this point I didn't have a "done deal," just a hand on the door. I still had to sell Larry on participating in my golf tournament. Larry quickly objected and volunteered his reasons. As a recovering alcoholic, he missed a lot of his family experience during earlier years, and now protects his family time, especially since he had a new baby granddaughter. He was also engaged in a demanding schedule of performances with his Gatlin Brothers music group.

I had profiled my prospect, and I knew he was not only a well-known entertainer but also a golf fanatic, recovering alcoholic, doting father, and financial provider. "We'll pay you $10,000" I said, knowing Larry's presence would generate far more than $10,000 for our cause. "Now you're talking," Larry replied.

Our hometown airline, Sun Country Airlines, already had donated ten airline tickets to be used at our discretion, and I quickly made an executive decision to play these chips. "What if we fly your daughter, your son-in-law, your wife, and your new baby granddaughter to Minneapolis? Everyone comes on our ticket!" His long pause and sudden laughter surprised me.

"Really? No one has ever offered that before!" WOW! I was hooking him with lavish and persuasive gifts and was only connected to him by phone. It wasn't long before he agreed to meet me for lunch the next day at the Grand Hotel where we could connect in person.

He was hooked at this point, but not completely sold. Hitting overdrive, I started ramping up my sales pitch so there would be no objection left unturned. Reflecting on his profile, I stopped first at The Minikahda Golf Club, where my charity tournament would be hosted. There was a buzz about a new Titleist Pro V1 golf ball that was so popular the entire city was out of supply. But I knew there had to be some Pro V1s somewhere, and my cause (product) was righteous.

Doug Nelson, the club pro didn't know when his next shipment might arrive, but I pleaded. (Most sales trainers don't teach begging and pleading, but sometimes ya gotta do what ya gotta do.) Doug surrendered, "I have a private stash. I hate to part with them—they really are that good—but for you and the event, you got me." He retrieved my golden box of golf balls. I bear-hugged Doug, and as I was about to leave the Pro Shop, I glimpsed a tiny pair of pink leather golf shoes for a newborn. PINK MAGIC! Those cute little shoes would fit my WOW strategy perfectly. Oblivious to the cost, I charged them to my account and raced to my next stop.

Recovering alcoholics must drink something, and I'd noticed many turn to coffee. But my special WOW package had to uniquely suit Larry Gatlin and reflect extra time and thought. The ordinary would not achieve the desired effect. A rare African blend, a Chateau Lafite-Rothschild of coffees, paired with a rare box of imported chocolates came immediately to mind. Off I raced to Gloria's Specialty Coffee Shop.

Back home, I located an extra copy of *Chicken Soup for the Golfer's Soul,* which included one of my stories. I autographed that page, and added one final note with the tiny pink baby golf shoes, "May you become as wonderful a golfer as your Granddaddy."

I had the gifts arranged in a mahogany wicker basket, shrink-wrapped, and with a few deep breaths, I hurried to the Grand Hotel for my first face-to-face sales meeting with Larry Gatlin. He already was predisposed to saying yes, but I wanted to seal the deal with a special acknowledgement of his acceptance.

And accept he did; Larry Gatlin did perform at our tournament. He performed spectacularly. His team won the event. And his warmth and generosity won over the 300 participants who attended his concert that night. Cancer research won, too, raising almost $270,000.

There are several lessons one can take from this story:

1. Search constantly for common ground; we relate best to those with whom we share an affinity. Common grounds are like windows to peer into new areas of discovery about another person.

2. Invest. Travel the extra miles and pay the extra dollars. *"You have to spend money to make money"* applies equally to sales. People respond positively to special treatment that is shown to them.

3. When you say please or thank you, say it unforgettably. Thank you always works as a form of politeness, but thank you accompanied with special thought and effort becomes a memory in the buyer's mind.

4. The greatest gift you offer is your time. It's simple: Most people are stingy with their time, so when you give your time, you stand out from the others. If your time is dedicated to aggrandizing another, the emotional response back to you will be their gratitude.

5. The greatest compliment you can pay is "I understand something that is deep in your heart." Now you are getting to the core values of a person; feeling that someone understands your core values is the greatest compliment one can receive. It has to be sincere and accurate.

———•·•———

Freelance writer Cynthia Lueck Sowden and realtor Chas Wilson, both from the Minnesota area, share with us a story about a real selling program that goes against the grain but creates a WOW experience for clients. Chas decided not to do the same thing with his real estate business that his competitors were doing, taking a gamble that people wanted something more. It wasn't long before the word got out, and Chas's business became a company that people gravitate toward.

———•·•———

GOING AGAINST THE GRAIN

CHAS WILSON AND CYNTHIA LUECK SOWDEN

My father-in-law talked me into a real estate career, even though I had never purchased a house myself. As a young man wanting a career, it sounded like a good idea. Soon I was selling houses the usual way—list the house, hold an open house, close the deal, and move on to the next house. This approach didn't appeal to me, and I looked for a better, more satisfying method—both for my sake and the benefit of my customers.

The usual way of selling homes relies heavily on the agent doing all the work. Most agents operate a one-person show . . . and most are breaking their backs trying to do a good job. To me, this selling process felt bland and tiresome for all concerned.

In 2003, I became the first Keller Williams real estate agent in Rochester, Minnesota, because I felt this organization allowed their agents to have more innovative leeway in the operation of their selling business. Rochester is comprised of many old-money families who don't like to spend freely. There is a large transient population, consisting mostly of doctors and their families who intern at the world famous Mayo clinic for two or three years, and then join the annual physician migration in and out of Rochester.

This community is fairly conservative, and change is slow to be accepted. But in my first seven months, I had a team of six people and 50 realtors associated with our office. In our first year, we sold 25 houses, but by the second year we were on track to sell more than 80 homes. We started changing things, and here's how we did it.

I decided from the start that I didn't want to do "business as usual." I also wanted time to spend with my family and to coach varsity football, which meant that I had to set up my business so it could run without me. While my face and name show up on our ads, much of the work is done by a team of people who all share the profits. Our sales team allows us to be in ten places at once and enhances the quality of our client service. We also employ cutting-edge technology that dramatically improves the speed, efficiency, and innovative capabilities of every aspect of our operation. Our mission is to provide extraordinary client services that are far above the usual offered by our competitors.

The homes we list *sell for more money in less time than any other agency,* which is shaking up the stodgy old real estate establishment. We're doing this through our commitment to "beyond-the-usual" customer service, some features of which include:

- We post a service guarantee on the real estate page, right next to our listed homes. For buyers, I offer peace of mind: "If you're not satisfied with your purchase in the first two years, I'll buy your house back." The guarantee for sellers was just as simple: "Your home sold in 120 days, or I'll buy it." Other real estate companies took notice of our guarantee and grumbled, but not many matched our commitment.

- Our company-owned moving van started making waves. It's free of charge to our clients. A real estate moving van service was unheard of in our city. The truck advertises our Chas Wilson Team and is on the road 20 days out of every month. Our team gets great exposure and huge goodwill with our customers. Along with lots of thank-you notes, we are mentioned as a preferred realtor more often by grateful recipients.

- We send 4,000–8,000 postcards out every week, inviting potential sellers for a free internet home evaluation. All they have to do is visit our web site (www.chaswilson.com) and sign up. In one three-month period, traffic to the site generated 449 requests for home evaluations. Team members call the homeowners to let them know their request was received and to determine the sellers' intent. If they're really serious about selling their homes, we arrange an in-home evaluation, and the customer is under no obligation to list with us. Our web site is loaded with informative articles on home buying and selling, while also showing off the latest listings.

- Each Friday, we run a spot called "Friday's Featured Home" on Rochester's largest radio station, KROC. We guarantee each of our sellers a 60-second commercial that will promote their home on-air at least five times on a Friday. This is just one more way we offer our listing customers more benefit through increased exposure of their home.

- Instead of the traditional open house program, we've opted for a Saturday Tour of Homes. Each Saturday we conduct one or two tours of six homes each. Tours are advertised and run between 1:00 and 3:15 P.M. There are lots of other buyers on the tour, and show times are exact. If buyers are interested in a particular house, they can arrange for a longer, private showing—often on the same day. Nobody else is doing this, and it's been wildly successful.

- We use more communication technology. I've invested in an automated calling system that gives sellers a call every 30 days. It delivers one of six pre-recorded messages from me (it sounds like a live phone call). It keeps me in front of them and saves me tons of time. If they have a question, they call me, and I call them back.

- Networking activities are embraced. I believe in keeping our company in front of as many people as possible, and I do this through the leveraged activity of networking. I belong to a BNI referral marketing chapter and am part of the Southeast Minnesota Association of Realtors. This helps me keep abreast of new trends in our industry and increases our marketing exposure through the BNI word-of-mouth referral system.

None of the above is really rocket science, and in some markets, it's already been done. But by doing things just a little bit differently, by going against the grain of how homes are usually bought and sold, we've quickly positioned the Chas Wilson Team as a major player in the Rochester area. Our clients feel our effort to provide spectacular service pays off, and they repay us by spreading the word about how our team is WOW-ing the customer, especially in comparison to our competitors. We believe customers like to feel special, and we want to make them feel that way.

We're expanding beyond the city limits into other southeastern Minnesota communities. Our competitors may not like it, but our customers love it . . . and we're here to stay!

Under-promising and WAY over-delivering is a fail-safe way to build up your respect and trust in the selling arena. This means attending to the way each person in the buying scenario wants to be treated, and following every step of the professional selling process to a "T." Chris Attwood is an expert in consultative sales, with more than three decades of sales and training experience operating at top echelon corporate levels. He shows us how to make significant client connections and WAY over-deliver, so that closing that client is virtually a non-issue.

SELLING DELL BY WAY OVER-DELIVERING

CHRIS ATTWOOD

It was 1998, and on the front page of *USA Today*'s Money section was a headline about Dell Computers: "Over $1 Million per Day In Online Sales." In those days, this was more money than *anyone* was making on the internet. Dell had cracked the code for e-commerce.

I was a new account executive for Human Factors International (HFI), in Fairfield, Iowa, a town of 10,000. HFI is the world's premier provider of software usability, consulting, and training services in the world. Even though it was barely a decade old, had only 35 employees, and was based in a small town, the company had developed an impressive list of clients, including General Motors, Ford Motor Company, Chase Bank, Motorola, Deloitte & Touche—and we were always eager to add to our blue chip list.

After reading the *USA Today* article and reviewing Dell's web site, I got excited. It might be making more money online than anyone else, but I could see some inefficiency issues in its webpage and thought we might be able to help Dell. I talked with my VP, and we both got excited by realizing how we could help Dell double its online sales results.

I didn't know anyone at Dell and had no referrals to the inner group. I knew it was located in Austin, Texas, and it had a phone. With a little help from directory assistance and the Dell corporate phone receptionist, I connected with the Dell executive listed in the *USA Today* article. Dell is a high technology company; it used voice mail.

Six unanswered voice mail messages and 30 days later, and despite my best voice mail pitch, I got nothing in response. It was time to give up or adopt a new strategy.

My VP and I brainstormed a new strategy. We decided to offer a free one-hour "expert phone review" of its site, featuring our CEO, who was the top usability specialist in the world. We'd give Dell some practical input and request no return obligation. Our company charged more than $3,500 per day for our CEO's services, so this represented a very generous (prospecting) offer.

I made my seventh call to the voice message machine. This time I focused on our CEO's credentials, big name clients, and our offer of a free hour consultation, during which he would give Dell concrete usability feedback with immediate application.

Surprise, we got a bite. The manager called me the next day. I asked for (and received) a phone appointment for a background call, during which I could ostensibly obtain useful parameters for our formal consultation call with the CEO. In actuality, the background call was to allow me the chance to get to know the manager a little and begin establishing rapport.

In planning our CEO's call, we decided to take an unusual approach of focusing on what we could give Dell and avoid any direct sales pitches. We were sure that Dell had plenty of vendors trying to get its business, so we crafted the call to provide very useful information and no sales pitch. We figured if the value we offered during our hour-long CEO presentation was thought to be useful, Dell would ask us for more help.

The call was set up with the original manager and two of his project managers. The CEO spent an hour dissecting the usability issues on just the web site home page, while explaining the principles and rationale for his suggestions.

A few polite questions were asked and the tone of the call seemed friendly enough, but I couldn't tell if this would be our last call or the first of many. As the call was finishing, the Dell senior manager said, "So, how does Human Factors make money anyway?" We had our opening!

We mentioned a few of our services that we felt were most relevant to the Dell situation, then said, "What will work best is for us to come to your office and do a walk-through of how we support companies like yours." The Dell manager said "Great!" We quickly made arrangements, hung up, and literally danced around the room.

My CEO and I made the trip together to Round Rock, Texas, and again decided on an unconventional approach. We were scheduled for a three-hour meeting, but we planned our direct input portion to last no more than 45 minutes. In other words, we wanted to spend most of the time asking questions.

We wanted the managers to talk as much as possible, while we would do our best to understand their environment, their challenges, and where they experienced their greatest pain. Our goal was to get Dell to hire us, even if just for work on a small project. A small project would allow us to lay foundations for a longer-term relationship. Prior to the trip, I spoke with the senior manager's assistant to make the arrangements, and asked her about other software initiatives in the company. Dell had an intranet in place headed up by another separate group, and the sales light bulb flashed in my head.

I called the head of the intranet group, and after explaining our upcoming visit to Dell, invited him and his team to meet us on the same day. He immediately agreed, and again we danced around the room because the hottest project in the Dell corporate offices at the time apparently was the intranet group.

Dell did contract with us for a modest $25,000 trial project, which included our putting on a three-day training course on usability. The course helped the entire intranet group understand the importance and basic principles of software usability, and cemented a long-term relationship between HFI and Dell.

The next year, Dell implemented a whole new e-commerce web site based on the software usability principles it'd learned during that initial

three-day workshop. It also had HFI completely redesign the site naviga-
tion. It turned out we hadn't been able to help Dell double its online sales
after all. Its sales went from $1 million per day to more than $40 million
dollars per day, and more than 50 percent of the company's revenues were
from online sales. Not all of its significant increase was due to the usability
enhancements, but certainly a significant piece was. HFI has now completed more than $1 million in consulting and training for Dell. This talks
volumes about over-delivering on a promise to help alleviate a buyer's pain
(or even mild discomfort).

There are some core lessons I learned from my Dell experience:

- *Persistence pays.* If you know you have something of great value for
  someone else, don't give up. No matter what.
- *Connect with the client's critical issues.* Dell's e-commerce group was
  its hot commodity, and had the budget for new initiatives. My sales
  research pointed me to this hot button, and through our discussion
  with its managers, we confirmed our suspicions. The Dell managers
  talked about the challenges they had, which were within our field of
  expertise. We then crafted our solution to match their critical
  needs.
- *Attraction is more powerful than selling.* By giving significant value
  for free, we attracted the manager's interest and built trust in our
  company's capability. We bridged the gap between our expertise
  and their trust in our company by spending most of our face-to-
  face time asking questions and probing their experience. As we
  spent more quality time together, they became more attracted to us.
  When it was time to discuss specific projects and budgets, they had
  bought in and we didn't have to "sell" them on our value.
- *Leverage your opportunities.* Once we had a foot in the door with the
  intranet group, we leveraged our growing reputation with other
  departments in the company and ended up working with most.
- *Long-term relationships provide the biggest paydays.* We could have
  pitched a big initial project, but by taking small steps and educating
  the client on our value, we created a bond of trust. It trusted that we
  would deliver on the bigger projects, and as we succeeded with

these larger jobs, word-of-mouth referrals were made to other departments within the company.

I now apply these principles learned years ago to our new company (visit www.healthywealthynwise.com), which is one of the largest online resources for personal growth, health, and wealth creation. We connect with, and become related to, powerful people like Stephen R. Covey, director David Lynch, Dr. Wayne Dyer, Mark Victor Hansen, Jack Canfield, Dennis Waitley, Jim Rohn, Stedman Graham, and Byron Katie. I never forget the lessons learned during that magical time with Dell Computers. It all started with a cold phone call and six more cold calling attempts. It reminds me that anything is possible when we keep our attention on the value we provide to others.

Conclusion

If you think about it, salespeople are critical to moving our world forward. With millions of inventors, artists, writers, professional services, companies, and manufacturers, someone has to get the product distributed to the end user. And this is the job of our salespeople. What many people may not know is that there are many opportunities within the sales profession to advance toward incredible personal goals. Within every industry—the sales industry included— there are those who are content to work at different levels of intensity, and selecting this aspiration level is highly dependent on the inner desire, attitude, and drive for achievement held by each person.

It really doesn't matter if the product is a life-saving medical device, a metal screw fastener, or envelopes such as those produced by Harvey MacKay's envelope company. The measurement of personal success is not in the greatness of the product, but in the significant effort expended by the manufacturer and then the seller. Once, Don Morgan was consulting for a small auto-parts manufacturer. The company was transitioning from making metal fenders to plastic fenders. Personnel in the company were actually ecstatic over the new plastic molding processes they were employing, which surprised Don. Then he realized what really was happening: The inherent value of a product to society matters less than the great personal satisfaction and pride felt when one completes a job well.

The new wave of selling professionals and sales trainers overwhelmingly stresses the importance of relationships to the selling scenario. Whether the sales arena is a box store, a corner grocery, direct sales, retail boutique, or major corporation, a relationship established between the seller and consumer will facilitate the first sale and encourage repeat business.

Of course, it is not possible for a new seller to graduate right to relationship sales without first going through Sales 101. Achieving greatness in any endeavor begins with mastering the fundamentals. Doing the prospecting, the meet and greet, qualifying the prospect, handling objections, and delivering a powerful product presentation that sells the benefits while explaining the features are crucial. Making certain to ask for the sale with an appropriate close and then following up are all part of the basic selling skill set, which must be integrated within the seller who wishes to move forward in this honorable career.

Referral marketing and network selling are being superimposed on the traditional sales paradigm, thereby making selling more appropriate to the characteristics of today's complex and competitive world. But moving from good selling to great selling requires an uncommon application of effort to refine and improve those areas most often difficult to master. These areas are the fine points that help forge powerful reciprocal relationships between individuals. At this point, we enter the realm of using communication tactics and strategies to enable one person to give value to the other. Today, selling is more about partnerships between buyers and sellers. Achieving partnership status demands carefully growing a relationship in which you, the seller, achieve a preferred vendor status for the buyer.

We all have experienced a time when we were treated as a very important person, and this moment is not quickly forgotten. Imagine if every one of our prospects and customers were made to feel very important. It didn't take much for Peggy Hunn, a CPA in Chicago, to train her reception staff to politely take the coat from a walk-in client, address each client respectfully by name, and offer a menu of drinks and light snacks and pleasant reading material while the client was waiting for the scheduled appointment. Needless to say, Peggy maintains her status as the preferred accountant for more and more clients each year.

We need to learn basic, time-tested sales lessons from the traditional Masters of Sales, and we also must be aware of what the new masters are beginning to discover and share with us. Selling is an interactive human endeavor, and we can never learn enough about how best to deal with humans. Technological advances of the day have always been an integral part of sales success, but a secret to masterful selling is treating each person in the way she or he wishes to be treated.

Thank you for owning this book.
We appreciate your business!

Whom do you know who might gain inspiration
from those who went before?

BNI, the world's largest business networking organization, was founded by Dr. Ivan Misner in 1985 as a way for business people to generate referrals in a structured, professional environment. The organization, now the world's largest referral business network, has thousands of chapters with tens of thousands of members on every populated continent of the world. Since its inception, members of BNI have passed millions of referrals, generating billions of dollars in business for the participants.

The primary purpose of the organization is to pass qualified business referrals to the members. The philosophy of BNI may be summed up in two simple words: Givers Gain®. If you give business to people, you will get business from them. BNI allows only one person per profession to join a chapter. The program is designed for businesspeople to develop long-term relationships, thereby creating a basis for trust and, inevitably, referrals. The mission of BNI is to help members increase their business through a structured, positive, and professional word-of-mouth program that enables them to develop long-term, meaningful relationships with quality business professionals.

To visit a chapter near you, contact BNI on the internet at bni@bni.com or visit its web site at www.bni.com.

Index